Global High-Tech Marketing
An Introduction for Technical Managers and Engineers

For a complete listing of the *Artech House Professional Development* Library,
turn to the back of this book.

Global High-Tech Marketing
An Introduction for Technical Managers and Engineers

Jules E. Kadish

Artech House
Boston • London

Library of Congress Cataloging-in-Publication Data

Kadish, Jules E.
Global high-tech marketing: an introduction for technical managers and engineers / Jules E. Kadish.
Includes bibliographical references and index.
ISBN 0-89006-704-X
1. High technology industries—Marketing. I. Title.
HC79.H53K33 1993   93-13320
620'.068'8—dc20   CIP

British Library Cataloguing in Publication Data

Kadish, Jules E.
Global High-Tech Marketing: Introduction for Technical Managers and Engineers.
(Professional Development Library)
I. Title II. Series
620.0068

ISBN 0-89006-704-X

© 1993 ARTECH HOUSE, INC.
685 Canton Street
Norwood, MA 02062

International Standard Book Number: 0-89006-704-X
Library of Congress Catalog Card Number: HC79.H53K33 1993

10 9 8 7 6 5 4 3 2 1

Contents

Preface

Early in 1990 Professor Saverio Rotella, a former colleague, asked me to organize a one-week course on international marketing for the Italian telecommunications graduate school Scuola Superiore G. Reiss Romoli. My course addressed the needs of technical people who wished to pursue management careers.

Most textbooks published in the field deal with domestic rather than international marketing and with consumer rather than high-tech products. Because I was unable to find an appropriate text for a brief course concerned mainly with international marketing of high technology, I decided to write this book. What can be taught in a such a course, when there is so much to cover that standard marketing courses normally last much longer? I elected to concentrate on strategy, organization, channels of distribution, and selling. To drive home related lessons, I felt it useful to have students study and discuss related cases.

Much of what is stated in the book about the selling aspects of marketing will seem simple common sense. The same can be said about employing obvious management principles—such as understanding that existence depends on serving customers well and respecting employees—to ensure that a company is successful. Likewise, good salesmanship is largely common sense, and I have sought to arrange in some order what should appear obvious. While marketing issues might require common sense approaches, nonetheless, solutions are not always immediately clear. I cite many real examples to illustrate how to apply these common sense strategies to the complexities of real life situations. Much in this book is based on decades of personal experience. Hopefully, some of the more successful aspects of that experience will rub off on students.

The course took place in September 1991, and students used the first version of this book. Afterwards, the book was revised to incorporate their suggestions. Appendix III, which covers financial aspects, is an addition. It was clear from the course that most students need assistance in this area.

My thanks are extended to Howard Crispin, Nick Wheeler, and Manfred Mack, who suggested changes to my original draft. My thanks are also extended to Dr. Attilia Properzi, a lecturer at the Scuola Superiore G. Reiss Romoli in L'Aquila Italy, who is mainly responsible for Chapter 2.

Introduction

This book is intended to serve as the text to an introductory course for students who are interested in a management career in international marketing. It differs from most marketing texts in that it is concerned mainly with international rather than domestic marketing, and the examples and case studies deal with high-tech rather than consumer products. There are substantial difference between export marketing of high technology and domestic marketing of consumer products. There is often much more uncertainty about market evolution in high technology, due to the rapidity of technological change. Other differences involve the extreme degree of expertise needed by marketers of high technology, and their close relationships to R&D and new product planning. Other differences involve the special attention that must be paid to selecting foreign channels of distribution and to resolving organizational issues. Still others relate to the type of selling used in high-tech firms and especially to the need for salespeople of the highest caliber, who can adapt to the different cultures of foreign countries.

A considerable portion of this brief book is devoted to issues of selling and salesmanship because of their importance in export marketing of high technology. Yet, there is a great deal of commonality in all types of marketing, and neglecting the basics could lead the marketer into serious problems. The book discusses many of these basics, but glosses over or even omits other issues, such as financial planning and budgeting, pricing, considerations of inflationary effects, problems related to currency exchange, the promotional mix, and exporting logistics.

The book is divided into two distinct portions, the first of which concerns the following four chapters:

Chapter 1, "Strategy and Organization"
Chapter 2, "The Profit Impact of Market Strategy"
Chapter 3, "Channels of Distribution"
Chapter 4, "Selling to Foreign Markets"

In the second portion of the book, three cases in marketing of high-tech products are presented. This "case method," which was originally developed at Harvard University, is widely used in schools that offer degrees in business administration.

The three cases chosen for study and analysis all deal with real business experiences and with topics covered by the course. The first case, entitled "Elektrolipa Marketing Channels in Scandinavia," was prepared by Dr Mitja Tavcar, vice-president of Iskra Commerce and part-time associate professor in the faculty of Economics and Business Administration, Maribor University. The key issue relates to choice of suitable channels for export marketing.

The second case, about a company called Interactive Computer Systems, was prepared by Mark Ulrich under the direction of Jean-Pierre Jeannet, associate professor of Marketing, Babson College, Wellesley, Massachusetts, US, and visiting professor at IMEDE Management Development Institute, Lausanne, Switzerland. The key issue relates to a typical conflict between various international organizations that are all part of the same corporation.

The third case, about a company called Telesat, involves a complex situation that focuses on overall marketing strategy for launch of a new high-tech product. It was prepared by Helen Steers, research assistant, and Professor Adrian B. Ryans of the School of Business Administration, University of Western Ontario, London, Ontario, Canada.

Four appendices are included at the end of this book. These are:

Appendix A, "Marketing Information Sources"
Appendix B, "A Typical Representative Agreement"
Appendix C, "An Introduction to Finance for Marketers"
Appendix D, "Suggested Readings"

Appendix C is included to assist students who are not familiar with the financial aspects of company management. Unless such aspects are quite familiar, students will have difficulty understanding the basis for many business decisions and deciding how to tackle the cases presented in the course.

Chapter 1

Strategy and Organization

This chapter discusses some fundamental marketing principles and their practical application and examines some approaches to international marketing organization. To a large degree, selection of a marketing strategy is independent of whether a product is high or low tech and whether marketing will be domestic or international. Where possible, however, the following discussion concentrates on international marketing of high-tech products.

1.1 THE EXPERIENCE CURVE

In the late 1960s, a well-known management consulting organization, the Boston Consulting Group, formulated an important theory about market share strategy. The basic theme was that market share was of crucial importance to a company, and its conclusions were based on a large collection of data from firms producing high- and low-tech products, including semiconductors, automobiles, insurance, primary commodities, eggs, and a host of others. The group's studies showed that the product unit cost for a company decreases some 20% to 30% every time the cumulative total quantity of that product doubles. Figure 1.1 illustrates what they called the "experience curve," plotted on a logarithmic scale.

To emphasize the significance of the experience curve, Figure 1.1 shows the relative unit cost for three competitors, the market leader and its two nearest rivals, and an assumed market price. To a first approximation, the market price and indeed the products themselves do not vary significantly from competitor to competitor. The difference between the unit market price and the unit cost is the gross margin, which is clearly higher for the market leader.

The reasoning behind the experience curve is easy to appreciate. It has to do with such aspects as amortization of development costs, the production learning curve, the marketing investment in a particular geographic area—aspects that are referred to as "economies of scale." But the point is dramatic. The company that is the market leader makes more money than its competitors and can therefore spend more on marketing, training, and

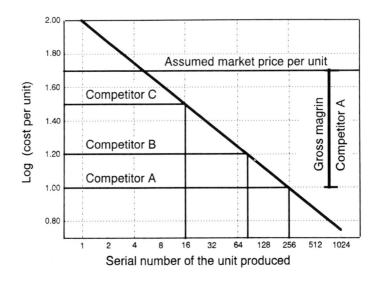

Figure 1.1 The production experience curve.

R&D than its competitors and keep ahead of them. In fact, the Boston Consulting Group study goes on to suggest that there is really only room for perhaps three successful competitors, and the remaining ones hang in there, making marginal returns or suffering losses.

In the same period as the Boston Consulting Group's study, the U.S. General Electric Company conducted an intensive study of businesses. One finding of that study suggested that companies with a greater than 30% market share are usually profitable, while those with a market share of less than 15% usually lose money. Yet, if firms with a market share of less than 15% lose money, how is it that so many small firms seem to prosper? The answer is that these companies probably have a substantial market share *in their market segment.*

The key to understanding these theories is understanding market segmentation. The study cannot be used to compare, for instance, the market share for Ferrari automobiles and the market share for LADA automobiles. The market segments for those two products are quite different. But it is that aspect, market segmentation, that is often overlooked by organizations attempting to determine market share. A company must seek to be one of the market leaders in its segment of business. The very first step, and one that must be reviewed continually, is to become thoroughly familiar with the market segment share of competitors and with their strengths and weaknesses.

A company that establishes market leadership for one of its product lines in a selected market segment must defend that position or be displaced. (Note: In what follows, the term "product" is meant to include both products and services.) To maintain leadership, the company must perform at least the following steps:

- Remain informed about state-of-the-art innovations related to the product;

- Keep abreast of likely moves by competitors and outmaneuver them;
- Maintain a superior marketing organization in countries in which it dominates;
- Resolve customer complaints expeditiously.

Of course, all this is easier said than done. Sometimes, when a company obtains the biggest market share, it relaxes efforts to retain that share and, instead, concentrates marketing efforts on other markets and products. If the company does not have the resources to defend market segment dominance while seeking other markets, it can become vulnerable to an aggressive competitor. That competitor might, in turn, exploit a technical innovation or create a better marketing organization and overtake the leader.

1.2 THE ECOLOGICAL VIEW

Hans Thorelli uses the expression "ecological view" in the book *International Marketing Strategy* to describe marketing efforts [1]. In Thorelli's usage, a company is a "living organism" and its "environment" is its market segment. The ecological view is the strategy by which a company directs its marketing efforts toward the segment it best fits and is best adapted to serve.

Thorelli suggests that there are at least three marketing viewpoints. The first viewpoint is, simply, to sell what you develop; companies that adopt this approach are said to be technology driven. The second viewpoint is to develop and sell what the market wants; companies with this viewpoint are market driven. The third approach is to develop and sell what the market wants, *taking into account what you are good at.*

Technology first developed as a driving force for companies during the industrial revolution and it continues to dominate as a marketing strategy for many firms today. The second approach, responding to market needs, evolved when competition became stronger and new firms displaced the former leaders. One reason displacement occurred was that new competitors were able to perceive weaknesses in reigning products that did not match market needs and develop better ones. Technological advances also provided aspiring competitors with the means to develop more economical or easier-to-use products that better matched market requirements. The market-driven approach spurred market researchers into determining what the market wanted. Of course, this research was devoted for the most part to consumer goods.

The development of the American railways is often cited to distinguish technology-driven and market-driven approaches. When a market for transportation was first perceived, the railway system quickly developed, with enormous investment in land, railway engines, and cars. Following the technology-driven approach, a product was developed and, in effect, sold with relatively little say from the users. This was fine for the investors for many decades. But advances in other forms of transportation, including road vehicles and aircraft, resulted in the eventual displacement of the railways as the primary means of transportation. Some analysts argue that if railway management had understood that they were in the transportation business rather than the railway business they could have averted displacement as the market leaders. They would have kept abreast of the times, investing in other forms of transportation, diversifying, and retaining their market lead. In other words, management should have developed and sold what the market needed.

The ecological viewpoint should, however, make those analysts question their analysis. There is absolutely no indication that managers of a railway system would be any good at all at managing other transportation systems, such as, for example, an airline system. Possibly, what management should have done was ask themselves what they were good at, and they might have concluded that, since they had enormous land investments and, of necessity, had to be good at managing those investments, perhaps they could put that skill to further use in the marketplace.

Just how does this discussion of market strategies apply to nonconsumer marketing? Is it not true that nonconsumer marketing is technology driven? Is not the strategy that dominates industrial marketing the first approach described above? Yes, many of the companies currently comprising the industrial market are technology driven, but if they are not also attuned to market needs, they risk being displaced by competition. The goal of a company must be to be a dominant player in its market segment. Unless a company matches its capabilities with that market segment, it risks failure. The marketing objective for a company would seem to be, then, to become and remain the market leader in the market segment that best matches its capabilities and make-up. Pursuing other market segments in which the company has no skills is risky and can lead to operational losses and to failure.

An organization's marketing group has a key role in selecting the market segment. Their first obvious responsibility is to help formulate product specifications for the selected market segment. A less obvious task is to select the geographic market. Even when a company is not the market leader, it can still seek to dominate certain geographic markets, such as those in developing countries. Once a company succeeds in penetrating a geographic market, customer knowledge, availability of service and parts, and established friendships can strengthen the company's overall position. Then, the high cost of entering that country might discourage a competitor's attempts.

The foregoing discussion might seem to be an oversimplification of the logic involved in choosing a marketing strategy. A small firm may seek to be a market leader in some segment and maintain that leadership by responding quickly to market demand with new, innovative products. A larger firm may not be able to react as quickly; however, it can use its greater resources to organize a larger and more effective marketing program to establish and maintain market leadership.

Regardless of the strategy, it should be obvious that all firms must be aware of and responsive to market needs. Engineers cannot remain isolated in their ivory tower laboratories. They must get out and talk to customers to understand their needs, rather than imagine, somewhat arrogantly, that they know better than the customers what is needed.

1.3 THE MARKET SEGMENT AND STRATEGY

It is clear that the experience curve relates to market share in a particular market segment. But it is not so clear how we can define a segment uniquely, to differentiate it from other segments. Type of product and type of market certainly are factors by which one segment differs from another. The same product offered by a competitor in a another geographic area might also factor into a definition of segment. Market segments can also overlap and when that happens real market share becomes difficult to measure. The objective of pursuing leadership in a market segment is clearly of paramount importance. But how should a company go about choosing the strategy to follow to achieve such leadership? Some answers to this question that are independent of market type include:

- Understand market needs. Why should customers purchase this product? What are the economic benefits of such a purchase?
- Identify market segmentation. Distinguish the characteristics of the various segments or groups of customers that comprise the entire market. Is product differentiation needed to penetrate individual segments?
- Determine the size of each market segment in the geographic area being served. What is the total market segment in terms of monetary amount?
- Identify the factors that determine annual growth or decline in market segment share. What is the annual volume of sales per market segment? What factors, such as technological advances, price changes, and regulatory changes, determine that volume?
- Know the competition. Who are these competitors? What differentiates their products, strengths, and weaknesses? What strategies do they follow and why? What changes in strategy can be expected from key competitors as time goes on?
- In light of the foregoing determinations, what market segment should be pursued? What is the best strategy for gaining leadership in that segment?

A simplified example involving the cable television industry illustrates the process described above. In the mid-1970s, the cable market in the United States was relatively small. One group of cable system operators helped householders in remote areas to receive TV programs without installing very costly antenna systems. Another group of cable operators provided viewers in densely populated areas with a larger choice of channels. They made their money by leasing a mix of channels to subscribers. Cable products included head-end equipment, such as antennas, receivers, professional VCRs; distribution equipment, such as coaxial cables, amplifiers, and filters; and subscriber products, such as the small converter that sits on top of the TV.

In this example, there are two customer segments in two geographic areas, a "rural" group and an "urban" group, and three product group segments. The number of potential subscribers in each segment was vastly different, as was the investment needed by the cable operators to serve each market. The rural segment was easier to serve and was expected to grow sooner than the urban segment, in which viewers already received some terrestrial channels and a higher capital investment was required. Clearly, though, the urban segment was much larger; it would grow later, but at a much steeper rate.

Availability of channels was a pacing factor, or "market driver," in the growth rate of either segment. The economic factor that impeded growth of the urban segment was the high cost of providing many channels in an inexpensive way to the cable operators. Because urban viewers were already receiving a number of terrestrial channels, operators needed to be able to attract them with a relatively large choice of channels. Using video tapes to accomplish this was proving difficult and expensive. At this time, geostationary satellites, which could carry many channels, were just starting to proliferate. If only a cable/satellite connection could be made, then the economics could become very attractive to the urban cable operator, and that market could take off.

TV receive only (TVRO) stations could be added to the head-end equipment, and satellite ground stations could "uplink" TV programs to the satellite transponders. If only programmers of TV programs could be convinced to use such uplinks, the cable operators who owned several cable networks could receive their programs via satellite, without the need to supply each headend with tapes.

Few competitors in the field were thinking of the potential of a satellite/cable connection. Here, then, was the key to a strategy for becoming a market leader in a new technology that would, in turn, stimulate the large urban segment's growth. But first, both television programmers and cable operators had to be convinced of the benefits of a cable/satellite connection, even if that meant the supplier must invest money in developing and demonstrating the new equipment. Sidney Topol, CEO of Scientific Atlanta, conceived this strategy and made the investment in equipment and marketing, and the firm quickly became market leader for the new satellite-related cable products. As a result of the cable/satellite connection, the entire cable television industry experienced an explosive growth, and today Scientific Atlanta is one of two firms that supply a majority of all cable television equipment to the whole market.

The cable television example also illustrates that companies do well to examine the market segments for products from several viewpoints when they are formulating marketing strategies. Matrices can be useful for such an examination. Examples are:

- Market segment versus customer's motivation for purchase;
- Market segment versus product segment;
- Market segment versus competition market share;
- Market segment versus total market size;
- Market segment versus annual market volume for that segment.

There are many ways to look at segmentation, and even an approximate analysis can be useful in strategy formulation. The most successful companies are those that are able to become market leaders in their chosen segments.

1.4 THE PRODUCT LIFE CYCLE

Provided they are accepted by the marketplace, most products go through a life cycle in which the factors of sales volume and time follow an S-shaped curve. This curve is often referred to as the product life cycle (PLC). Sales increase slowly during the introduction phase, grow more rapidly during the growth phase until they hit a peak, and then flatten during the maturity stage and start to decline (Figure 1.2).

Figure 1.2 A product life cycle.

During a product's introduction phase, expenditures are likely to be far higher than revenues, and money must be invested in the product. This is the time when the company should invest heavily in marketing, including product promotion. If the product is successful, sales will increase at a rapid rate. During the growth stage, sales will continue to increase at a rapid rate. Although the product may begin to show a profit, any cash generated is likely to be ploughed back into the product to pay for expansion. However, toward the end of the growth period, the sales rate will be decreasing, and profits might begin to generate cash that is no longer required to fund sales expansion.

When the product reaches the maturity stage, sales are relatively stable. If the product is a winner and has captured a substantial, possibly major, share of the market, profits should be high. Cash generated by these profits should fund R&D to develop new products to replace this one. Depending on the length of time required for development, such R&D might have to commence long before product maturity, so that by the time the product sales start to decline, new products are available to replace it.

During the early part of the decline stage, profits might still be realized, but the time will come when losses start to pile up. The company then faces a critical decision. What should happen to this product? How should it be phased out? On the one hand, too early an introduction of the replacement product might cause sales of the declining product to plummet, and the company might find itself with a lot of unsaleable inventory. Writing off that inventory will result in substantial losses. On the other hand, too late an introduction of the replacement product might permit entry of a competitor whose product might quickly capture a substantial market share. Displacing that competitor could prove extremely difficult. Timing is of the utmost importance.

1.5 PRODUCT PORTFOLIO

A company might start out in life with only one product, but soon enough it will have to offer a portfolio of products to compete in the marketplace. Each of these products will be at a stage in its own product life cycle. Each product will have a measurable growth rate (even if it is zero or negative) and a measurable market share.

Figure 1.3 illustrates a hypothetical company with a product portfolio of ten products. The products are represented by small circles distributed on a graph of relative market share versus annual sales growth rate. The area of each circle is proportional to the product's annual sales.

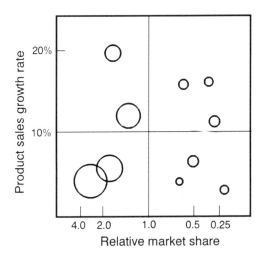

Figure 1.3 A portfolio product mix.

The two products in the upper left quadrant of Figure 1.3 can be thought of as "stars." They are both market leaders in a high growth stage of their life cycles. Two more products, in the lower left quadrant, are also market leaders, but sales growth is small. Such products can be milked, like cows, for their cash. The future of the three products located in the upper right quadrant is questionable. The sales growth rate is relatively high, but whether or not they can capture a substantial market share is not clear. The market share is low, and it is likely that they are losing money as well. The products in the lower right quadrant are clearly in trouble. Their sales growth rate is slow (maybe even negative), and they have a low market share. It would be surprising if they were not the cause of substantial losses.

Bruce Henderson of the Boston Consulting Group (see Appendix D) popularized the product portfolio matrix shown in Figure 1.4. Henderson calls products whose success is uncertain or unstable "problem children," and he calls unsuccessful products "dogs" (an American colloquial expression for something unsatisfactory or inferior).

Ideally, as stars mature, they slip into the lower left quadrant to join other cash cows. Companies would no doubt like to move problem children into the upper left quadrant, but that might take more investment in marketing or product improvement. One strategy, illus-

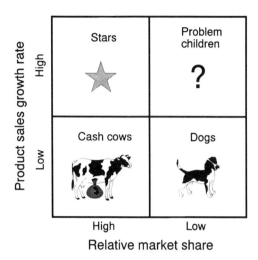

Figure 1.4 The product portfolio matrix.

trated in the "success sequence" in Figure 1.5, is to invest cash generated by cash cows in problem children.

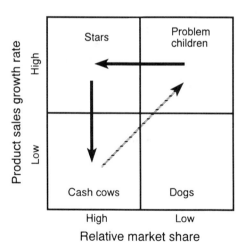

Figure 1.5 The success sequence.

The "disaster sequence" could well occur (Figure 1.6) if R&D is not continuous and funded properly, if the product portfolio is not examined carefully to ensure that the appropriate strategy is applied to individual products, or if money is not ploughed back into the business. Dogs can eat up this money very rapidly.

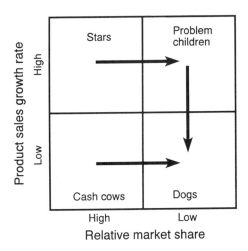

Figure 1.6 The disaster sequence.

Companies should try to maintain a balanced portfolio of products. When there are too few cash cows, the cash generated by the company might be insufficient for its needs, and cash cows gradually slip into the right quadrant as they approach the stage of decline. Stars are needed too, as well as problem children that can be elevated to stars through marketing or product improvements. The existence of some dogs is almost inevitable, and companies must watch these carefully. Henderson ends Chapter 5 of his remarkable book with the observation, "'Dogs' are not necessary. They are evidence of failure either to obtain a leadership position during the growth phase or to get out and cut the losses" [2].

The portfolio and the PLC approaches have received many critical reviews; however, though neither provides the complete answer to the question of marketing strategy choice, both have proven to be very useful. (For an example, see *International Marketing Planning & Strategy*, Chapter 10, listed in Appendix D.) There are other approaches, but either of the approaches discussed above, combined with imaginative and creative thinking about marketing basics (mentioned fleetingly in Section 1.1) and attention to competition, are essential for good marketing. Companies judged to be excellent pay a lot of attention to marketing basics and achieve product portfolios that include a number of market leaders. Section 1.6 discusses some of these successful companies.

1.6 THE EXCELLENT COMPANIES

In 1982, a book published in the United States had a profound impact on the views of many managers. The book was *In Search of Excellence* (see Appendix D). In it, authors Thomas Peters and Robert Waterman surveyed 62 American companies, many of them considered to be innovative and excellent by an informed group of business scene observers. Each company's performance over a 20-year period was measured against a set of six well-defined financial criteria. To be included in the category "excellent," a company had to be in the top half of its industry in at least four of the six measurement criteria throughout the entire 20-year period. The study included six market categories: high tech, consumer goods, general industrial products, services, project management consultants, and resource suppliers. The following are excellent companies in the high tech group that passed all—not just four of the six—criteria:

- Allen-Bradley
- Amdahl
- Data General
- Digital Equipment
- Emerson Electric
- Hewlett-Packard
- Hughes Aircraft

- IBM
- Intel
- National Semiconductor
- Raychem
- Schlumberger
- Texas Instruments
- Wang Labs

That some of these companies have slipped from prominence or are experiencing difficulties today does not alter the conclusions reached by the authors. Each of these companies certainly carved out an important market share in its segment. They grew throughout the measurement period and consolidated that market share, so they must have been doing something right. Each must have had a clear-sighted approach to marketing strategy. Obviously, one facet of each company's strategy was to become a market leader, and, not surprisingly, the authors found that there was much more to becoming a market leader than simply deciding what segment to pursue.

The authors found a common thread in the corporate culture of each of these companies, which was a common-sense approach to everyday management. In each case, ordinary employees of the companies had pleasant and, to them, exciting stories to tell about their firm and their place in it. The companies cared about their employees and showed it, and so the employees were proud to belong. Also in each case, the companies asked for and obtained extraordinary performance from all employees. And, finally, each company considered their customers' views and requirements to be of supreme importance. The authors praise their discovery of common-sense management practices:

> Our findings were a pleasant surprise. The project showed, more clearly than could have been hoped for, that excellent companies were, above all, brilliant on the basics. Tools didn't substitute for thinking. Intellect didn't overpower wisdom. Analysis didn't impede action. Rather, these companies worked hard to keep things simple in a complex world. They persisted. They insisted on top quality. They fawned on their customers. They listened to their employees and treated them like adults. They allowed their innovative product and service "champions" long tethers. They allowed some chaos in return for quick action and regular experimentation.[3]

Eight attributes characterized these excellent companies at the time. Each company

1. *Favors action.* Senior management finds an answer to a problem and implements it without delay. For example, instead of 250 engineers working in isolation for fifteen months on a new product, bands of five to 25 engineers test ideas out on customers, often with inexpensive prototypes, within a matter of weeks.
2. *Respects customers.* Everyone in the company regards the customer as king.
3. *Encourages autonomy and entrepreneurship.* Rather than acting as a stifling bureaucracy, the company encourages entrepreneurs and practical risk taking.
4. *Sees productivity in people.* The company has high respect for individuals and regards all employees as being the source of quality and productivity gain.
5. *Favors hands-on, value-driven practices.* Members of very top management believe that they themselves must be involved in all parts of the company and that they must work to ensure that employees understand the values the company holds as important.
6. *Sticks to what they know.* The company practices the philosophy of never acquiring a business it doesn't know how to run and stays reasonably close to the business it knows.
7. *Achieves a simple form, a lean staff.* The structure and organization of an excellent company is elegantly simple, with a small, efficient, motivated staff.
8. *Maintains simultaneously loose and tight properties.* An excellent company is both centralized and decentralized.

As can be concluded from these attributes, it takes more than strategic market planning to arrive at a state of excellence. Many of the attributes do, however, apply to the marketing department of a company. For example, no chosen marketing strategy can be pursued with dramatic success without a highly motivated group of employees who feel part of a team, believe it can succeed, and *know* the customer is the key to success. Likewise, a team can't succeed unless it includes entrepreneurs who can help the company forge ahead. And, as the companies listed above exemplify, the best results are obtained by organizations whose top management participates in marketing.

1.7 THE ROLE OF TOP MANAGEMENT

Two of the attributes of an excellent company described above–favoring hands-on, value-driven practices and achieving a simple form and a lean staff–relate specifically to the responsibilities of top management. In a well-run company, even the CEO is involved in encouraging employees to achieve results, and the organization is simple, with a sparse staff and very few layers between the CEO and the bottom rank.

A thought-provoking book about business organization was first published in 1970. Although it is written in a humorous style, *Up the Organization* is also quite serious. The author, Robert Townsend, wrote the book just after he left his job as CEO of the car rental company Avis, several years after converting Avis from a loss-making organization into a highly profitable one. The book is actually a unique management handbook; its chapters are short, alphabetically arranged discussions of common management issues, such as marketing, advertising, budgets, and conflicts within the organization. The book received widespread publicity, not only because of its humor, but also because so much of it makes down-to-earth sense, (as does so much of *In Search of Excellence*).

Townsend's entire chapter on marketing is reprinted below.

> "Marketing" departments—like planning departments, personnel departments, management development departments, advertising departments, and public relations departments—are usually camouflage designed to cover up for lazy or worn-out chief executives. Marketing, in the fullest sense of the word, is the name of the game. So it had better be handled by the boss and his line, not by staff hecklers. Once or twice a year for three or four days the boss takes ten, twenty, or thirty of his key people, including some from the ad agency and the controller's office, away to some secluded spot. On average they spend twelve hours a day asking unaskable questions, rethinking the business (What are we selling? To whom? At what prices? How do we get it to him? In what form?), four hours a day for relaxing and exercising, and eight hours a day sleeping. It's hard work. But more good marketing changes will come out of such meetings than out of any year-round staff department of "experts" with "marketing" signs on the door.[4]

This description is possibly a little exaggerated, but not in its insistence that "marketing is the name of the game" and the chief executive had better be intimately involved in marketing strategy and organization. *Up the Organization* might not be a recipe book that, if followed, automatically results in a super organization, but it does highlight some key management points. Dave Packard, cofounder of Hewlett-Packard, said that marketing is too important to be left to the marketing department, echoing this insistence on participation by the CEO.

If a marketing manager finds that top management is not participating sufficiently in marketing, he has a responsibility to investigate and rectify the problem; otherwise, his company will find it extremely difficult to join the ranks of the excellent. Of course, such a problem might exist because a CEO is unaware of how powerful his influence can be in the marketing process (including selling). If this is so, the marketing manager can greatly increase his measure of success by involving the CEO in marketing activities. Conversely, a good way to risk failure is for marketing managers to assume that they can solve whatever problems arise, without help from the top.

1.8 PLANNING AND THE MARKETING PROGRAM

Financial planning is an integral part of every company's activity. These plans are often three-year programs, with the first year considered to be a budget. Some companies, extend their plans to cover five-year programs.

The marketing department must play a central role in financial planning. Decisions about what new products are needed and what markets should be entered must be based on detailed examination of the company's strengths and weaknesses, market trends, and the competition. The objectives for each product line must be realistic and, at the same time, challenging. The objectives must also be quantified into forecasts for orders and sales as well as for resources needed (i.e., people and facilities). Comparing the cost of resources needed to income available from forecasted sales is an inevitably reiterative process.

Planning isn't everything, but without plans a marketing organization has nothing. When we talk about a marketing program, we are really talking about a set of actions consequent to a study of the marketing objective. The objective might be to supply Russia and the new Soviet republics with modern air traffic control equipment or to become the dominant supplier of shaker-control test instrumentation for India, for use in its space program. Whatever the goal, it must be an achievable objective that is consistent not only with the company's marketing strategy but also with its marketing program. Achieving and defending the desired market share requires more than good strategy and an enthusiastic, well-knit team; it requires a clearly defined set of actions.

William Davidow, who directed the marketing organization of Intel when it decided to become the world leader in the 16-bit microprocessor market, wrote a remarkable book entitled *Marketing High Technology—An Insider's View* [5]. In it he describes the clearly defined set of actions he undertook in a crucial campaign to "crush the opposition" and gain the dominant share of 16-bit microprocessors in the large, emerging PC market. The strongest opposition came from Motorola and Zilog, both with microprocessors that were in some ways superior to the Intel 8086. IBM's launch of the PC was imminent; when it came, IBM captured the biggest PC market share. The list of competitors poised to attack the market included firms that were much larger than Intel, such as Texas Instruments, Motorola, National Semiconductor, Philips, Siemens, NEC, Hitachi, and Fujitsu. There were others, including Zilog, a small but technologically advanced company.

When Davidow took over marketing responsibility for the 8086 family, he had to focus on the objective, which was to dominate the upcoming PC market. He put together a task force that examined, in a short time (days, not weeks), Intel's strengths and weaknesses. Following that, the task force had to decide on a plan of action. These are the weaknesses the task force found:

- A dispirited, demoralized team, accustomed to failing with customers;
- Strong opposition from Motorola and Zilog, each with better processors;
- Potential opposition from the giants in the industry;
- No management plan for achieving the objective, with time running out.

These are the strengths the task force found:

- A fine image as a technology leader;
- A more complete product family than their competitors, with advanced plans to enhance that line;

- Better performance at system level than competition when a number of devices were combined;
- A well-focused and superbly trained technical sales force (specialists, in contrast to the generalists in the Motorola sales force);
- Much better field support than Motorola, whose customers were experiencing difficulties in getting help to overcome problems with the chips.

A campaign was needed almost immediately or the competition would win. There was no time for the engineering department to develop new devices. The marketing department had to take the existing devices and "invent" the product.

This new "product" was a combination of the following:

- The 8086 16-bit microprocessor;
- The 8087 math floating point coprocessor;
- The peripheral circuits;
- Application notes on how to use the devices;
- Customer support from the marketing people;
- Software support;
- A catalog of future developments of the devices.

Refining the application notes and writing the "futures" catalog required a massive amount of work. The team decided that their objective had to be changed from achieving market leadership to crushing the competition; if they did that, they would automatically achieve their original objective. The organizers even called their campaign "crush the competition." The name spread like wildfire through the company. The marketing team spent hours discussing why some sales were lost to the competition and some were won. Gradually, enthusiasm crept into the team. They presented a strategy to the sales force that incorporated what was considered to be an extremely high goal: each sales representative had to make one sale per month. The team stressed to the sales force the importance of the strategy to the company's future, and the strategy earned the sales force's approval. Davidow stresses the importance of that approval; the strategy was not imposed on the sales force.

The rest of the story is history. Intel now has by far the largest market share, which they won with the 8086 and maintained with the 80286; the 32-bit 80386; the 32-bit 80486 processor, with its higher speed, built-in coprocessors (for the DX version); and the Pentium, a 486 successor with a 64-bit chip. (As of the date of this book, AMD, IBM, and Chips & Technology all produce versions of a 386 chip that eat into Intel's market share. In addition, some Intel competitors might come out with their own 486 chips.)

Intel is a good example, not only because it is one of the companies judged to be excellent by Peters and Waterman, but also because its marketing plan incorporated several of the attributes that characterize an excellent company. The plan

- *Favored action*, setting the objective and swinging into action in a short time to achieve it;

- *Respected the customer*, in sales, in service, in every imaginable way;
- *Encouraged autonomy and entrepreneurship*, inventing the product and developing the "crush the opposition" campaign;
- *Saw productivity in people*—the sales force was "sold" the campaign, it was not imposed on them;
- *Favored hands-on, value-driven practices*, with top management playing a direct part in the campaign;
- *Stuck to what they knew*—Davidow himself has a PhD in electrical engineering and specialized in microchips, and the entire sales and service force was composed of technical specialists.

Intel probably also possessed, at the time, a simple form and lean staff and simultaneously loose and tight properties—the final two of the eight attributes that Peters and Waterman believe characterize excellent companies. But the point here is that Intel's marketing strategy and marketing program were consistent with the common attributes of excellent companies.

1.9 ORGANIZATION

This section discusses the types of organizations that are engaged in international marketing. These companies can be technology driven, in which case they develop products that derive primarily from internal ideas and feedback from the market is of secondary importance, or they can be market driven, in which case feedback from the market assumes greater importance. They can also be either highly decentralized or highly centralized.

1.9.1 Organization Types

This section is derived largely from a book by Michael Z. Brooke entitled *Centralization and Autonomy: A Study in Organization Behavior* [6]. Figure 1.7, taken from the book, lists five types of organizations that operate foreign subsidiaries and indicates the degree of centralization found in each type. "Centralization" relates to the extent to which the organizations control subsidiaries from the home office.

1. *Direct.* Senior staff members of the home company have a direct relationship with the foreign subsidiary. The Swedish ball bearing firm SKF, which has the largest share of its market segment, is headquartered in Sweden. However, most of its operations are outside of Sweden, and SKF manufactures and sells its products from subsidiary companies all over the world. SKF has traditionally operated in this direct fashion. As Figure 1.7 indicates, companies of this type seem to operate with different degrees of centralization.
2. *Geographic.* Geographic managers are responsible for operations (including marketing) in their territories. Most of these companies operate with a medium

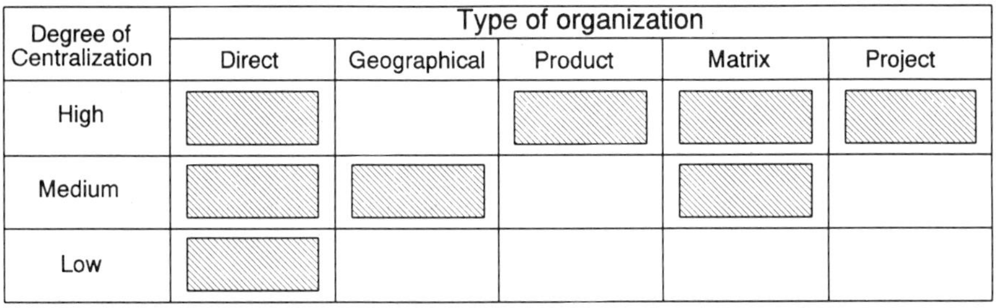

Degree of Centralization	Type of organization				
	Direct	Geographical	Product	Matrix	Project
High	▨		▨	▨	▨
Medium	▨	▨		▨	
Low	▨				

Figure 1.7 Organization types.

amount of centralization. A territory might include a number of countries in which key customers are multinationals.

3. *Product.* A product-line manager usually works in the company's home country, and the portion of the foreign subsidiary that markets the particular product line reports directly to the product-line manager. As can be expected, there is a high degree of centralization in this type of organization.

4. *Matrix.* Subsidiary managers are responsible for a range of the company's products in their geographic territory. They report to a regional manager who, in turn, reports to top management. Subsidiary managers do not report to a product-line manager, even though the product-line manager oversees marketing in their territories. There seems to be a tendency for high to medium centralization in these companies.

5. *Project.* These organizations are responsible for large projects, such as the design, manufacture, and sale of the Airbus. As can be expected, centralization is high.

Which type of organization is best fitted to the high-tech firm? Companies differ substantially from one another, and there is no simple answer. If the company is in a highly concentrated market sector, direct and product-based organization seem best, because these types of organization avoid some of the problems of geographic-based and matrix-based organization. Project-based organization is very specialized and is adaptable to few companies.

A company might start its foreign operations with a direct or product-based organization, and then migrate toward geographic-based or matrix-based organization as it diversifies. There is often a combination of the latter two—a geographic manager, responsible to the home company CEO, is placed in charge of a number of matrix-type subsidiaries.

In an article in the *Harvard Business Review*, Weichmann and Pringle include a list of problems that companies practicing geographic- and matrix-based organization might experience [7]. Table 1.1 summarizes these problems.

Another vexing problem not mentioned in Table 1.1 is the establishment of equitable transfer prices, or commissions, between product-line divisions and the subsidiaries. All of these problems result from decentralization and are the penalties companies must pay for

Table 1.1
Headquarters' and Subsidiary's Views of Problems

Key Problems—Headquarters' View	Key Problems—Subsidiary's View
Lack of qualified international personnel	Excessive control of procedure by headquarters
Lack of strategic thinking and long-range planning at the subsidiary level	Excessive financial and marketing constraints
Lack of marketing expertise at the subsidiary level	Insufficient utilization of multinational marketing experience
Too little relevant communication between headquarters and the subsidiary	Insensitivity of headquarters to local market differences
Insufficient participation of subsidiary in product decisions	Shortage of useful information from headquarters
	Lack of multinational orientation at headquarters

decentralization's advantages. Companies are likely to experience many of the problems, and the wise CEO will contain them by recognizing them and by ensuring frequent communication between product-line and subsidiary managers.

1.9.2 The Marketing Organization

In its simplest form, a marketing organization supports product-line managers. The product-line managers are responsible for every aspect of their product lines, from development, to manufacturing, to marketing, to finance. Marketing includes the following functions:

- Market research
- Financial control
- Technical support
- Sales
- Marketing management

1.9.2.1 Market Research

Without insight into its customers and its competitors, even high-tech firms can quickly lose touch with market needs. The whole marketing department need not devote all its attention to market research; however, the product-line manager must conduct research constantly, possibly with the aid of field sales and service engineers. They must constantly ask questions that reveal the quality standards of customers and the competition. Often, outside consultants can perform this research more effectively, by seeming to carry on "independent" surveys of customer opinion. Such surveys can help reveal company weaknesses, which might not be discovered easily by the company itself.

Products have life cycles and these life cycles are often reflected in annual sales over time. New products should emerge from a company at a rate that ensures that, as total sales for one product pass the peak and decline, total sales for a follow-up product are building. Market research plays a key role in the determination of what these products should be and when they should hit the market.

1.9.2.2 Financial Control

If it is a large department, the marketing organization often includes a section that is responsible for financial control. If the marketing organization is a subsidiary company, it always includes such a section. Unless the financial activities of a company are quantified, they cannot be measured easily. Financial control involves quantifying and forecasting budgets for financial activities and then, on a weekly or at least monthly basis, assessing budget forecasts against actuals. These financial components must be quantified and routinely measured:

- *Backlog*, that is, orders that have yet to be delivered;
- *Orders* for products, the lifeblood of the organization;
- *Sales*, or the delivery and invoicing of products ordered;
- *Gross margin*, which is the difference between the product price and product cost;
- *Expenses*, which include the administrative cost and sales cost of doing business;
- *Interest* paid on business loans;
- *Profit before tax*, or the difference between gross margin and the sum of expenses and interest.

1.9.2.3 Technical Support

Customer service is another vital aspect of marketing and provides both technical support to the sales force and installation, repair, and maintenance services to customers. Technical support for the sales force might include product demonstrations, presale resolution of customers' technical problems, and predelivery inspection of products. This technical support is a part of the expense of selling. The service department can also perform warranty repairs and, to do this, must maintain an adequate supply of parts and assemblies. Warranty repairs are normally charged back to the manufacturing organization, as are any installation costs.

Service departments can be very profitable. As the number of products sold in any country increases, so does the need for repair and maintenance. Quite apart from the fact that locally available service is of fundamental importance to customers, repair and maintenance contracts can be very lucrative. Likewise, a service department can often be a powerful stimulus to sales, particularly in multinational situations that involve great distances. Service representatives might have far more contact with customers than sales representatives and, therefore, might have opportunities to discuss new sales. (Service is such an important topic that some aspects are discussed further in Chapter 4.)

1.9.2.4 Sales

The sales department is possibly the most important function in a high-tech marketing organization. Usually, the sales force is well trained technically. (The sales function is covered at greater length in Chapter 4.)

1.9.2.5 Marketing Management

Marketing managers are responsible for coordinating the whole marketing effort. Together with the product-line managers, they set the objectives and decide on the strategies that will be used to achieve those objectives. With the help of the marketing team, they subdivide the objectives and strategies into manageable chunks. Then they manage the members of the team, who carry out the objectives. To be successful then, marketing managers must be good people managers. In many firms, marketing managers decide where, what, and when to advertise and which trade shows to participate in, basing these decisions on the chosen marketing strategy. Marketing managers also oversee special marketing campaigns (e.g., the "crush the competition" campaign).

A marketing department might include a market research specialist (if the firm deems that one is needed), a technical services manager, a financial services manager, and the key sales managers or sales representatives. If less than five employees report directly to the marketing manager, that manager is probably delegating too many responsibilities. On the other hand, it is doubtful that a manager can manage directly more than eight employees.

1.10 MULTINATIONALS

A discussion of multinational companies touches the core of the organizational issue, which relates to centralization versus decentralization and standardization of global marketing versus local control.

Tracing the typical evolution of a high-tech company from a relatively small domestic company to a multinational organization with sales and service subsidiaries and, possibly, manufacturing plants in many parts of the world facilitates an understanding of the concept of centralization. In the first phase, the young, technology-driven company sells its products only in its home country. When the company has established an important place in its market segment, management (or the product-line manager) decides to export some products. The company studies export markets, decides on certain territorial priorities, and tries to sell products by sending sales representatives to these territories or by using agents, distributors, or even export organizations located domestically.

The company might then subdivide the marketing department into domestic and export groups, though still maintaining both groups in its home country. If the company is successful in its exports, it will seek to build on this success and will probably establish a more widespread network of representatives (agents and distributors). Up to this point, company management maintains direct control over all phases of export marketing from its domestic base and, thus, operation is centralized.

In some countries, sales might grow until it becomes worthwhile to establish a wholly owned subsidiary, possibly to replace the representatives. If the company operates in a sharply defined market niche, the subsidiaries can continue to report to a domestically located export marketing group. The product-line manager will consider the subsidiary to be an extension of the domestic marketing group. Centralized control, in that instance, still makes good sense.

The subsidiary company, which might have been founded to serve one of the parent company's product-line divisions, can be expanded to serve other product-line divisions. Such expansion seems worthwhile; it can result in spreading the marketing costs over increased sales, thus increasing overall profitability. However, if there are several product ranges, each with its own product-line manager and marketing group, a problem arises. Does each product-line manager set up a representative or subsidiary? It does happen, when the product line is strong enough to represent a large portion of the company. Or should one representative or subsidiary handle all the product lines in one territory? If there is an export marketing manager, should the product-line managers funnel their requirements through that individual to the foreign representatives and the sales and service subsidiaries?

Product-line managers who have complete control of domestic and foreign marketing in early phases of the company's evolution will not want to relinquish control of foreign marketing. On the other hand, if there are several product-line managers, it is difficult to conceive of any organization in which they are all in charge. This dilemma leads to geographic- and matrix-based organization. The degree of centralization becomes largely dependent upon the central corporate role in moderating between the requirements of product-line managers and the geographic manager.

And what happens if, at a later stage in this evolution, the company decides to establish a joint venture, license a foreign manufacturer, or establish a manufacturing subsidiary? How much independence should a manufacturing subsidiary have? Should it be centralized, with a global approach to marketing whereby the company dictates products and policies? Or should it be decentralized, with a good measure of local control? These are not easy questions. However, true "globalization" certainly can lead to dramatic success, as noted below.

1.11 GLOBAL MARKETING

In *Multinational Marketing Management,* Buzzell and Quelch devote several chapters and a number of case studies to an analysis of global marketing [9].

Buzzell and Quelch define a *multinational* company as having substantial operations outside its home country. They define a *multidomestic* company as being a multinational company that pursues different strategies in different countries, with the different operations being essentially autonomous. A *global* company is a multinational company whose competitive position in one country is affected significantly by its position in another country and vice versa.

A global strategy is so powerful that multinational companies threatened by the global strategies of competitors must either modify their strategies or risk losing market share. As Buzzel and Quelch point out,

> An industry's pattern of competition usually does not evolve from multidomestic to global in a gradual fashion. Rather, one or a few competitors within the industry see an opportunity for market growth and so adopt a so-called global strategy to take advantage of it. They may design products/services to appeal to reasonably large market segments in some (or all) major national markets; mechanize their manufacturing or operations activities; set prices based on an expectation of rapid growth in output; and promote their offerings aggressively. This was the pattern of Japanese producers in a variety of industries during the 1970s and 1980s, including automobiles, motorcycles, microwave ovens, VCRs, cameras, television sets, and machine tools.
>
> In industries that shift from multidomestic to global, the established competitors usually find it difficult to respond to the challenge presented by the new competitive pattern. Often their response to the challenge is a pattern of de facto withdrawal from the market, one segment at a time. [8]

High-tech companies that operate with a global strategy include Siemens; General Electric; Mitsubishi, in heavy electrical equipment; L.M. Ericsson, in telecommunications; Sony, in entertainment products; Hewlett-Packard, in electronic instrumentation; and IBM, in computers. The global approach involves a substantial amount of centralization, even if the company establishes large manufacturing organizations in countries far removed from one another, like Sony did in Japan, the United States, Great Britain, and elsewhere. The design is common, the manufacturing and sales techniques are common, and even the advertising in various countries shares commonality. Another example of globalization is when the home company decides that one subsidiary should produce only part of or one product line, exchanging products or product lines with subsidiaries in other countries.

Jacques Maisonrouge, who retired as chairman of IBM World Trade in 1984, discusses the cost impact on IBM of shifting from multidomestic to global operation [9]. In *Inside IBM*, he explains how IBM rationalized production in Europe. After reorganization, each of its 14 factories had a specific role and manufactured one particular product for all markets in Europe, the Middle East, and Africa. Because product quantities were substantial, when duplication of production was eliminated, costs fell dramatically. Costs eventually fell until they were lower in Europe (in U.S. dollars) than in the United States. This is an excellent example of the power of a global approach.

Many subsidiary managers oppose attempts to centralize decision making. Country managers resent diminishing autonomy and nationalistic feelings are aroused. Some subsidiary managers argue that competitive conditions differ so much from country to country that global marketing is not practical. Even if the home office decides that it must change its strategy and organization to a global one, if a smooth transition is not planned, chaos can result. However, there are so many advantages to globalization that many industries adopt this approach. Buzzell suggests these advantages:

- Standardizing product design and manufacturing techniques offers substantial cost savings.
- Consistency in product style, sales, customer service, brand names, and packaging project a uniform image to customers and offer a powerful means of increasing sales.
- Multinational customers often insist that their suppliers standardize on products and even on prices and terms of sale.
- Good marketing ideas and people are hard to find and should therefore be used as widely as possible.
- Consistent, standardized advertising results in greater customer impact and lower costs.

1.12 INTERNATIONAL MARKETING AND COMPETITION

The advantages of marketing internationally attract many companies. Costs of international business are greater than costs of domestic business, but the advantages of economies of scale resulting from expanded sales might offset this. To be successful internationally, a company must adopt a strategy and form the type of organization that will give it some competitive advantage. We have seen how global marketing and a global organization can lead to this competitive advantage. A global company gains this advantage by integrating its worldwide activities. But what exactly do we mean by integration and what activities are integrated? Professor Michael Porter of the Harvard Business School has written extensively about this matter, and this section draws from some of his writings, in particular, *Competition in Global Industries* [10].

Porter uses what he calls a "value chain" to examine which activities of a company are integrated (Figure 1.8) [11]. Regardless of its organizational structure, a firm pursues a number of identifiable activities. For domestic companies, these activities all occur in one country. For international companies, the activities take place in a number of countries and they are not necessarily collocated in the same country.

The value chain in Figure 1.8 identifies nine activities, comprising the totality of the company. Five of the activities can be segregated as relatively independent and are termed "primary." Four additional activities support these five. Support activities comprise the firm infrastructure, which includes top management; the human resources department serves the entire organization, as does technology development and procurement.

The total cost of these nine activities amounts to the total cost and expenses of the entire company. What remains is its "margin," which any company seeks to maximize. In its international strategy, a firm tries to maximize that margin by gaining competitive edge, which results in a higher market share. Its approach to achieving this is to integrate the ac-

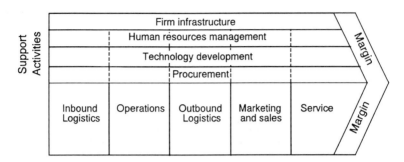

Primary activities

Figure 1.8 The value chain. *Source*: Michael Porter, *Competition in Global Industries*, Harvard University Press, 1986. Reproduced with permission.

tivities in some way. This integration involves both *configuration* issues and *coordination* issues (Table 1.2).

Table 1.2
Configuration and Coordination Issues by Category of Activity [12]

Value Activity	Configuration Issue	Coordination Issue
Operations	Location of production facilities for component and end products	Allocation of production tasks among dispersed facilities, networking of international plants, transferring of process technology and production know-how among plants
Marketing and sales	Product line selection, country (market) selection, location of advertising and promotion efforts	Commonality of brand name worldwide, coordination of sales to multinational accounts, similarity of channels and product positioning worldwide, coordination of pricing in different countries
Service	Location of the service organization	Similarity of service standards and procedures worldwide
Technology development	Number and location of R&D centers	Allocation of research tasks among dispersed R&D centers, interchange among R&D centers, development of products responsive to marketing needs in many countries, sequence of product introduction around the world
Procurement	Location of the purchasing function	Locating and managing suppliers in different countries, transferring knowledge about input markets, coordinating purchases of common items

The marketing activity can be partially centralized or completely centralized, as it is in some high-tech firms (e.g., aircraft), even when customers are located in other countries. Usually, however, marketing and sales efforts have to be located near the customer.

Apart from its location, marketing has a key role in international strategy. Porter and Takeuchi describe three roles of international marketing in global strategy [12]. Two are mentioned in Table 1.2. The first involves configuring marketing activities worldwide, the second involves coordinating these configurations, and the third involves establishing links between the configuration and coordination of other activities in the value chain.

How can marketing be configured in an international company? As noted earlier, marketing and sales activities usually occur close to customers. Competitive advantage results from the responsiveness perceived by customers when these activities are performed close to them. Is there any competitive advantage to be derived from centralizing marketing activities, other than in the special case in which there is partial or total centralization? The authors suggest six activities for which centralization would be advantageous.

1. *Central production of promotional materials.* While it is often necessary to adapt promotional materials to the language and cultural environment of a country, graphics, many publications, and video materials can be produced centrally with consequent economies of scale.
2. *Central sales force.* It is rarely the case that *all* selling can be done worldwide from one central location. Nevertheless, in a high-tech industry in which the technical complexity of the selling task is high, specialists from a central location can bolster the efforts of the local sales force.
3. *Centralized service support.* Especially in the case of high-tech firms, highly skilled, centrally located service engineers can travel to countries to supervise installations, resolve difficult service problems, and train local service people. In addition, an inventory of expensive parts, which is not economically justifiable for individual countries to possess, can be maintained at a central depot.
4. *Centralized training.* All training need not occur in one location, but the benefits of face-to-face contact cannot be overemphasized. Teleconferencing permits centralization; preparation of training materials can also be centralized.
5. *Global advertising.* There is probably no way to supplant the need for local advertising; however, global advertising in respected, internationally circulated publications can complement and augment local advertising.
6. *International marketing coalitions.* Medium- or long-term alliances can allow a firm into a market that is otherwise difficult (or even impossible) to penetrate.

Porter and Takeuchi suggest four ways that central coordination of international activities can provide competitive advantage:

1. *Employ similar marketing methods in different countries.* Common brand names, common service standards and warranties, standardized sales force training, and standardized distributor selection can all be centrally coordinated.

2. *Share knowledge across countries.* As an example, a centrally organized newsletter or routine meeting can disseminate marketing information.
3. *Sequence marketing programs.* Decisions about sequencing the introduction of new products to different countries can be centrally coordinated.
4. *Integrate efforts across countries.* A common example is the assignment of one marketing account executive to handle the accounts of an international company with branches in different countries.

Marketing links to nonmarketing activities are of particular importance to high-tech firms. Will a standard product be offered worldwide, regardless of national preferences? Such a move could promise powerful economic benefits. If the product has to be adapted to local requirements in some way, how can it be tailored to meet these requirements, while still maintaining a significant degree of standardization? Close links between marketing and international customers are required to answer these questions. In addition, the link between marketing, R&D, and production must be tight to ensure that products meet the needs of customers. There is an obvious need for integrating marketing activities on a worldwide basis, to achieve the competitive edge a company needs to capture a sizable portion of the market in its chosen segment.

1.13 HIGH-TECH VERSUS LOW-TECH MARKETING

Many high-tech marketers dismiss the idea that there could be commonality between high-tech and low-tech marketing. But, is there a difference between how high-tech and low-tech companies plan strategic approaches to the market or in how they approach such issues as market share, ecological view, market segmentation, product life cycle, and product portfolio? No mention was made of the degree of technology when we examined these issues. What then is the difference between high- and low-tech marketing? This question might not have an easy answer, and there is no consensus on a definition, but the technology industry does seem to agree on these general points:

- A high-tech industry has a much greater number of technical employees, and many more of those technical people are in marketing.
- There is a much tighter coupling of marketing and R&D in a high-tech industry.
- High-tech employees (including sales representatives) are often of a higher technical caliber than low-tech employees.
- The rapid pace of technological change results in much greater uncertainty about the high-tech market than the low-tech one, so that market forecasting tends to be more uncertain.

There can be a tendency for high-tech marketers to become so involved in the advanced technology that they forget some marketing fundamentals. These fundamentals include identifying the customer base, finding a market niche in which the needs of these customers are not met by the competition, specifying a product that will meet those needs, and determining the mix of product, price, promotion, and distribution.

The Macintosh computer, a high-tech product, provides a good illustration of how to balance technical knowledge with marketing principles. This example underscores the fact that it is not the high technology of a product that is important to its success, but the marketer's sound approach to the fundamentals of marketing. Regis McKenna tells the story very well in his excellent book *Relationship Marketing* [13]. The story concerns the problem Apple Computing faced in positioning the Macintosh computer in the marketplace, defining its functionality, and promoting its image.

Small computers had gained widespread acceptance in the financial community and were ubiquitous in accounting departments. Other sectors included a scientific and engineering market, an evolving home computer market, and an evolving word processing market. IBM dominated the PC market, and trying to obtain a relatively small share of that did not seem worthwhile. The Macintosh was designed to be very user friendly and, with a graphic user interface, it could have widespread appeal, especially in the creation of graphics. But in which market niche did it fit? Instead of simply trying to carve out a slightly larger share of the PC market, Apple went after a completely new market segment, which they called the "desktop publishing" market.

Up to that time, no one had conceived of a desktop publishing market, but advances in the graphics capabilities of computers and the potential of the computer to perform the tasks of traditional typesetters, along with the Macintosh's graphic orientation, made this new market a natural for Apple. Apple enlisted the software firm Adobe to create a product called PostScript, which converts computer-generated data into a language that describes the printed page for a laser printer. Enhanced by a laser engine from Canon, the Apple Laserprinter prints offset-quality documents that are created right on the user's "desktop" computer. A software package from Aldus called PageMaker further enhanced users' capabilities to design and produce professional documents, such as books, newsletters, and custom letterhead.

Corporate users who created brochures and reports could certainly use a system that allowed them to design and produce text and graphics quickly, easily, attractively, and economically. The desktop system eliminated the need to enlist typists, graphic artists, and photographers to assemble a publication; the computer could combine it all. That market niche certainly did exist, in almost any commercial enterprise or government office.

Apple made a powerful advance on the desktop publishing market—with widespread advertising, promotion at trade shows, seminars, and demonstrations—and soon achieved a significant penetration. In 1990 that market amounted to nearly $3 billion and Apple utterly controlled it.

1.14 SUMMARY

There are very few universal truths or strategies to guarantee international marketing success and, while we can identify a few organizational approaches, they must, of necessity, change from company to company, from country to country, and as technology continues to advance. Technological changes result in the obsolescence of products, manufacturing techniques, strategies, and organizational approaches and, consequently, companies, like empires, rise and fall. There is little doubt, however, that establishing a dominant position in a domestic market segment or niche, defending that position, and expanding internationally, or globally, if possible, is the correct objective to pursue.

REFERENCES

[1]   Thorelli, Hans, and Helmut Becker, *International Marketing Strategy*, revised edition, Oxford: Pergamon Press, 1988, pp. 5–20.

[2]   Henderson, Bruce D., *Henderson on Corporate Strategy*, Cambridge: Abt Books, 1979, p. 166.

[3]   Peters, Thomas J., and Robert H. Waterman, Jr., *In Search of Excellence*, New York: Harper and Row, 1982.

[4]   Townsend, Robert, *Up the Organization*, New York: The Free Press, 1987.

[5]   Davidow, William H., *Marketing High Technology—An Insider's View*, New York: The Free Press, 1986.

[6]   Brooke, Michael Z., *Centralization and Autonomy: A Study in Organization Behavior*, Holt-Rinehart-Winston, 1984.

[7]   Weichmann, Ulrich, and Lewis Pringle, "Problems that Plague Multinational Marketers," *Harvard Business Review*, 1979.

[8]   Buzzell, Robert D., and John A. Quelch, *Multinational Marketing Management*, Reading: Addison Wesley Publishing Company, 1988.

[9]   Maisonrouge, Jacques, *Inside IBM—The European Story*, London: Harper Collins, 1988.

[10]   Porter, Michael E., ed., *Competition in Global Industries*, Boston: Harvard Business School Press, 1986.

[11]   Porter, Michael E., ed., *Competition in Global Industries*, Boston: Harvard Business School Press, 1986, Part I, Chapter 1.

[12]   Porter, Michael E., ed., *Competition in Global Industries*, Boston: Harvard Business School Press, 1986, Part II, Chapter 4.

[13]   McKenna, Regis, *Relationship Marketing*, London: Random House, 1991, pp. 209–210.

Chapter 2

The Profit Impact of Marketing Strategy

Chapter 1 established the importance of the goals of achieving a high market share and keeping a company focused on doing what it knows. It also discussed the role of market segmentation in product life cycle and portfolio management and explored internationalization as a means of keeping ahead of the competition. It should be obvious that companies with high market share are more profitable, but is there a way to determine, qualitatively, the effect of market share on profitability? It should also be obvious that high-quality products are more saleable than low-quality ones, but the fact that quality affects profitability is not so obvious. Is there a way to determine, quantitatively, the effect of quality issues on profitability? Indeed there is, and the beauty of the measurement of the profit impact of marketing strategy (PIMS) is that it permits the profit impact of many factors to be explored in great depth.

The Strategic Planning Institute (SPI), in the United States, manages PIMS. The institute maintains an extensive database that covers the early 1970s through today and holds information about times of recession and times of expansion. That data has been gathered from approximately 3,000 strategic business units (SBUs) in the industrial sectors, consumer goods sectors, and service sectors of North American and Europe. Analyzing different combinations of PIMS data permits examination of the profit impact of a variety of marketing strategies. (Although company names are normally confidential, high-tech companies that have made their membership public knowledge include Westinghouse, Xerox, Philips, and Siemens, in the electronics field; General Electric and Montedison; and AT&T, GTE, and Wisconsin Bell in the service field.)

2.1 ORIGINS

The PIMS methodology originated in the 1960s as a result of work done at the large American corporation General Electric. Out of this work developed an economic model for management in highly competitive environments. The model, called the profit optimization model (PROM), was primarily intended to evaluate the effect of a number of factors

---

on the profitability of a business. In 1972 PROM was ceded to the Marketing Sciences Institute at Harvard University. This organization further developed the model with the help of a number of scholars, notably, Robert Buzzell, Bradley Gale, Ralph Sultan, and Sidney Schoeffler. The result was the renamed PIMS model.

In 1975 SPI, a nonprofit organization, was formed to gather and disseminate information about the PIMS methodology. Private organizations paid for access to the data; for academic research, access was free. In the late 1970s, SPI formed an industry consultant group called PIMS Associates. An affiliated but independent group was also formed in Europe, with offices in the United Kingdom, Sweden, Germany, Italy, and Austria. Today companies access the PIMS database through PIMS Associates, who also offer consulting services on such topics as benchmark setting, margin control, and strategies for industrial marketing, international marketing, productivity, and start-ups.

In 1987 Buzzell and Gale published a very lucid book entitled *The PIMS Principles* [1]. (Both authors are very active in SPI.) The principles derive from a study of the actual experiences of many businesses represented in the PIMS database. The authors set out to explain the strategic relationship of profitability and all the important factors that affect it. Interestingly, many of the effects of these factors are the same for just about any type of business. The authors were able, though, to compare similar businesses so that they could focus on the probable effects of choosing a particular strategy. Many but not all of the factors are closely related to marketing strategy; others are related to corporate strategy. The authors first explore the relationships statistically using PIMS data and then provide compellingly logical discussion of the rationale for these relationships.

Much of what follows is taken from *The PIMS Principles*. Many management experts believe that the PIMS principles for business strategy are so effective and consistent (not only those principles related to marketing) that they should be part of the basic education of any manager in a free-enterprise system.

2.2 THE PIMS DATABASE

The PIMS database holds information about the financial performance, market conditions, and competitive position of a large number of business units. A *strategic business unit* (SBU), in PIMS terminology, is a self-managed, strategic portion of a company. It is defined by the company's internal characteristics and competitive position in the market and by the product or service with which it is concerned. SBUs are often but not necessarily profit centers; consequently, a company might be composed of multiple SBUs, but PIMS data is maintained only for SBUs that are of financial consequence.

The SBU is a logical reference point for analyzing company performance. PIMS data includes financial extracts from the company on market position, competition, and the type and quality of products. The data is gathered from SBU general managers and management teams, who respond to extensive questionnaires. Then it is filtered and reworked in accordance with the PIMS methodology so it can be compared to SBU data from other companies. The PIMS questionnaire extracts information about:

- Products, services, customers, and relationships with other businesses;
- Financial results;
- Details about the market and the competition;
- Details that characterize the type of business;
- Forecasts for turnover, prices, and costs.

To ensure that the information is a reasonably accurate reflection of the SBU's situation, data is gathered over several years of operation. Experience with the database has shown that a period of four financial years is generally sufficient for this determination. Every SBU is defined by 200 factors, which can be grouped under these headings:

- Growth and innovation rates of the industry and its related markets;
- Market share of the SBU and its major competitors;
- How the SBU's products differ from those of its competitors;
- Capital structure of the SBU;
- Production processes of the SBU;
- Ratio of budget allocations to sales, R&D, marketing, etc.;
- Customer, channel, and supplier characteristics.

The validity of the choice of these factors for analysis has been verified empirically in thousands of recorded cases.

2.3 ANALYSIS TECHNIQUES

Strategic characteristics and financial results for the SBUs are stored in the PIMS databases. A multiple correlation method is used to select relevant data for analysis. The strategic characteristics are evaluated quantitatively. Their relative position at the time of analysis and the probability of variation are both measured. For example, these characteristics are measured for an SBU and for its principle competitors: 1) the index and variations in the index of product quality and 2) sales of new products as a percentage of total sales, as well as variations in the percentages [2].

How is performance measured? The object of the PIMS model is to relate performance to strategy and market factors. It uses such indicators as: return on investment (ROI), or the ratio of profit before tax and interest to investment; return on sales (ROS), which is the same index but as a ratio to sales; cash flow; and market capitalization. Of those indicators, ROI is possibly the most important.

But ROI by itself does not take account of long-term effects of a policy that favors short-term profit. For this reason, if the data is available, the "enhanced value" of an SBU at the end of a 7-year period is compared to its estimated book value at the end of a 2-year period. The fact is that short-term profitability and long-term value enhancement usually go together, which suggests that many of the strategic factors that improve short-term performance also improve long-term performance. To quote from *The PIMS Principles*,

Businesses with strong competitive positions, above-average employee productivity, and efficient use of assets tend to maintain and improve their high performance levels. Conversely, strategically weak businesses typically remain weak, at least over time spans of 7 years . . . [3]

2.4 OBJECTIVES

The principal objective of the PIMS model is to correlate SBU strategy and profitability. The vastness of the database permits correlations that combine a large variety of factors. For example, the relationship between market share, perceived product quality, and SBU profitability can be determined for strategically similar SBUs. With that information, the profit performance of the individual SBUs can be assessed. Figure 2.1 presents the actual configuration of the PIMS competitive strategy paradigm.

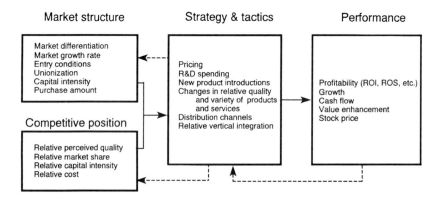

Figure 2.1 The PIMS competitive strategy paradigm. *Source*: Buzzell and Gale, *The PIMS Principles*, The Free Press, 1987. Reproduced with permission.

The diagram shows that market structure and competitive position guide SBU strategy and tactics, and strategy and tactics determine performance. The solid lines that connect the blocks in the diagram show direct effects, while the dashed lines show the regenerative relationship between the blocks. The relationships between all these factors are obtained statistically. In fact, PIMS database statistics show that profit is principally determined by

- The market situation (whether the market is growing, whether demand is growing, the stage of the product in its life cycle, the rate of inflation);
- The intensity of the investment;
- The competition (in particular, market shares and perceived product quality).

Any manager knows intuitively that these factors have an important influence on the SBU profit. The large amount of data that comprises the PIMS model allows quantitative relationships to be obtained for all these factors and the SBU profitability.

2.5 METHODOLOGY

The first step in the PIMS methodology is to isolate all the factors that influence economic results and increase the value of the business and, therefore, affect the expected profitability of the SBU. The second step consists of measuring how much these factors influence profitability and growth. To summarize then, the first two phases of the PIMS methodology are: (1) identify the factors that correlate positively or negatively to SBU performance and (2) measure the impact of each factor on performance.

PIMS data allows researchers to isolate the factors that influence, either positively or negatively the profitability and growth of an SBU. Data can be selected and measured consequent to certain choices. The analysis employs multiple linear regression to determine how all the factors combine to impact profitability. Thus it shows not only how certain factors influence profitability but also how the relationships of certain factors to each other exert influence.

High market share correlates positively to ROI. At a given market share, a given ROI can be expected, and marketing expenditures should reflect this market share. Spending too little can mean the objective of making the product known is not attained and the sales turnover forecast is not achieved. Excessive marketing expenditure, beyond achievement of the marketing objective, can only result in a worsening ROI. (A misdirected expenditure might bring no benefit at all; in this case, the effectiveness of the expenditure must also be evaluated.) The PIMS methodology takes into account the complexity of the combined effect of isolated factors.

Long-term analysis of PIMS data has identified three categories of important factors. These categories are: (1) the market structure, (2) the competitive position, and (3) the operating structure. Figure 2.2 details these factors. All the variables in these three categories in combination account for approximately two thirds of the differences (either in ROI or ROS) among PIMS businesses. Figure 2.3 shows the effect of market share.

The factors listed in Figure 2.2 can have positive or negative influence. Market share, perceived quality, plant productivity, and utilized capacity all have a positive correlation with ROI.

Achieving a high market share is an objective, not a strategy. What strategy should companies implement to obtain a high market share? Buzzell and Gale point out that a strategy based on improving product quality until the product is perceived by customers as being the best might be the best way of gaining top market share. Figure 2.4 shows the dramatic impact of high market share and quality on ROI.

Even if high quality correlated positively with ROI, high expenditures for marketing and other factors do not. (See Figure 2.5.)

Buzzell and Gale's analysis shows the effects of various factors on profit, and their explanation of these effects culminates in a useful set of general management principles.

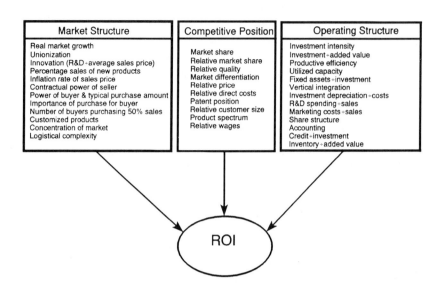

Figure 2.2 Structural factors that determine two-thirds of profit.

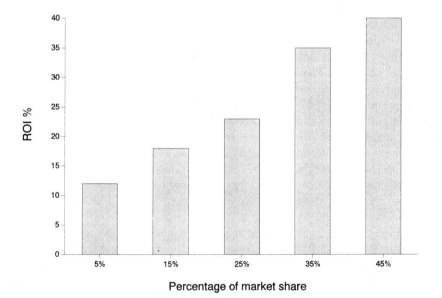

Figure 2.3 Market share versus ROI. *Source*: Buzzell and Gale, *The PIMS Principles*, The Free Press, 1987. Reproduced with permission.

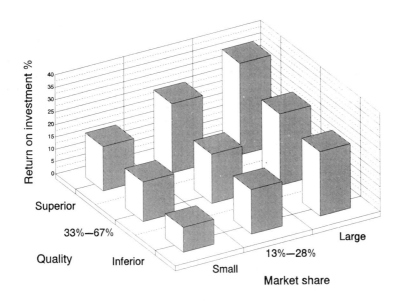

Figure 2.4 Quality, market share, and ROI. *Source:* Buzzell and Gale, *The PIMS Principles*, The Free Press, 1987. Reproduced with permission.

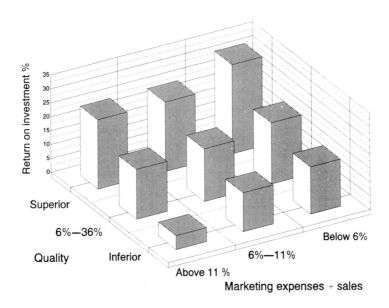

Figure 2.5 Quality, marketing expenses, and ROI. *Source:* Buzzell and Gale, *The PIMS Principles*, The Free Press, 1987. Reproduced with permission.

One interesting principle derives from analysis of the level of fixed capital on profitability. Many managers might imagine that high intensity investment (investing ahead of the market to establish preemptive capacity, increased use of robots to reduce labor costs, etc.) enhances profitability. Such investment sometimes pays, but the strongly negative correlation between the investment/sales ratio with ROI should encourage managers to analyze carefully the risks involved in increasing investment. Figures 2.6 and 2.7 show investment results for all businesses in the PIMS database.

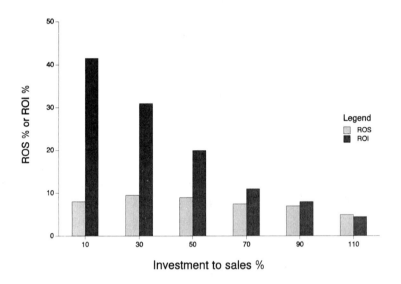

Figure 2.6 Negative effect of investment on ROI/ROS. *Source:* Buzzell and Gale, *The PIMS Principles*, The Free Press, 1987. Reproduced with permission.

Table 2.1 is an overview of relationships between a number of factors that influence market and industry profit and the impact of those factors on profitability.

2.6 SOME GENERAL PIMS PRINCIPLES

Analysis of the operating performance of many hundreds of SBUs does show that different types of businesses experience differences in the influences on profitability. In general, however, the primary profit influences, such as market share, relative quality, and capital intensity, affect almost all businesses in a similar way.

Managers might feel that their business simply cannot be analyzed in the same manner as others, because it is special in many ways. There certainly are exceptions, but research has shown that a general set of strategy principles govern most businesses. Some of the key linkages between strategy and performance derived from this research on the PIMS database are noted below. The linkages are general and, with some exceptions,

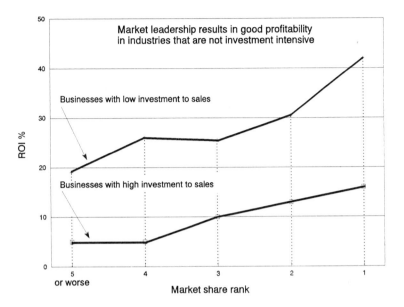

Figure 2.7 Capital intensity hurts profitability. *Source:* Buzzell and Gale, *The PIMS Principles*, The Free Press, 1987. Reproduced with permission.

apply broadly to all businesses. They cannot be used mechanistically, but can assist in focusing a study of any business. These linkages, set forth in *The PIMS Principles*, are [4]:

1. In the long run, the most important factor affecting a business unit's performance is the quality of its products and services, relative to those of competitors.
2. Market share and profitability are strongly related.
3. High investment intensity acts as a powerful drag on profitability.
4. Many so-called "dog" and "question mark" businesses generate cash, while many "cash cows" are dry.[1]
5. Vertical integration is a profitable strategy for some businesses but not others.
6. Most of the strategic factors that boost ROI also contribute to long-term value.

In contrast to less successful businesses, businesses that perform well and maintain long-term growth spend more on R&D and marketing, achieve higher quality levels, and maintain lower costs than competitors. A paper entitled "Perceived Veracity of PIMS Strategy Principles in Japan," presented a list of strategies, most of which both Japanese and American executives agreed apply to their countries [5]. The strategies included:

- First entrants in the marketplace will have higher levels of ROI.

---

1.   PIMS includes many more variables than growth rate and market share.

Table 2.1
Market/Industry Profit Influence

Market/Industry Influence on Profitability; an Overview of Major Relationships	*Impact on Profitability*	
	ROI + or −	*ROS + or −*
Real market growth rate (annual %)	+	+
Stage of market evolution:		
• Growth stage	+	+
• Decline stage	−	−
Rate of inflation in selling prices	+	+
Typical customer purchase amount:		
• Small	+	+
• Large	−	−
Importance of product purchase to customer		
• Low	+	+
• High	−	−
Percentage of employees unionized	−	−
Standard products (versus custom products)	+	+

Competitive Position, Strategy, and Profitability		
Market share	+	+
Relative product/service quality	+	+
New products, % of sales	−	−
R&D expense, % of sales	−	−
Marketing expense, % of sales	−	−
Newness of plant and equipment	+	+
Labor productivity	+	+
Inventories, % of sales	−	−
Capacity utilization rate	+	+

Source: Buzzell and Gale, *The PIMS Principles*, The Free Press, 1987.
Reproduced with permission.

- Firms with higher levels of market share are more profitable.
- Firms with higher levels of *relative* market share (defined as a firm's share in comparison with the combined market share of the three largest firms in the market) are more profitable.
- Low market share firms must offer high value to achieve profitability.

- Late entrants into a market must offer high levels of value (quality for the price) to achieve high profitability.
- New products (introduced in the last three years) improve profitability.
- Firms that introduce new products gain in profitability if they were in a strong market position to begin with, otherwise not.
- Firms with marketing programs shared by two or more business units are profitable.
- Firms with sales to customers by more than one unit of the company are profitable.

2.7 THE STRATEGIC BUSINESS UNIT AND PAR ROI

An important feature of the PIMS model is that it can be used to evaluate the probable evolution of a specific type of business. Knowledge of the characteristics of a business, combined with knowledge of the competitive situation and market characteristics, make possible a prediction of the "normal" profitability of an SBU. By combining all the factors known to significantly influence ROI and assigning specific values for a particular business, speculators can determine the profit that business should realize can be determined. This profit is defined in PIMS as the "par ROI." Figure 2.8 shows a graph of actual versus par ROI.

Par ROI is not the average ROI of a business sector, nor is it the average ROI in the database; it is the ROI that a business should achieve, given its structure and competitive position and taking into account the characteristics of its market. Par ROI, therefore, is an important benchmark for a firm; it identifies a reasonable business result and permits realistic forecasting. Companies should use actual versus par ROI results to validate the internal consistency of financial and strategic data and to confirm market definition.

If the data was correctly determined in terms of the market share, quality, competitive position, etc., then, if an SBU has a substantial gap between actual ROI and par ROI, its manager should explain the difference, and intervene with corrective measures.

Figure 2.8 provides several interesting observations. The actual ROI and par ROI of business 2 are equal; however, the profitability is low, and the business might have to be repositioned to obtain a higher return. On the other hand, business 3 has a high par ROI but a low actual ROI. Internal and competitive characteristics favor increased profitability. In this case, increasing the operating effectiveness might be required to accelerate the conversion of actual ROI to potential ROI. Business 1 might have the least optimistic future. It seems to be earning a higher profit than warranted, but the prediction is that this profit will slide downward. In this case, the intervention might have to be a change in strategy.

2.8 COMPARING SBUs: STRATEGIC LOOK-ALIKES

A principal feature of the PIMS model is its diagnostic capability. In addition, because it can reconstruct the winning strategic paths of profitable SBUs, the model permits compa-

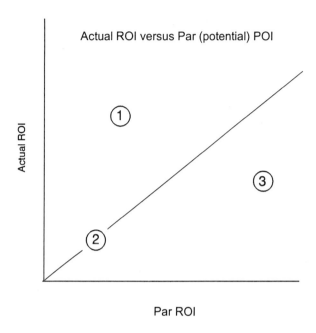

Figure 2.8 Actual versus potential, or par, ROI. *Source*: Buzzell and Gale, *The PIMS Principles*, The Free Press, 1987. Reproduced with permission.

nies to base their strategy plans on the successes of similar businesses. In other words, it allows companies to identify "strategic look-alikes." Figure 2.9 illustrates the process of look-alike selection. The businesses defined as strategic look-alikes face the same strategic problems, particularly in the following areas:

- Market segment
- Market growth
- Quality/price ratio
- Channels of distribution
- Amount of marketing expenditure
- Capital intensity and application
- Productivity
- Degree of vertical integration

A company might, for example, define its strategic look-alikes as possessing these characteristics:

- Factors concerning customers are similar in terms of needs, volume of purchases, channels of distribution, and type of promotion;

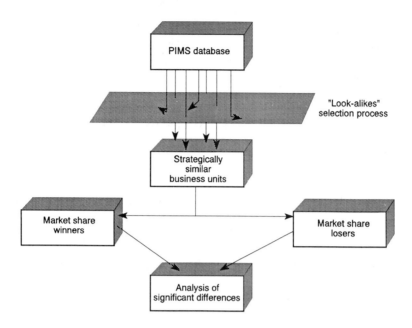

Figure 2.9 Look-alike analysis. *Source*: Buzzell and Gale, *The PIMS Principles*, The Free Press, 1987. Reproduced with permission.

- Factors concerning material purchases are similar in terms of volume and cost, the effect of inflation on costs, the ratio of material purchases to sales, and relations with suppliers;
- Factors concerning production are similar in terms of mix and capital intensity, plant productivity, and plant utilization.

Once strategic look-alikes are identified, their chosen strategy and resulting performance can be analyzed. Benchmarks can be formulated to measure financial profiles. Par ROI can be compared to actual ROI. The factors that determine the relative success of the strategies chosen by the strategic look-alikes can be identified.

2.9 THE COURSE OF ACTION SUGGESTED BY PIMS

Effective use of the PIMS methodology calls for a sequence of actions.[2] The first phase involves analyzing the actual financial performance of the SBU. The second phase involves

2. PIMS is one analysis method companies can employ to resolve marketing issues. The empirical nature that characterizes the PIMS model differentiates the method from other analysis methods. For a comparison of analysis methods, see *Strategic Market Planning* by D. F. Abell and J. S. Hammond, Prentice-Hall, 1979.

determining what the normal profit (par ROI) of the business should be. The third phase should be an analysis of strategic look-alikes, which will determine the potential of the SBU and, hopefully, uncover some winning strategic moves. The fourth phase is development and implementation of a plan of action.

2.10 THE RELATIONSHIP BETWEEN BUSINESS FACTORS AND PROFIT

PIMS data suggests that several business factors have a strong effect on profitability. These factors include:

- The (real) rate of growth of the market and its evolution (age of the products, stage in the product life cycle);
- The rate of inflation of sales prices;
- The degree of concentration of suppliers;
- The importance of the product for the client and the average value of the individual purchase;
- The degree of unionization.

The PIMS model can simulate the weight of each of these factors on the profit level. The resulting effects are grouped for three business types: attractive, average, unattractive. Table 2.2 shows the effects of the factors in more detail.

Analysis of these three business types (with all unlisted strategic factors fixed at an average level) shows an enormous expected ROI difference of 25%. A business operating in an unattractive market sector might have an ROI of approximately 10%, while a business in an attractive market sector might have an ROI of approximately 35%. The biggest differences are in the average value of individual purchases. This might be because higher priced products are often the subject of intense competition and customer bargaining, with consequent effect on SBU margin. The next biggest difference is in unionization. Unions might bring many benefits to their members, but they also depress profitability.

Section 2.5 discussed product quality or, more precisely, *product quality as perceived by the customer*. The pursuit of quality is an essential ingredient for success. The concept of quality, about which there is much debate, might seem vague and not easily measurable, but the PIMS model actually provides a method for analyzing and quantifying product quality. It is possible, for every product, to construct a chart that contains all the variables that can influence purchase. These variables are defined, via questionnaire, by SBU management teams. Based on their answers, products receive a score. The teams are also asked to evaluate competitive products. All the information is used in a comparison of competing product prices (see Figure 2.10).

As Figure 2.11 illustrates, most products cluster around a diagonal line, which represents a sort of elastic measure of demand in terms of the price/quality ratio. Comparison of the SBU team evaluations to actual prices allows identification of a position (on the graph) for every product.

Table 2.2
Combined Effect of Market/Industry Factors on Profitability

Factor	Unattractive		Average		Attractive	
	Level	Impact on ROI (%)	Level	Impact on ROI (%)	Level	Impact on ROI (%)
Market growth rate (%)	−4	−1.2	4	0	11	1.1
Inflation rate (%)	4	−1.0	8	0	12	1.0
Purchases from top 3 suppliers (%)	7	−0.8	42	0	70	0.8
Unionization (%)	75	−2.4	42	0	0	2.9
Purchase importance (%)	5+	−3.0	1–5	0	<1	1.8
Purchase amounts	$10K+	−4.0	$1–10K	0	<$1K	5.2
Exports:imports	0:6	−0.4	5:3	0	10:0	0.7
Total impact (%)		−12.6		22.4		13.5
All other profit influences (%)		22.4		22.4		22.4
Expected ROI (%)		9.6				35.9

Source: Buzzell and Gale, *The PIMS Principles*, The Free Press, 1987. Reproduced with permission.

Figure 2.10 Relative price versus relative quality. *Source*: Buzzell and Gale, *The PIMS Principles*, The Free Press, 1987. Reproduced with permission.

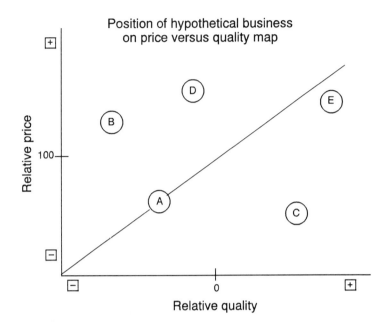

Figure 2.11 Position of hypothetical business on price versus quality map. *Source*: Buzzell and Gale, *The PIMS Principles*, The Free Press, 1987. Reproduced with permission.

The products that fall along the diagonal possess reasonable price/quality ratios. A position higher than the diagonal represents relatively low quality at a relatively high price. A position below the diagonal and to the right represents, to the customer, a very attractive product. This diagram can help an SBU understand the reason for low order intake and identify the need for product or price improvement.

Enterprises that offer what customers perceive to be superior quality derive a series of advantages, including: strong customer loyalty; less vulnerability to price wars and, hence, the chance to ask a higher price without losing market share; lower marketing costs; and a higher market share.

A concentrated effort on quality improvement can give rise to a chain reaction. Improved quality results in higher market share, which, in turn, increases the productivity of investment and of employees. This means that relative marketing expenses are reduced (as are production costs, as a result of economies of scale), which results in lower product costs. Since customers are willing to pay a higher price for higher quality products, the double impact on profitability can be very significant.

2.11 PORTFOLIO MANAGEMENT

Figure 2.8 showed how par ROI can be plotted against actual ROI. Companies that possess multiple SBUs might find it useful to plot the position of each SBU on one graph. Well-positioned clusters would fall in the upper portion of the diagonal, where the ROI is greatest. These companies might also wonder if there are particular strategic moves they can make to facilitate upward migration of SBU clusters. Companies can, in fact, evolve strategies for creating sustainable competitive advantage in their market segments. If a company's SBUs can be synergistic and reinforce one another, their product costs can be lower, their quality higher, and their market share greater. How can SBUs be synergistic? The following are some strategies that a company's SBUs can adopt to ensure synergism:

- Share resources, such as R&D, production, procurement, and common sales forces, to achieve scale economies;
- Exploit indirect benefits from the marketing and R&D expenditures of sister SBUs (e.g., General Electric research into turbines helped its aircraft engine business);
- Share technical and managerial skill, especially in high-tech industries, where specialized marketing skills are needed;
- Share perceived high quality images with sister SBUs.

Evaluating PIMS data can help companies assess the potential for synergy between SBUs and, indeed, might suggest related start-up businesses that can take advantage of synergy.

2.12 PIMS AND GLOBAL STRATEGY

The market share and the relative size of the served market have a major influence on the SBU profitability and are therefore primary growth objectives. A company can pursue these objectives by choosing a market that is well suited to its structural characteristics and output. A combination of economic good sense and statistical analysis of PIMS data can help in the choice of suitable markets.

If a company pursues a strategy whereby its competitive situation in one country affects its situation in another country, its outlook becomes global. A company that moves toward a global market is driven by various forces. These include market, cost, and environmental and competitive factors (see Figure 2.12).

Market factors include homogeneous market needs, the existence of global customers and global channels of distribution, and transferable marketing skills. Cost factors include economies of scale in production, amortization of the learning curve over a larger market, increased efficiency of sourcing, logistics of sourcing and distribution, lower labor or material costs in a geographic area, and lower development costs in a geographic area. Environmental factors include favorable trade policies, with respect to customs duty or export credits, together with compatible technical and marketing standards. Competitive factors include competitive interdependence among countries or matching (or even preempting) competitor moves.

Global companies link industries in different geographic locations, concentrating one part of the production chain in one country and other parts of the chain in other countries. They benefit from significantly increased production, with attendant economies of

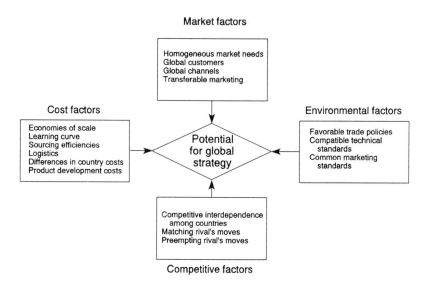

Figure 2.12 Global market drivers. *Source:* Strategic Planning Institute.

scale and shortened lines of communication (as discussed in Chapter 1). A global strategy is thus very powerful. Questions that companies moving toward a global strategy should ask themselves include:

(a) What is the best strategy for the company's characteristics?
(b) What markets can really interest the business?
(c) How should the product be presented in different countries?
(d) How should international policies be coordinated?
(e) What are the competitive levers most suited to the company?
(f) What are the benefits and costs? What are the risks and opportunities?

PIMS can assist companies in answering these questions. PIMS data, combined with analysis of companies operating in different geographic markets, can aid delineation of a global strategy. But, ultimately, the answers that companies give to the subsequent questions help them to answer question (a). The PIMS model can help companies answer question (b). The motivation, or driver, for internationalization guides the search for this answer (see Figure 2.12). If the motivation is competitive, choice of a market should be dictated by the moves of competitors, though without undervaluing economic perturbations or future growth (question (f)). If the motivation is a cost driver, PIMS can help carve the competitive area into one in which such internal factors as capacity, competence, and knowledge can be usefully managed. If the motivations are drivers from the market or the environment, these factors should be investigated in detail.

Whatever the driving force, as soon as the market of interest is identified, the company should gather all information about local conditions, needs of the customers, culture, traditions, and existing local competition. This information should be assessed in light of the company's capabilities. Again, PIMS data can help delineate the potentialities of a company moving toward globalization, and study of strategic look-alikes lends realism to the evaluation. The vast accumulation of PIMS information is very useful tool in decision making, especially in a global marketplace.

2.13 SUMMARY

Chapter 1 discusses the importance of a number of topics leading to selection of a suitable market strategy. These include high market share, the product life cycle, portfolio management, and multinationals and global marketing. Chapter 2 shows how these related factors (and others) impinge upon the ultimate financial goals of a company, and what the qualitative results of their interaction could be. PIMS is one of many tools that can aid a company in marketing strategy, albeit a very powerful one.

The subject of channels of distribution, which is touched on briefly in this chapter, is explored more fully in Chapter 3.

REFERENCES

[1]   Buzzell, Robert D., and Bradley T. Gale, *The PIMS Principles*, New York: The Free Press, 1987.
[2]   Buzzell, Robert D., and Bradley T. Gale, *The PIMS Principles*, New York: The Free Press, 1987, Appendices A and B.
[3]   Buzzell, Robert D., and Bradley T. Gale, *The PIMS Principles*, New York: The Free Press, 1987.
[4]   Buzzell, Robert D., and Bradley T. Gale, *The PIMS Principles*, New York: The Free Press, 1987, pp. 7–15.
[5]   Kotabe, Duhan, Smith, and Wilson, *The Journal of Marketing*, Vol. 55, No. 1, pp. 26–41.

Chapter 3

Channels of Distribution

Channels of distribution for selling products into foreign markets are limited. This chapter examines these channels and lists some of the problems and advantages associated with them. The channels are

- Direct export;
- Selling through distributors or agents;
- Selling through a wholly owned subsidiary company in the foreign territory;
- Selling through a joint venture.

Licensing a third party in the foreign market is another possibility, discussed in the section on joint ventures.

3.1 FINANCIAL CONSIDERATIONS

A company should choose the distribution channel that will enable it to maximize long-term incremental profitability. One measure of that profitability is incremental ROI, or the incremental return on investment for incremental sales. For the purpose of this discussion, incremental ROI is defined as the difference between a company's ROI with and without export sales. The incremental return is the difference between the operating profit with and without these export sales. (For a more complete discussion of financial considerations, see Appendix C.)

Companies selling to foreign markets have to invest in increased assets for export sales, and there are also expenses associated with sale of the products. The end result should be an incremental operating profit (return) whose ratio to the total company investment is maximized. Table 3.1 quantifies these financial considerations. The table summarizes a number of income statement and balance sheet items for each of the four distribution channels. Note that the table begins with sales (in the foreign territory) and ends with the incremental ROI. It is the last item that a company seeks to maximize.

Table 3.1
Financial Considerations for Export Channels

Item	Direct Export	Agent or Distributor	Owned Subsidiary	Joint Venture
Incremental sales	100	250	1,000	1,500
Gross margin	60	150	600	900
Home expenses	5	15	15	15
Foreign expenses	25	63	250	325
Foreign profit/loss	–	–	0	0
Total expense	30	78	265	340
Gross margin minus total expense	30	72	335	560
Operating profit, no export	200	200	200	200
Total operating profit	230	272	535	760
Home investment	1,000	1,000	1,000	1,000
Foreign investment, less A/R	0	0	100	1,000
Foreign A/R	25	63	250	375
Total investment	1,025	1,063	1,350	2,375
Total ROI	22.4%	25.6%	39.6%	32.0%
Incremental ROI	2.4%	5.6%	19.6%	12.0%

Table 3.1 illustrates a useful exercise for companies evaluating the different channels of distribution, although it is useful only to the extent that the various parameters can be estimated with any accuracy. Once a channel of distribution has been decided and sales statistics determined, this accounting exercise can be performed with more precision—regrettably, after the choice is made. Before that choice is made, companies should, at the very least, make their best estimates concerning the likely choices. This is particularly important for companies that are considering replacing a foreign representative with a wholly owned sales and service subsidiary.

(Note that this discussion does not take into account the "opportunity cost" of investment, i.e., the cost resulting from the fact that the investment in foreign distribution *might* have been used elsewhere, possibly producing a higher ROI. This consideration is outside the scope of this discussion, but should be examined by top management before the investment is made.)

Calculation of the elements listed in Table 3.1 will provide the incremental ROI that results from foreign sales. We shall assume, for the purposes of this example, that the operating profit without foreign sales is 200 and the investment without foreign sales is 1000, so that the ROI with no foreign sales is 20%. We shall assume also that the gross margin is always 60%.

Home marketing expenses vary considerably for the different channels. For example, if the channel is direct export through the purchasing agency of the foreign client or an exporting company located in the home territory, expenses might be low. If no other channel of distribution exists, the company might decide to send its sales representatives to the foreign country despite the high expenses.

Expenses for most channels of distribution also vary, but a figure of 25% of sales is probably a pretty good guess. For the sake of convenience, let us guess that 25% of the sales price is reasonably close to the foreign marketing expense. If the channel of distribution is a wholly owned subsidiary or a joint venture company, the company might make a profit on sale and service of the mother company's products or might lose money. Upon consolidation of that company's income statement with that of the mother company, that profit or loss must be accounted for. In Table 3.1, it is assumed that this company has neither profit nor loss in the sale and service of the mother company's products and, for the sake of this accounting exercise, this amount (foreign profit/loss, zero in our case) is considered an overall marketing expense.

There are two portions to the incremental investment. One portion is associated with the increased company assets needed to create the foreign company, and this only occurs in the case of the wholly owned subsidiary or the joint venture. Neglecting any inventory, most of the other portion is associated with the increase in assets (and therefore investment) due to the accounts receivable (A/R) resulting from sales. For the sake of this exercise, we shall assume that A/R are equivalent to three months of sales, that is, 25% of the annual sales volume.

The total ROI is given by the total operating profit divided by the total investment, foreign plus home. Subtracting from this total ROI the 20% ROI for domestic sales, we obtain the incremental ROI. Approximate as they are, with a given sales volume, it is not too difficult to estimate the figures needed to arrive at the "bottom line," that is, at the incremental ROI. But what is the sales volume with various channels of distribution? This is not too easy to estimate, but crude "guestimates" can and should be made in preparing a plan for foreign sales. Should the expenses involved in any channel of distribution be too high, then the incremental ROI could even be negative. It is possible that several or all of the incremental ROIs are negative, but the company might still decide to pursue foreign sales. In this case, the maximum incremental ROI is probably still the best choice.

From the figures in Table 3.1, it might be concluded that the subsidiary is the correct channel to choose. The foreign sales turnover does increase from channel to channel as suggested, but the incremental ROI might not necessarily follow this pattern. Furthermore, there might not be an option available for the establishment of a subsidiary or joint venture. There might even be other long-term considerations that lead the company to change the choice from that determined above. Let us examine the various options more carefully.

3.2 DIRECT EXPORT

This channel requires the least investment, but probably also yields the least amount of incremental sales and incremental ROI. Nevertheless, it is a relatively painless way of selling into foreign countries. Direct export involves selling directly into the foreign territory without the use of intermediaries. This can be done from the company's home country through such activities as advertising, attending trade shows, and making direct visits. Direct export can also be accomplished via purchasing organizations, which many foreign customers maintain in major western countries. In the case of military equipment, this could be to the foreign country's military attaché. Large military systems are often sold in this manner.

Another form of direct export, often chosen by small companies, is an exporter located in the home country. That exporter will have contacts in the foreign country and might purchase directly from the company's marketing group, attending to all the export and credit arrangements and collection of the accounts receivable.

A key problem in direct export is the inability of the company to provide service for it's products in the foreign country. Another problem is the limited exposure the company has for sale to foreign customers. Still another problem is the difficulty of communications between foreign customers and the company, a problem that can be resolved if the customers can deal with representatives in their own countries. These problems can be serious enough to limit sales growth. The annual sales for the direct export channel shown in Table 3.1 was deliberately made a relatively small amount to highlight this limit, although in special cases the small annual sales suggested for this channel of distribution might be misleading.

3.3 AGENTS AND DISTRIBUTORS

The terms agent and distributor are often treated loosely in discussions about foreign representatives. For the purpose of this discussion, an *agent* is a person (or organization) who receives a commission as compensation when a sale is effected. The sale actually occurs between the company and the foreign customer. The company takes the credit risk and collects receivables from the foreign customer. A *distributor*, on the other hand, purchases the company's product, marks up the price, and sells the product directly to the foreign customer. The distributor takes the credit risk and collects receivables from the foreign customer. In this case, the company sale is between the company and the distributor. Also for the purposes of this discussion, *foreign representative* is used to refer to either agents or distributors and either a single individual or an organization.

Most companies use agents or distributors in foreign countries to further their sales efforts. There are no fixed costs associated with this channel of distribution, because all expenses are borne by the agent or distributor. When the value of a sale is substantially higher than the net worth of the foreign representative, that representative usually acts as an agent. In countries that enforce fiscal currency control regulations or have a high import duty tax, the representative might be constrained to be an agent, and the customer must arrange for importation and pay the duty. That agent might still act as a distributor when, for example, the local representative is required to purchase and maintain an inventory of spare parts. The same legal contract can be used for both situations, as explained later.

Customers might prefer to deal with a distributor rather than an agent. Payment terms are often much more stringent if the customer's contract is directly with the company, and the company might also insist on a letter of credit to be exercised at the time of shipment. If customers are substantially bigger than the distributor, they can impose their own payment terms, withholding payment until their expectations for the product are met.

3.3.1 Finding a Foreign Representative

Mistakes made in choosing a foreign representative to act as an agent or distributor can be expensive. In many countries, terminating a representative can result in costly legal claims, even if the contract appears to allow termination with only a small compensation to the representative. A poor choice can also damage a company's reputation and result in lost business opportunities and wasted training efforts. On the other hand, a good choice of foreign representative can help a company increase exports substantially. How then does one find a good foreign representative?

- *First, check existing files.* Several good leads might have been filed away because the company was not ready when the prospective agent or distributor wrote.
- *Look in trade directories and yellow pages.* Today, trade directories are available for every country in the world, and most major cities have yellow page listings for key businesses. (Appendix A supplies some sources from which a company can compile a mailing list tailored to its needs.)
- *Attend international trade shows.* In addition to providing an easy and important way for companies to promote their products overseas, shows are good places to find agents and distributors.
- *Advertise in local papers.* Though slightly more expensive, this is a very effective method.
- *Try industry associations and trade journals.* Almost every industry has an association and associations often have foreign members. Trade journals are often mailed to foreign readers, hence, mailing lists are available from the publishers. In addition, competitors or manufacturers of complementary products often advertise in trade journals, providing useful lists of foreign representatives.
- *Query the international chamber of commerce.* Virtually every country possesses a chamber of commerce. Many publish newsletters, and these might print business opportunity listings.
- *Enlist the aid of an international banks.* Many banks today offer consulting services in international trade and/or can be cultivated to initiate contacts with potential agents and distributors in foreign countries.
- *Hire a consultant.* Such companies as Frost & Sullivan, Dun & Bradstreet, and Business International offer consulting services for identifying agents and distributors. Services are also available from leading consulting companies and accounting firms.
- *Participate in a trade mission.* Many governments organize trade missions to foreign countries.
- *Query your foreign-based embassy.* Commercial attaches can be helpful in providing lists of candidates and, sometimes, opinions about them.

- *Talk to customers.* Sales representatives can ask customers in the territory about the preferred foreign representatives.
- *Talk to colleagues.* Colleagues in associated but noncompeting industrial organizations might have advice about finding leads in the country.

3.3.2 Important Criteria for Selecting a Foreign Representative

In addition to knowing how to find foreign representatives, companies must know how to recognize *good* foreign representatives. The following questions will aid that selection:

- Is the prospective representative well connected, especially with the key customers, and respected in the community?
- Is there a key individual within his organization—someone (whom we'll call the "champion") who possesses the necessary technical expertise, can be trained, and can be relied on to further your sales objectives?
- Does the prospective representative know your company's products and the market for your products and have positive ideas about how to penetrate that market?
- If you plan to subcontract work (e.g., civil works or the supply of prime power, telephone, or water), can the prospective representative find the most qualified local organizations available to do the work?
- Does the prospective representative have the required financial resources? A service organization that can maintain your products? A reliable means of communication (e.g., fax, telex, e-mail, answering service), especially for remote time zones?
- Does the prospective representative have the managerial capabilities necessary to fulfill his obligations?
- How long has the representative's organization been in business? How many people does it employ? A large company may not always be the best: your products can be buried in a pile of other products they cannot sell because "the price wasn't right"!
- How eager is the prospective representative to sell your products? Is it just that your logo will look good on the representative's letterhead?
- Is the prospective representative willing to set sales goals with you?

It is always wise to poll some prospective customers before selecting a particular foreign representative. As in most cases in which references are sought, more than one source should be consulted. After narrowing the choice, the company's representative (often a member of the sales force) should conduct indepth interviews of candidates.

3.3.3 What Foreign Representatives Must Do for Companies

Effective foreign representatives must perform these tasks:

- Create a marketing plan;
- Provide competitive information;

- Provide market research data;
- Offer after-sales service, if necessary;
- Advertise and promote the products in a manner that is consistent with your company's approach;
- If a distributor, continue to be a good credit risk; if an agent, assist in collection efforts;
- Participate in trade shows;
- Attend sales meetings.

3.3.4 What Companies Must Do for Foreign Representatives

Companies that employ foreign representatives also have a responsibility to support and manage them. Duties include:

- Provide catalogs, technical manuals, etc.;
- Provide technical training and assistance;
- Provide sales training and assistance;
- Organize periodic sales meetings;
- Set yearly sales quotas.

3.3.5 Motivating Foreign Representatives

Foreign representatives will continue to sell your products only if they realize profits; hence, they must be motivated to develop business for mutual advantage. Possible incentives include:

- *Commissions and discounts.* Offering reasonable commissions or discounts suggests to representatives that they can make more money for themselves and, therefore, your company.
- *Sales meetings.* Paying for overseas representatives to attend sales meetings is expensive but worth considering.
- *Training.* Foreign representatives should receive training comparable to your own sales force.
- *Support.* Paying attention and responding quickly to representatives avoids frustration and ensures that they concentrate on your products.
- *Follow-up.* Keep in constant touch with the representatives and follow up on agreed-upon actions.
- *Visits.* When company sales representatives visit foreign representatives, they have little choice but to pay undivided attention to your company's needs. Visits to foreign representatives and customers should occur as often as business needs dictate and certainly no less than once a year.
- *Personal relationship.* Develop a close relationship, especially with a champion in the representative's organization.

3.3.6 Legal Considerations

A formal legal contract should do much more than indicate what can be done in case of disagreement. It should define clearly and unambiguously the responsibilities of both parties. Although the agreement is drawn up by lawyers, it is important that the involved members of the foreign representative's sales force be intimately familiar with its details. Appendix B contains a sample foreign representative agreement. At the very least, the following matters should be covered:

- The territory to be served, and the exclusivity of the appointment;
- If the appointment is to be exclusive, a clear statement prohibiting the foreign representative from representing competitive products;
- The products that might be sold by the foreign representative and the products (if any) that are excluded;
- A clear statement of the sales and service responsibilities of the foreign representative and the responsibilities of the company;
- Payment terms;
- If the foreign representative is a distributor, the applicable discount schedule, from the export list price; if an agent, the commission granted for sales;
- If the foreign representative acts as an agent, the clear-split commission policy;
- The date the contract comes into effect and the date it terminates;
- The legal mechanism through which any disagreement will be settled.

Exclusive representation is not necessarily desirable for marketing consumer goods, but it is desirable for high-tech products. Such exclusivity should be on both sides. Failure to make this clear can only result in confusion for potential customers, who might be approached by several organizations claiming to represent the same company.

Companies that possess multiple SBUs sometimes employ multiple foreign representatives in the same territory to represent their different products. This can happen when the product lines are completely different and intended for different customers. It can also happen when one company acquires a second company that already employs its own foreign representatives.

Although possible in exceptional cases, for several reasons it is generally a poor idea to use more than one foreign representative in a given territory. Costs per sales representative multiply, resulting in lower efficiency and higher prices. Customer confusion can result—a situation always to be avoided. Legal and marketing costs are higher. Using a single representative ensures that his sales efforts can be more lucrative, so he is more likely to be helpful to the company. At the same time, arranging for one foreign representative to represent all SBU product lines also affords a company more leverage over that representative.

Certain categories of sales are commonly excluded from an agreement. For example, a company might sell some of its products to a third party, who incorporates them into the larger systems that it also sells in the foreign territory. If the third party uses a different foreign representative, a conflict could result if it isn't made clear which foreign representative is responsible.

A foreign representative can act as either an agent or a distributor on a case by case basis. An agent's compensation can be the same percentage of the export price as the discount percentage that a distributor receives. Thus one agreement can allow for both roles and still remain simple and probably equitable.

Agreements often place an upper limit on commissions for very large orders. Both parties can increase this limit by mutual agreement; but companies must be allowed to decide on commissions for very high-value sales for which the sales effort might not have exceeded the effort expended for much lower-value sales. This limit would be particularly important in situations that involved competitive bids in which any amount over the limit might represent an important contribution to the company's profit for the sale.

Problems might arise over sales for which the company believes the representative did little or nothing to warrant a compensation. For instance, the product might be purchased in the company's home territory and then imported into the representative's territory. Endless arguments can result if the company claims that the representative does not merit compensation. The usual way to avoid this problem is to agree a priori that the representative receives full commission for any products not excluded from the agreement that are sold in the territory. And there still might arise a situation in which the representative is entitled to at least partial if not full compensation. A clear and unambiguous split commission policy, acceptable to both parties, should be included in the agreement.

The date an agreement comes into effect is usually easy to stipulate; the duration of an agreement is not as easy to decide. Agreements that are renewed automatically unless there is notice of termination can pose risks to the company unless a specific clause allows termination without cause by either party within a time limit (e.g., 90 days after the first year of agreement). On the other hand, agreements that automatically expire unless renewed by both parties can also be troublesome, because they demand tracking and seemingly arbitrarily timed action (to renew or not to renew). For this reason, many companies opt for a long-term (multiyear) agreement that can be terminated at the convenience of either party. Ultimately, they can differ in many ways, but all agreements must provide both parties with the right to break the agreement immediately for fault (as defined in the agreement) by either party.

3.4 WORKING WITH AGENTS AND DISTRIBUTORS

After an agent or distributor is selected and a formal agreement signed, much of whatever success is thereafter achieved depends on the company and its sales force. Regular and frequent training meetings should be organized. Sales literature should be supplied in sufficient quantity and updated as needed. In fact, substantial sales efforts are required to convince the foreign representative of how saleable the products are. The champion in the foreign representative's organization, who will be responsible for key customers, must receive frequent communication. Without this champion, chances of success in the foreign territory are limited. The company sales representative assigned to the territory should make especial efforts to develop a good relationship with this individual.

Above all, an annual sales plan should set out specific actions for the company representative and for the foreign representative and forecast (budgeted) results. Routine communication and scheduled visits by both parties must be used to cement relations and provide opportunities for measuring results against the plan, defining revised strategies and actions, and refining forecasts for future sales.

If, for some unfortunate reason, a foreign representative must be terminated, it should be done quickly and in as friendly and smooth a manner as possible. The company would do well to be generous in awarding any compensation, because this will make the break easier to effect and help avoid legal complications. Both parties will be damaged in the process, and the resulting transient will take time to settle.

3.5 SUBSIDIARIES

When sales turnover in a geographic territory reaches a volume that makes attractive the establishment of a sales and service subsidiary, a company should respond to the opportunity. (Section 3.1 discusses how companies can determine if such a decision is attractive in quantitative financial terms.) The fundamental argument in favor of establishing a subsidiary is that, if the market is large enough to support it, the subsidiary can sell more than an independent representative, bringing economy of scale and a higher incremental ROI to the company. It is not difficult to understand why this should be so, and firm after successful firm has taken this path (IBM, Hewlett-Packard, Digital Equipment Corporation, Scientific Atlanta, Intel, and a host of others). The reasons are:

- Foreign representatives are in business primarily for profit and therefore need a substantial gross margin to cover expenses and interest and make a profit. (Typically, in the electronic instrumentation business, this is about 35%.) A subsidiary has as its primary goal the maximization of sales in a territory and, therefore, it can accept a lower gross margin, typically on the order of 25%. A subsidiary can accept a fairly small profit on sale of company products and, consequently, can be more competitive than the representative. (On the other hand, the subsidiary must aim to make an acceptably high ROI on service and on any noncompany products it might sell.) Note that local tax authorities normally expect a subsidiary to trade profitably; if profits are not realized, an arbitrary tax assessment might be made.
- Foreign representatives are constrained to support the products of a number of principals and, therefore, cannot concentrate their efforts on one company's products in the same way a subsidiary's sales force can. Consequently, foreign representatives are less successful at capturing a substantial share of market in the territory.
- Beyond the terms of the representative agreement, companies have no legal power to dictate the actions of a foreign representative. Subsidiary employees, on the other hand, are bound by the company's directives. For example, they can be instructed to

do a lot of marketing long before a product is available, to create or consolidate a market position.

- A company might be willing to invest in the creation of a subsidiary or in assets needed by a subsidiary (e.g., to invest in a large spare parts inventory) and wait for several years before the investment pays off. A foreign representative is not normally willing to make such an investment.
- Subsidiary personnel can support subsidiary organizations in other territories. Such support would normally be difficult to get from a foreign representative legally bound to service only one territory.
- Foreign customers are likely to identify a subsidiary with its parent company, thus making the subsidiary's sales force more welcome than that of a foreign representative.

The fact that customers identify a subsidiary with its parent company is of paramount importance to securing orders. However, this association is only fruitful when customers receive timely answers and help from the subsidiary. Customers and their purchasing staff want to speak to suppliers in their own language, they want suppliers to be relatively close by, and they want access to experts who can answer technical questions. If they don't receive these services, customers are likely to look elsewhere.

Another advantage subsidiaries have is the availability of local service and spares, which is so important that it can easily swing a decision to purchase. Because of the convenience of local representatives and local service, customers will often choose paying a premium to the subsidiary over paying to import the products directly.

Because it costs companies more to export products than to sell them domestically, export prices are usually higher than domestic prices, often by as much as 15%. Customers can elect to import products themselves, but normally they will have to pay export prices rather than domestic prices. Furthermore, they usually have to pay by letter of credit, in advance of shipment. Transfer prices to a subsidiary are normally close to domestic prices, and the gross margin takes into account these factors, so there is little advantage to customers in importing products themselves.

Companies that establish subsidiaries typically experience a doubling, tripling, and quadrupling of annual sales in a very short period. Of course, when a subsidiary takes over from a representative, it is important that the takeover be friendly and smooth, or there will be an unwelcome transient in the company's business in the country.

A company may decide to establish a subsidiary in a foreign country, with its own financial, engineering, manufacturing, and marketing groups. If that company makes products that complement a product made by SBUs in the parent company, it makes sense to use the new marketing infrastructure to market products of other SBUs in that country.

3.5.1 The Inherent Conflict in Matrix Organizations

With such a rosy description of the benefits of establishing a subsidiary when the market size warrants it, why on earth should there ever be a conflict? One reason is that communication is much more difficult when the distance between the company and its subsidiary is great, for example, more than a very few hours travel time. Travel becomes expensive and time-consuming, so that personal contact tends to be far less frequent and misunderstandings can arise much more easily. Delays in responses to queries tend to cause friction and, with time, can cause demoralization in the subsidiary and frustration in the company. This might also be true of the relationship between a company and its foreign representative, but in that case, the company has the upper hand and can terminate the representative if the relationship deteriorates too much, regardless of who is at fault. The representative can also decide to terminate a relationship. The subsidiary cannot terminate or be terminated in the same way.

When a subsidiary handles the product line of only one SBU, the potential conflict can normally be avoided or controlled. That subsidiary is in effect an extension of the company's SBU within the foreign territory and follows the direction of the SBU. The situation is quite different, however, when a subsidiary handles the products of several SBUs. In such a matrix organization, shown in Figure 3.1, each SBU marketing manager is responsible for sale of products in *all territories*, and each subsidiary manager is responsible for sale of products of *all SBUs* in one territory. There is a built-in conflict, which must be understood and controlled to achieve successful overall results.

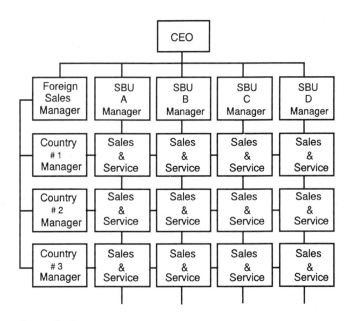

Figure 3.1 A matrix organization.

The idealized income statement in Table 3.1 can be calculated at the corporate level but not at the SBU or subsidiary level. Whether or not it is rigidly enforced by the laws of the country in which it is registered, a subsidiary is constrained by the fiscal authorities to be a profit-making organization. In a decentralized company, an SBU is usually allocated profit and loss responsibility and it too is required to make a profit. Normally, neither the subsidiary manager nor the SBU manager study or even see the other's financial results.

An SBU needs the highest gross margin possible to develop new products, pay for marketing and administration, pay for interest on borrowed money, and show the company corporate group (and the shareholders) an acceptable level of ROI. A subsidiary only needs its gross margin to pay for marketing and administration and to pay interest on borrowed money. Ideally, it need only break even, although, under the fiscal laws of the country in which it operates, it is probably expected to be profitable.

Because neither the SBU manager nor the subsidiary manager is responsible for the financial "bottom line" of the other, friction between the two can easily lead to an instability in the relationship. The SBU manager will often press for lower subsidiary markups and more sales support. In either case, acceding to SBU pressure will result in a lower gross margin for the subsidiary, with consequent corporate dissatisfaction with the subsidiary's financial performance. The subsidiary manager will often press for higher commissions (or a lower transfer price from the SBU) and more technical support. In either case, acceding to subsidiary pressure will result in lower gross margin for the SBU, again with consequent corporate dissatisfaction with financial performance.

If either subsidiary or SBU financial results are not satisfactory, the party experiencing financial problems might seek to push some of the blame onto the other party. If the financial performances of both parties is unsatisfactory, conflict is almost inevitable. The SBU might imagine that life would be far easier with a foreign representative reporting directly to it. The subsidiary might try to correct its financial shortfalls by selling products for many more third parties, diluting the sales help available to the SBUs. Conflict can be moderated by close relations between subsidiary and SBU managers, but at a cost of frequent travel and expense. Organizational changes can often cause havoc, with relationships having to be established anew.

3.5.2 Conflict Resolution

A well-run, experienced company can stem the potential conflicts described above. Closer relations and communications between SBU managers and the subsidiary manager can help, but only the actions of a strong corporate group, to whom both the SBU managers and subsidiary manager report, can wield control. What exactly can a corporate group do? It can recognize its responsibility to understand the conflicts, arrive at resolutions, implement action plans, and routinely monitor results. There are really only four actions the corporate group can implement, but implement them it must or it is asking for trouble. These actions are:

1. Ensure that its objectives in foreign marketing are well and truly understood and pursued by all its managers.
2. Formalize the rules governing the relationship between corporate, SBUs, and subsidiaries. Such rules must recognize the needs of both the SBUs and the

subsidiary. Corporate must set a commission and transfer price schedule that is consistent with the industry and with the offerings of the SBUs' most favored distributors.

3. Arbitrate any disputes and chair regular meetings between SBU managers, the subsidiary manager, and the operations manager, to whom the subsidiary manager reports.

4. Instruct the corporate financial group to set up a management accounting system that eliminates financially based conflict between SBU and subsidiary managers.

On a case by case basis, when the SBUs or the subsidiary believe that higher commissions or higher subsidiary markups can be granted, for the good of the company as a whole, they should be encouraged to pursue this path. If an SBU believes that pricing is critical and must be kept as low as possible, a lower commission (or subsidiary markup) than normal might be required. A formal rule should exist to allow the SBUs to impose this request. However, in this case, there could also be a mechanism in corporate's management accounting system to allow both the SBU and the subsidiary to claim credit for the full gross margin as allowed by the standard rules. The double gross margin figures must be reconciled in corporate consolidation. The subsidiary manager, SBU managers, and international sales manager all have budgets to meet. For each, reputation and perhaps bonus are at stake. Removing these potential sources of conflict makes it easier for both managers to do what is best for the company.

Failure of the company CEO or corporate director of marketing to implement formalized agreements between subsidiaries and SBUs can damage the entire company.

3.6 CONSORTIA

There are many examples of companies that form temporary agreements to bid for an international program or to market a product in other countries. The Concorde aircraft, sponsored jointly by the French and British governments, is an early example. Airbus Industrie is another. The F104 Starfighter and the F16 were manufactured by different companies who formed consortia, as was the NATO HAWK missile. The NATO Air Defense Ground Environment (NADGE) program was bid on by international groupings of companies who formed consortia specifically for that purpose. The winning consortium participated in the development and manufacture of various portions of the system.

Political factors often enter into this sort of marketing. Large international programs usually involve government expenditure commitments. There is generally some offset purchasing formula required by each government that specifies that industries in its country receive contracts from the successful consortium in direct proportion to the country's contribution to the overall program.

Companies that wish to participate in these international programs must be aware of governmental requirements and of the likely international contenders long before the request to bid. They could also profit from a detailed study of what the various international contenders might offer, along with an analysis of who has the best chance to win. At this point, they should focus selling efforts on the contenders, to convince them to form the consortium. The company must apply this pressure quickly and expertly or lose its chance to be part of the best consortium or even to participate at all.

After performing this research, the participating consortium of companies forms an international team to determine the marketing effort required in each country (including efforts to influence specifications), assign marketing tasks, and decide on how work will be divided should the contract be awarded. All these activities are so important that only the most senior marketing people should participate on the team. The work might also require the active participation of CEOs.

3.7 JOINT VENTURES

For the purposes of this discussion, a *joint venture* is a company set up by two companies in different countries. Specifically, this new company is set up in a foreign market by a company already located there and another company wishing to export into that foreign market. What advantages do joint ventures offer?

Some governments do not permit foreign companies to create subsidiaries in their countries (whether for sales and service only or for manufacture as well). To such governments, this foreign investment and control is seen as a form of industrial colonization and resisted. However, they might permit and even encourage joint ventures, because joint ventures can aid the industrialization process. Even if a government does permit subsidiaries, the difficulties of penetrating the market without substantial local know-how and connections can be overwhelming. Rather than invest the time and money needed to acquire know-how and connections, many companies decide to seek out foreign companies with whom to create joint ventures.

As might be expected, there are potential problems. The chances of two companies with totally different cultures being able to function together smoothly may be slim. And even if the joint venture starts to operate smoothly, can it achieve an acceptable incremental ROI? If it can, can the profits be repatriated?

What are the alternatives to creating a joint venture in a country in which good foreign representatives cannot be found and local know-how is indispensable to penetrating the market? In Eastern European countries, for example, only recently emerged from the tightly centralized control exercised in communist countries, market needs and potential might be enormous, even though financial resources are slim. Can a foreign high-tech company from a Western country really hope to establish itself successfully without close collaboration with an existing company?

Establishing a joint venture might be one stage in the evolution of two companies who benefit from the union for a period and then dissolve it. Entering into a joint venture might involve manufacture of some of the company's product in the foreign country as well as the transfer of know-how. The end result might be that the joint venture prospers, matures, and even becomes a competitor. However, if the period is sufficiently long, and the opportunity to create a joint venture is missed, both partners might lose the prospect of an entrenched position in the market—a position that others are always there to seize.

Experts have studied successful joint ventures in India and Pakistan [1]. Four stages in the investment environment are quoted below, and Paliwoda [2] suggests that the chronology has universal application.

1. *Unilateral antagonism.* The host nation fears danger of economic imperialism.
2. *Mutual suspicion.* Both foreign investors and capital-importing governments might have considerable doubt over the mutuality of their interests. There is concern over the stimulus of economic development with scarce resources, so both foreign capital and technology are required. Imports are paid for by earnings from extractive industry exports. Entry conditions for foreign capital and labor are relaxed but still constrained.
3. *Joint acceptance.* The social benefits are seen to exceed the social costs and, as the needs of development create their own self-generating momentum, their relaxation continues.
4. *Sophisticated integration.* The logical extension of the relaxation mentioned. Foreign investors might be permitted entry in any form of operation they desire. In so far as local collaboration and participation are felt to be desirable or even necessary, they might well be promoted through discriminatory fiscal and financial incentives, rather than through legislative prohibitions.

Studies conducted several decades ago (Stopford and Wells, 1972 [3], and Franko, 1972 [4]) established an analytic framework for examining joint ventures between multinationals and local partners. (See Michael Porter's *Competition in Global Industries*, listed as a suggested reading in Appendix D.) Stopford and Wells concluded from results of an extensive questionnaire that

> . . . firms that aimed to adapt their products to local markets, that could retain control of all vertical stages in their industry by dominating one stage, or that had an exceptional need to spread the risk of their expansion, were all more likely to participate in joint ventures with local partners. [5]

This conclusion suggests a reasonable approach for joint ventures. The company that believes it has products for a foreign market might find adapting the products to the market a good approach. Retaining control of one of the key stages in the process (by controlling the design or granting a restricted license to the joint venture, for example) gives the company leverage to maintain equality with its foreign partner.

3.8 LICENSING

Licensing is another effective means a company can choose to distribute its products in a foreign market. Unlike a company entering a joint venture, a company that licenses the right to manufacture and sell its products might grant this privilege to a completely independent firm. The benefit of a licensing arrangement to the licensor is temporary because, if the know-how transfer is successful, the licensed company matures and might eventually become a competitor. A joint venture, on the other hand, tends to prolong the benefit because the licensor continues to own part of the venture. For this reason joint ventures, licensing, and even licensing to third parties share many characteristics.

Licensing usually involves a down payment for transfer of designs and drawings; payment for technical assistance, or transfer of know-how; and a royalty payment that is a percentage of the value of the licensed product sold. The monetary amounts are highly variable, but a royalty on the order of 5% is common. Because the benefits to the licensor are of limited duration, licensing should be seen as a temporary and short-duration strategy. Nevertheless, licensing might be the only way a company can penetrate a specific foreign market, and it does offer some advantages:

- The level of investment needed is very low;
- Funds might be repatriated when currency control regulations allow it;
- For a small but technologically advanced company with relatively short development cycles, royalties might help fund new R&D;
- The licensed product receives a lot of exposure, which might stimulate further sales for the company;
- While building up capacity to produce the licensed product, the licensee often imports a substantial portion of the product's components and assemblies (in fact, many licensees underestimate the duration of this process and licensors continue to export the product);
- A successful relationship can lead to other licenses and to an expansion of the licensor's sales into that territory.

Licensing has much to recommend it despite the pitfalls. Some of the benefits in the sales process are discussed in the next chapter.

3.9 SUMMARY

Chapter 3 examined the basis for choice and the alternatives for the channels of distribution available to a high-tech company that seeks to sell nonconsumer products in foreign countries. Chapter 4 discusses the selling aspect of marketing in some detail.

REFERENCES

[1]   *Matric Organization of Complex Business*, Elsevier, 1983.

[2]   Paliwoda, Stanley, *International Marketing*, Oxford: Heinemann Professional Publishing Ltd., 1990, pp. 71–79.

[3]   Stopford, J. M., and L. T. Wells, *Managing Multinational Enterprise: Organization of the Firm and Ownership of the Subsidiaries*, New York: Basic Books, 1972.

[4]   Franko, L. G., *Joint Venture Survival in Multinational Corporations*, Praeger, 1972.

[5]   Stopford, J. M., and L. T. Wells, *Managing Multinational Enterprise: Organization of the Firm and Ownership of the Subsidiaries*, New York: Basic Books, 1972.

Chapter 4

Selling to Foreign Markets

So much attention is paid to the term "marketing" that the fact that a key aspect of marketing is "selling" is sometimes forgotten. In high-tech companies, sales engineers are experts. They are the front-line people in closest touch with customers and in the best position to influence sales, as well as to understand and make market needs known to the company. This chapter concentrates on the characteristics that distinguish good sales technique and selling.

4.1 HIGH-TECH SALES ENGINEERS

Selling high technology into foreign markets differs from selling other products in several important ways. But first, the following list summarizes attributes good high-tech sales engineers must possess regardless of where sales take place. To be effective, high-tech sales engineers must

- Possess a sufficiently high level of technical understanding of their products and their customers' needs;
- Know a lot about the competition;
- Believe they are selling the best product;
- Possess a strong will to succeed and the tenacity to win sales;
- Possess the ability to listen carefully and really understand the needs of customers;
- Be able to communicate clearly and succinctly to customers and the company;
- Recognize when they need to ask for help from superiors.

Selling technical products and services in a foreign country requires special considerations, and companies do well to choose sales engineers who possess the fundamental attributes needed to assure success. Problems that might be resolved easily when customers are domestic become more acute when customers are foreign.

Language differences result in communications difficulties. Telephone and fax facilities in a foreign country might not allow quick and easy communications with the

---

home office. This isolation means that sales engineers take on a much larger share of the responsibility of selling and negotiating than they do in the domestic market.

Costs of selling are higher, not only because of travel expenses but also because of the commissions for foreign agents. This extra cost means that the sales productivity (sales achieved divided by the costs of achieving the sales) might well be lower for selling abroad than for selling domestically. To compensate, only very capable sales engineers should be enlisted to sell in foreign markets.

An important characteristic that sales engineers chosen for foreign markets must possess is an openness to different cultures. Adventurous sales engineers who are eager to sample the differences—whether they be in customs, cuisine, or lifestyle—and willing to learn about the history and culture of the country are often rewarded with a more ready acceptance by foreign customers.

Professional sales engineers do their homework before approaching potential customers. They study the targeted organization and determine probable needs *before* they visit. The scope of such homework is more extensive in foreign selling than in domestic selling, because it also involves gaining familiarity with the potential customer's background and the country's history, politics, and classical literature.

No matter how much homework sales engineers do, they can never know nearly as much about these subjects as the customers. Therefore, they do well to be humble and modest in their display of knowledge and to show willingness to learn. It is surprising how approachable customers are when sales engineers have done their homework. It should not be surprising if customers are cold and indifferent to sales engineers who are unprepared.

4.2 LANGUAGE

One of the most obvious requirements for sales engineers is fluency either in the customer's language or in a language they both share. Sales engineers must be able to communicate with customers' decision makers and with any other personnel who typically interact with them. Lack of such fluency can be a considerable impediment to successful selling, although interpreters might be used as a last resort.

Fluency in a foreign customer's language is an asset, but, ironically, sales engineers who are natives of the customer's country and for whom the language is their mother tongue might find this common bond a detriment. It might seem neither logical nor correct, but sometimes customers assume that foreigners are more open, frank, and even honest than natives. This is not a clear-cut case for avoiding native sales engineers, however, because individuals might possess overwhelmingly positive compensating characteristics.

Fluency in a common language is nearly as acceptable as fluency in the foreign language. In Eastern Europe, the lingua franca is often German (or Russian), and in South America, it is Spanish or Portuguese. In North and West Africa, it is French. However, the most widely used language in foreign marketing is English.

Even France, with its strong nationalistic feelings, recognizes the importance of English for international communications. INSEAD is one of the foremost business schools in Europe, located in Fontainebleau, not far from Paris. Fluency in English and French is among the entrance qualifications to this institute, which grants an MBA degree. Ninety percent of the courses, many of them in marketing, are in English. Students cannot graduate without passing an exam in a third language. Students cannot graduate from the famous École Supérieure des Telecommunications of the French PTT without passing an exam in three languages, one of which must be English.

John Harvey-Jones, the former chairman of the British ICI, wrote a book called *Making it Happen*. He devotes a full chapter ("Do We Want to Be International?") to problems of language communications. In it, he comments,

> I am always amazed at how admiring American people are of the verbal facility of many Britons, the wider range of vocabulary and the, to them, more elegant construction of the language. But the British using more words in an elegant way does not make for better understanding between our nations. Even in companies which pride themselves on their internationalism, and ICI is one, it is amazing how frequently misunderstandings arise between the British and American branches. Because we apparently speak the same language we tend to believe that we think in the same way, and that the words convey the same message. It is, of course, a peculiarly British characteristic to think that every man is the same under the skin . . . [1]

(An amusing sidelight occurred at a conference at the École Supérieure des Telecommunications in May 1991. In front of a distinguished international audience, the majority of whom were French, the French chairman said jokingly that the meeting would be conducted in broken American, which he felt sure everyone understood well except the English!)

It is true that even between the British and Americans language can occasionally pose a problem. If misunderstandings can arise between two people whose mother tongue is English, imagine how much more easily misunderstandings can occur between two people for whom English is a second language. Sales engineers must pay particular attention to choosing words carefully, enunciating clearly, avoiding colloquial expressions, and asking questions frequently, to ensure that they are communicating well. If the response to questions is a blank stare, they must try again and try harder.

4.3 ASSESSING THE COMPETITION

Regardless of what sales engineers are selling, they must be thoroughly informed about the competition. Even in situations in which there is demand for the product and seemingly no competitor, there still exists competition. For example, the customer might be weighing need for the product against spending the money to satisfy a completely different need.

When sales engineers visit a foreign customer, they must have a clear objective for the visit. If the visit is to sell products or services, success will be determined to a large extent by the competition. Engineers seldom have the time or resources to study what the competition has to offer during a visit. They must do their homework before the visit so they are prepared to find strategies to defeat the competition. If possible, a sales visit should occur long before the competition becomes entrenched. If the customer has already issued a purchase specification, it might be too late for the sales engineer to enter into the fight to win. The competition might already have influenced the specifications to an extent that precludes the sales engineer's bid and proposal receiving serious consideration. The lesson to be learned is that sales engineers have the greatest chance of success if they get to the customer ahead of the competition.

L. M. Ericsson, of Sweden, is a good example of a company that got in ahead of the competition. The company exploited its development of modular electronic switching and concentrated its attention in certain carefully chosen developing countries. Often, before competitors realized that a good sales opportunity existed, Ericsson had already tied up the market.

Even when sales engineers are responding to invitations to bid for the opportunity to provide a product or service, they might still be able to influence customers away from the competition with a convincing presentation. An example from real life illustrates this effort. This example, as well as the other examples used in this chapter, is based on actual experience. The customer names and countries are not given, but otherwise the situation is undistorted.

- A country in the Far East was developing a fighter aircraft at a company located on an airfield. The company wished to purchase a radar that was as inexpensive as possible, but would enable it to "see" the aircraft on the ground as it taxied, as well as in the air, for a distance of at least 50 nautical miles. The aircraft company had a relatively limited budget for this program.
- The long-range radar would need moving target indication (MTI) capability, so it could detect the aircraft and pick out the aircraft radar echo from ground-reflected echoes. The requirement to see the fighter aircraft as it taxied (runway surveillance) was not too critical, but was nevertheless important because from time to time mist descended on the runway.
- The aircraft company wrote a specification that was rather general but did stress the long-range capability, the MTI need, and the requirement to detect the aircraft on the runway. This latter was a feature that was not available to an acceptable extent in the normal long-range MTI radar. Several companies replied to the specification, proposing two radars that cost substantially more than the company's budget allowed.
- A sales engineer from a well-known Italian company decided to visit the customer to understand better what the requirements really were. He had done his homework and was quite sure of the cost of competitive radars and what they could do. His company had two radars that in combination could satisfy the written requirement, but the total cost would be high.
- During his discussions with the customer, the sales engineer established that the real competition was not with other radar companies (although they were in a good position), but with other projects in the aircraft company that were competing for budget

money. He also clarified in his own mind that the requirement for runway surveillance, though necessary, was secondary in importance.

- The sales engineer therefore proposed a unique solution in which an extremely inexpensive ship radar would be used for runway surveillance rather than a much more expensive runway surveillance radar, even though the required specifications would not be entirely met. He prepared a proposal and bid during the visit and even helped the project officer plan details of where to site the radars.

- The company was awarded the contract. As expected, the requirement for runway surveillance proved to be secondary, and the inexpensive radar was adequate for the rare occasions when it was needed. The company's long-range radar proved to be so reliable and performed so well that it became the standard for future procurement in that country. The Italian company later granted a license to a company in that Far East country to manufacture the radar. (Licensing is discussed later in this chapter.) Tens of millions of dollars of business resulted from the initial encounter in which the sales engineer sought to outwit the competition.

Sales engineers might learn of some weakness in a competitor's product or discover some negative attributes related to the competition and be tempted to use this information to influence the customer. To do so is very unwise; a little reflection is all that is needed to understand why. There are ethical and possibly legal reasons that mitigate against this practice. Sales engineers who wish to be respected should accord respect to their competitor, as well as to customers, whose intelligence they might impugn by using underhanded arguments. The dividing line between what might be considered fair criticism of a competitor and unfair or even unethical criticism is very blurred. A good general rule is to refrain from negative criticism and rely instead on positive arguments in favor of one's own equipment or services to convince the customer.

4.4 ESTABLISHING TRUST

The conventional wisdom is that, given a choice of products or services, customers base decisions on purely logical grounds. However, the factors that influence a logical choice are so complex that it is often too difficult to define the basis of the "logic." For example, what importance does the customer place on the product's price versus other factors, such as advanced technology, availability of good service, reputation of the seller's organization? Weighting these factors is so difficult that, in the end, emotion rather than logic might play the dominant role in the decision process. The choice is very often made subconsciously by the customer, based upon these emotional factors, and then the "logical" justification is made by weighting the logical factors to fit that decision! A book published in 1991 addresses this question of logical versus emotional choice rather completely. The book is entitled *Rethinking Business to Business Marketing*, and the author is Paul Sherlock, director of Strategic Marketing for Corporate Technology at Raychem. Sherlock gives an example of an aircraft servo motor evaluation, listing characteristics of two competitive products. The engineer at the aircraft factory is required to choose between these two products. After listing the specifications of each, as well as such considerations as price, delivery, supplier reputation, and experience with service from the two suppliers, the author goes on to say,

> How do you "logically" approach this, since either product would work? Ah, simple. You might say, "First array the factors in order of importance." But is cost more important than size? Just how much is size worth? You can give a value to weight in terms of fuel savings, but over what life of the product and at what fuel price? Once you have them arrayed, how do you factor them? Is cost twice as important as size? For a value factor, is a 10% reduction in size weighted 1/10 or is it so important that it should be multiplied by a scaling factor? If so, should this be linear, logarithmic, or something else?
>
> If you think this is a simple decision, imagine trying to follow this procedure in comparing two similar computer installations or in choosing between a Boeing 767 or an Airbus A310 for an airline. [2]

The lesson to be learned from this is that the relationship between sales engineers and customers, even the "chemistry" of that relationship, plays a most important part in influencing the "logic" of a customer's decisions. This does not mean that sales engineers should try to influence customers to choose wrongly. However, the rapport they establish with customers goes a long way in helping selling efforts. Good sales engineers know that selling themselves to customers is of vital importance to their success. Another example illustrates that point.

- Some years ago, a well-known European company that was very successful in selling equipment to a government organization in a South American country sent one of its key sales engineers to the country to participate in the sales effort. Unfortunately, the engineer committed an indiscretion in the country (that a good foreign representative could have helped him avoid), was declared persona nongrata, and was forced to leave. The company sent a replacement engineer but, unaware of the details of the indiscretion, did not inform the replacement of the difficulties with the key customer. The new employee asked for an appointment with the customer. When they met, the customer representative stated flatly that his organization would never purchase anything again from the company and made the employee understand that he was most unwelcome.
- How could that newly arrived engineer possibly make himself acceptable to the customer under these circumstances? What he did to "sell himself" at that point is an excellent example. After apologizing for his predecessor, he explained that he was totally ignorant of what had occurred (the truth) and that he had not been sent primarily to sell equipment at all (not the complete truth). He explained that he was an engineer whose primary job was to ensure that purchased equipment functioned to the complete satisfaction of the customer. He added that, because it was technically complex, the equipment the customer purchased often had problems. He wanted to

investigate those problems and see how they could best be resolved. He asked to be introduced to end users.

- The result was a complete change in the attitude of the customer. The customer and engineer's conversation immediately became a friendly one. The newcomer was trusted and proceeded to do what he said he would do. The end of this true story came several years later. The engineer was leaving the country to return to Europe, after he had sold a large quantity of equipment to the very customer who had told him that he would never purchase again from the company. The customer, who was a high government official, accorded the sales engineer the distinctive honor of hosting the going-away party himself.

The object of selling oneself is to create a bond of trust. Such a bond is not easy to create, and, once created, it must be nurtured if it is to flourish. Sales engineers must know substantially more than their customers about key features of their products. When they cannot answer a question about a product, they must not try to guess. Instead, they should promise to find out the answer and state when they will deliver that answer. They must thereafter keep their word.

It might appear at first glance that the advice given above is the same for domestic and foreign selling. Certainly selling oneself is important for all sales people. However, there are often key differences in a foreign country that require that the creation of trust be pursued carefully. Despite the example cited above, in general, sales engineers have relatively infrequent contact with foreign customers. These contacts are by correspondence (fax, letters), by telephone, or by visits. It is primarily during visits that sales engineers must establish the bond of trust, and they must thereafter maintain this bond via action or correspondence.

Frequency of contact is equally important for customers. Sometimes customers are wholly dependent on sales engineers they come to trust, even for explanations of problems they must resolve. This is especially true in developing countries. Such dependence can assist sales engineers' goals immeasurably. It is often the case that sales engineers arrive at a point where, together with the customer, they write the specifications for the product that will be purchased. Good sales engineers ensure that those specifications allow for a measure of competition. Needless to say, sales engineers who establish a bond of trust that allows them to assist in writing specifications can enjoy great advantages over the competition.

Highly professional sales engineers will appear in front of customers convinced that they represent their company totally and will convince customers that they can negotiate reasonable deals on behalf of the company. That customers must perceive that sales engineers possess such authority cannot be stressed sufficiently. Sales engineers must convey this level of responsibility and control, as well as establish a strong bond of trust with customers. If they achieve such a level of trust, they must strive to maintain it during all subsequent dealings and never betray it. They must never promise anything they are not sure they can maintain and must provide whatever they promise to deliver.

4.5 TECHNICAL SELLING

One way customers of sophisticated technical equipment differ from others is in the number of people involved in the purchase decision, which is normally greater than it is for simpler equipment. In addition, the decision often involves a substantial amount of money. The money normally comes from a government body or an organization that can afford the expenditure. The decision maker in the group is often nontechnical, but almost invariably has the advice of a technical consultant. Sales engineers therefore have somewhat complex selling tasks. They must convince both the technical adviser and the decision maker to purchase the product, even if the decision maker has only a superficial understanding of the product's technical aspects.

Good technical sales engineers must know much more than the technical features of their product. They must know how to sell the product. They must

- Understand the customer's problem;
- Understand the key technical features that distinguish the product from competitors' products;
- Understand the level of technical sophistication of the customers, including the decision maker;
- Prepare a good technical proposal.

4.5.1 Understanding the Customer's Problem

Even if customers have problems that will be resolved if they purchase the product, there is no assurance that they are even aware that a problem exists. The first task of a sales engineer in this case is to convince the customer that a problem exists. The sales engineer must convince the decision maker or at least someone within the customer group who can convince the decision maker. This can be accomplished only if the solution is economically justifiable within the legal and political constraints of the country. Sales engineers must therefore be aware of the legal, political, and economic aspects of the problem, including a best estimate of the payback period for the purchase.

For example, the problem might be that the customer must establish telephone communications between two locations, and the sales engineer is selling satellite communications equipment. Can the customer purchase and operate such equipment within the legal constraints of the country? What are the payback periods if the customer chooses connection by cable, by microwave link, by radio, by satellite? These questions can be difficult to answer. In a remote area, especially in a developing country, connection by cable or microwave link might take too long to establish and connection by radio might be unsatisfactory for other reasons. In such cases, connection by satellite might provide a good answer, but does the payback period justify the expenditure? If the answer is obviously negative, the sales engineer might be wasting time pursuing the sale. Again, sales engineers must do their homework before they try to sell.

An example from an actual sales experience illustrates how understanding the problem helped one sales engineer sell far more equipment than the customer originally planned to purchase.

- An American company designs and manufactures a line of antenna measuring equipment. A customer in a Far Eastern country requested help in resolving a production problem.
- The customer had received a contract from the country's armed forces to manufacture a quantity of antennas within a certain period. The specifications for side-lobe level and antenna gain were quite stringent. The military end user required that the antenna performance be measured for each antenna and that all measurements be carried out in secure areas. This meant that the customer could not use his outdoor antenna range for the measurements.
- The customer had a problem. He had to construct a special room in which the antennas could be mounted and their characteristics measured. That room had to be militarily secure. The customer also had time constraints in arriving at a suitable solution, since manufacturing was proceeding rapidly, with an increasing number of antennas accumulating, awaiting tests. He planned to perform the measurements in an enclosed room that was militarily secure and would allow technicians to work in good or bad weather and during the night as well.
- At this point, the customer should have obtained expert advice on how to resolve the problem. Instead, he decided to have his production engineer design a solution. Unfortunately, while the engineer did know something of electronics, he did not seek more expert advice and proceeded to design a chamber, called an anechoic chamber, in an available room. Unfortunately, the room was too short to allow for antenna measurements in the antenna far field. The room design and construction were complete when the company's foreign representative convinced the customer to purchase the antenna measurement equipment and requested a visit from the company's sales engineer.
- The customer had a problem, but he was not even aware of that problem. He thought that for an expenditure of about $50,000 he could purchase all the antenna measurement equipment he needed. He was not aware of the fact that to use his small room, he would have to purchase near-field equipment that would cost him at least five times that amount. The sales engineer, however, quickly understood the problem and knew that if he sold the customer the equipment he wanted the problem would persist.
- That sales engineer had to use all his technical selling skills to

1. Determine what the problem was and devise the correct technical solution.
2. Determine whether the solution could be paid for by the time (and money) saved in production testing.
3. Convince the customer that finding the extra money for the costly ($300,000) solution was the least expensive alternative.

4. Find a way for the customer to save face—this was the most difficult task of all! He did this by helping the customer to present the solution to the armed forces and convince them to pay extra money for a valuable facility that would have years of useful life.

- Our sales engineer succeeded in this challenging sales effort, with the end result that a very unhappy customer became a happy one, who willingly purchased far more equipment than either he or the foreign representative originally anticipated.

4.5.2 Understanding the Technical Features of the Product

Sometimes a new product is developed or a standard product is modified specifically to suit a customer's requirements. In this case, unless they have only a minor role in a technical sales team, sales engineers must be intimately acquainted with the technical features of the product.

Usually, companies sell only standard products and, while they might consider minor modifications, their strong preference is standard products. Novice technical sales engineers, unsure of themselves, are sometimes drawn into fruitless discussions with technical customer representatives who want substantial specification changes. Those sales engineers might then return to their companies convinced that if only the products were modified they could sell them. On rare occasions, a company might be willing to consider the change, but the more likely answer to these sales engineers is that they should expend their efforts in selling the products the company has.

Novice sales engineers also tend to assume, because of their lack of experience, that they must know all the technical features of their products in profound detail. This is seldom required, although it is undeniable that the deeper their knowledge, the easier sales engineers find their selling task. The more important point is that sales engineers must learn how to describe key technical features in a concise and lucid manner.

As well as knowing the technical features of their products, as explained earlier, sales engineers must also do their homework, so they understand the customer's problem. They are then in a position to discuss how purchasing the product will resolve the customer's problem. They must describe what the product does and how it does it. They must describe the physical appearance of the product, using photographs, drawings, or sketches. They must describe how users operate the product and how the product interfaces with other equipment. Features that make the product easy to install or very user friendly should be described in detail. After describing the product, they should discuss interesting technical features, not necessarily in great depth but certainly expanding on what the customer already knows about the product.

Again, an example illustrates this selling process.

- In the early days of communication by satellite with ships at sea, there were few competitors, and customers had to be convinced that products were reliable. Customers were aware that equipment aboard a ship was subject to a rough environment and that the antenna had to perform correctly not only when the ship rolled and pitched violently but also when it was pounded by a heavy sea or suddenly fell heavily to the bottom of a large wave trough. A key question they might have posed was how would the antenna perform under such conditions. Would it remain pointed at the satellite?

- A sales engineer who sold satellite communications equipment for ships decided he would answer that question before it was posed. As it happened, the antenna design was a novel one, and even if the solution to the problem was relatively simple, it was not obvious. The solution was to design the antenna so that its center of rotation about the pitch and roll axes coincided perfectly with the center of gravity of the portion of the antenna that rotated about these axes. Therefore, any sudden ship movement would not result in perturbation of the antenna's angle. Rather than display a photograph or drawing of the design, the sales engineer learned to describe it by sketching the design on a blackboard, explaining it simply and clearly as he drew.

- The result was that the customer was pleased at learning something new, and the sales engineer established the reputation of knowing a considerable amount about his product, far more, in fact, than he actually knew!

Some of the complex technical features of a product might be relatively unimportant in terms of salability, but other features might be important. If there are important features, sales engineers must understand them so completely that they can describe the features clearly and simply, even to nontechnical customers. A technical friend whom I shall call Bill gave me an excellent example of the importance of this, which anyone with a good mathematical background can appreciate.

- Bill was with his wife, driving his car in Washington, looking for a particular street name. His wife had happened to notice that earlier that day Bill had been writing a technical paper in which he used the word "cross-correlation" several times, and she asked him what the term meant.

- Although Bill's wife is highly intelligent, she has a limited mathematical background. Rather than enter into a long explanation, which his wife might not even understand, Bill used an analogy to explain what cross-correlation meant. He used the street name they were looking for. He pointed out that the street names, which were affixed to signs at the corner of every important intersection, could not be read clearly because of the speed at which they were traveling.

- The names passed in a blur, and they could only make out part of what was written on the sign as they passed it. However, the two of them had a priori knowledge of the correct street name. Using this a priori knowledge, they could quickly distinguish whether the street name "cross-correlated" with the name they were seeking. They could pick out the correct name from the blur of incorrect names (extraneous noise) by this cross-correlation process.

This is an example of how something fairly technical can be explained simply. Other examples abound, but the important lesson is that sales engineers must capture a customer's attention concerning key features of the product by using clear and simple explanations, while, at the same time, creating the impression that they know their products in detail. Clearly, it is not enough to be superficially informed. It is important to know more than the customer, but not very much more. It is equally important that sales engineers, if they don't know the answer to a customer's question, be able to obtain the answer quickly, so they don't imply ignorance of any key product feature.

4.5.3 Understanding the Technical Level of the Customer

Sales engineers must learn quickly their customers' levels of technical understanding and direct their sales efforts accordingly. There is little purpose served in "selling" to those who are neither decision makers nor in a position to influence decision makers. This often eliminates more junior technical people, who are usually very curious about the product's technical features. Sales engineers should deal with those people politely but avoid wasting time on them. However, customer representatives who are technical and are in a position to influence decision makers (or who are themselves decision makers) are usually broader in outlook. Their questions seldom probe for details, which are often of little consequence to the prospects of a successful purchase. Sales engineers should be in a position to answer questions from such people and to judge the level of technical detail the reply requires.

It is far more important that answers be simple, concise, lucid, and to the point than overly detailed. The greater the detail the less clarity is a fairly general rule and a true one.

4.5.4 Preparing the Technical Proposal

If the product is not simply and completely described by a standard brochure, a technical proposal might be needed. And if a standard brochure exists, it might still be included as part of a proposal. This section does not describe the contents of a technical proposal in detail, but it does discuss the following important points:

- Language and clarity;
- Form versus substance;
- The summary;
- Organization.

The proposal should be written in a language that is understood by all who participate in the purchase decision. It should also be written in a language that is understood by those who must present the proposal. Sometimes, this might mean that the proposal is translated twice. It is first translated into a language that is understood by some or all of the customer personnel and by the writers themselves. (This is typically English or, less often, French or Spanish.) Then, if some of the important customer personnel do not understand this common language, and winning the sale is worth the expense, the proposal should be translated into the language of the customer (for example, into Arabic).

The quality of the translation must be good. If the translation is sloppy and full of grammatical or spelling errors, it might give an impression that the quality of the product is inferior or that the seller is inconsiderate of the customer's language and culture.

The importance of the form of the proposal cannot be overstressed. In some ways, form is even more important than substance, although the substance must be correct and as complete as needed. Many will skim through the proposal rather than study it in detail, so, to create a good lasting impression, the form must be well prepared.

If the sale is sufficiently important, the cover should state clearly what the proposal is about and who the customer is. As much as possible, the proposal should include clear, informative, and imaginative illustrations and drawings. A common but true saying in this regard is that a picture is worth a thousand words. The print and graphics should be professional and tidy.

There will often be several levels of customer personnel who look at the proposal. A summary, as simple, concise, and lucid as possible, should appear at the beginning of the proposal. It might be the only part the decision maker reads and could therefore prove extremely important. It should be followed by a brief introduction, a main body, and then conclusions.

Appendices to the proposal should be used wherever possible to avoid inclusion of detail that might interrupt the smooth flow of the description in the main body. Where a table of compliance to the specification is requested, it should be contained in an appendix. The specification should be included in this table, rather than simply referred to, to facilitate reading. Appendices should also be used to describe the company, its related experience, its organization, and how the contract would be managed, and to show any detailed calculations.

There are no strict rules for preparing a technical proposal, but it is a good idea to study several, including some from competitors, before writing one.

4.6 THE SALES CYCLE

The techniques described here in abbreviated form might be studied in more detail in various books on marketing, such as *Rethinking Business to Business Marketing* by Paul Sherlock (see Appendix D).

Unless the list of qualified customers is so small that they can commit the lot to memory, it is prudent for sales engineers to generate a database of customers, which they can update and refine periodically and frequently. The key objective of the sales cycle, described in Figure 4.1, is to book orders ("book" is a term widely used for receipt of an order, whereas "sales" is reserved for invoicing), which is why "book orders" is placed at the center of the diagram. The contents of the database might be determined purely by market research, as a result of market stimulation and responses from customers, or as a result of referrals by customers.

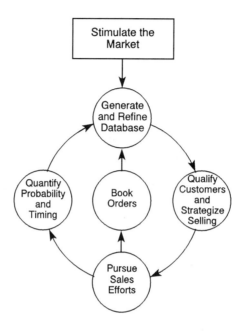

Figure 4.1 The sales cycle.

Sales engineers study their databases and, using the criteria appropriate to the particular industry, "qualify" potential customers. Then they strategize their approaches to customers and implement those strategies. Some success might (hopefully) result and orders will be booked. Even if they do not book orders in a very short time, the knowledge sales engineers gather during selling will enable them to quantify their forecast of probability of success and the timing of orders, and they can use this new data to refine the information in their databases.

The sales cycle is never ending, as sales engineers expand their databases, refine them, study data to qualify those customers from whom they believe they have a good chance of obtaining orders, and strategize their approaches. The sections below discuss this cycle in some detail.

4.6.1 Stimulating the Market

Some products are the result of inspiration, and no amount of market research could have predicted their success. Akito Morita, chairman of the Sony Corporation, was the person who conceived the Sony Walkman. Before launching or even perfecting the product, he was advised by all the "experts" he consulted that the market for such a gadget was extremely limited. He persisted in his belief that the product would achieve widespread acceptance, and the resulting phenomenal growth of the Sony Corporation is legendary [3].

In the usual case, however, product development results from feedback from the market itself. Ideally, new products are defined as a result of a sales engineer's contacts and study of the market, complemented by a parallel study by a marketing group. This is a cyclical process, like the sales cycle, and is part of another closed-loop cycle of study, selling, feedback to product design teams, and design of new products. At the end of a cycle, a new product is introduced into the market to "stimulate" it.

The objective of such stimulation is to elicit interest from customers. The market can be stimulated in a number of ways. Some methods are much more costly than others, and there is no easy way to decide what combination of methods, or promotion mix, is best for a particular company. Sometimes more money is spent on analyzing which method is most cost effective than the result justifies! The list below, while not exhaustive, contains the key single or combined methods that companies can employ.

- Products, services, or both can be advertised in magazines and journals dedicated to the specific market segment. Promotion can be in the form of direct advertisements, new product announcements, or technical articles.
- A sales campaign can be conducted in which a letter and pertinent literature are sent to the prospective customers in the database.
- Prospective customers in the database can be solicited by telephone.
- Products can be displayed at appropriate trade shows.
- Key customers can be invited to view products at convenient locations (hotel conference rooms, for example).
- Key customers can be invited to attend seminars at convenient locations.
- Demonstration tours or slide or video presentations can show products at work at customer locations.

Advertising and sales campaigns might be very effective means for identifying customers. These campaigns should target the periodicals that are most influential in each foreign market. The company's foreign representative can be most helpful in this regard. On the other hand, if there are only a few potential customers and they are easily identified, advertising might not be worth the cost.

Exhibiting at trade shows can be very important for several reasons. An important trade show, even in the company's own country, might attract key foreign customers. Failure to exhibit at trade shows at which competitors exhibit might send an negative message to customers. Simultaneous exposure to many customers can be effected at these shows. Furthermore, shows are good places for sales engineers to get to know the competition and their products. The cost of exhibiting at important trade shows is high, so shows must be chosen carefully for maximum impact on the targeted customers. American Business Consultants publishes a useful pamphlet on trade shows.[1]

---

1. *Ways to Sell at Trade Shows*, by M. Roderic Sponck, 1987, approximately $6 (U.S.). Available from American Business Consultants, Inc., P.O. Box 5221, New Jersey 08809, U.S.A.

Companies that organize frequent seminars soon establish importance in the field. Further, if those companies encourage engineers and technical sales engineers to publish technical papers frequently, that image of importance is enhanced. The sales engineers in such companies often find it easy to be accepted by prospective customers.

Whatever method is chosen to stimulate the market, literature must be prepared carefully. Sales engineers should play a key role in literature preparation because they are in the best position to know what customers want to read. Literature should use meaningful photographs and diagrams. It should include key specifications, but not in such detail that it weakens the overall impact. The text should be clearly and simply written, keeping in mind that the company might be communicating in a language that is not its mother tongue to a foreign customer who might also have some difficulty with the language. Sales engineers should strive to include something in the literature that will stand out in the customer's memory. Above all, the literature should be of high quality in its presentation, diagrams, photographs, and accuracy.

4.6.2 Generating and Refining a Database

A database should contain the names, titles, addresses, and any other pertinent information for all potential customers. It should also include the types of products each customer is interested in. This data comes to a company as a result of its market stimulation, as well as from many other sources, and the information should be updated as frequently as possible. A database's basic purpose is to enable sales engineers to send literature or other information to customers and to contact them.

Companies frequently use databases in combination with word processing programs so they can send the same document to many customers, accompanied by a letter customized with the correct name, address, and heading. If the database includes preferred language, individual letters can be generated in those languages (provided, of course, that letters are first prepared in the different languages). The database can also be used to print out envelope labels. No one likes to receive a letter in which their name is misspelled or, even worse, in a language they cannot understand. It is important then, to keep the database updated and accurate.

Companies should also maintain a second database in which they gather information collected as a result of the market stimulation. This information relates specifically to potential orders from customers who, for example, expressed interest during a visit to a trade show in having a demonstration of equipment.

What sort of information should be included in the second database? The simple answer could be, enough to allow sales engineers to strategize their selling efforts. Because high-tech sales engineers selling to foreign markets seldom deal with many customers simultaneously, it can be argued that they can strategize effectively by keeping good notes. However, if the information is in a database, other employees can also access it, such as, for example, the manager of a different sales group who needs the information to manage the group and allocate resources efficiently. The information is also needed by the company's top management and by the financial department, which uses it in assessing overall company needs (e.g., capital, production capacity, human resources).

The customer data that the second databases should contain is largely determined by the industry and the specific company. The following is a partial list of general information that all industry and company types would find useful.

- Record number
- Country
- Customer
- Product line
- Equipment description
- Initial enquiry date
- Order amount

- Date for any responsible sales representatives
- Probability of an order
- Expected date of order
- Decision maker's name
- Details concerning the competition
- Next action and its date

Forecasts have to be made of the probability of winning orders from each prospective customer, which in turn can be used by the production department, along with other market information, to plan production. Ideally, the production plan should result in timely deliveries to customers, early enough to give the company an advantage over its competition. On the other hand, overproduction and the resultant buildup of inventory can be very detrimental to a company's finances. Forecasting, then, is of considerable importance.

Sales engineers can carry portions of a centralized database in small laptop computers. They can access a central database remotely by modem and, if they possess the appropriate software, enter updated information.

4.6.3 Qualifying Customers and Determining Selling Strategies

After establishing a database of prospective customers, the next step in the sales cycle is to qualify customers and strategize selling. It would seem an easy enough matter to peruse this database and extract information from it. But what does "qualifying" customers mean? In this context, it means selecting a subset of prospective customers from the database for whom an aggressive sales strategy will be planned. Criteria is required to perform this selection. The criteria differ from company to company, but clearly, the expected value of the sale and the assessed probability of success should be included, along with timing.

After the customer qualification process is completed, a strategy is set for each prospective sales effort. Which sales engineer should be assigned? How should that sales engineer proceed? A two-pronged selling effort is often required—one at a technical level and the other at an executive level. Should the same sales engineer be assigned to both tasks? If the product is highly complex and expensive equipment, should a selling team be assigned to the customer? Who should be on that team? Who should lead it? Other factors that must be studied to strategize these sales efforts include:

- A study of the competition and their weak and strong points;
- A carefully considered comparison of company and competitor strengths;

- A careful study of the customer's organization that identifies the decision maker and how the decision will be made.

In the case of equipment of relatively small value (for example, instrumentation), some of this study comes automatically and is performed almost subconsciously. In the case of very costly equipment, the study should be more thorough.

4.6.4 Selling Efforts

Sales engineers are not always able to answer all the questions that determine an appropriate strategy before they make the preliminary visit to the customer. By this time, though, they have truly entered into the sales cycle, and they will either make the sale, learn that they must "dequalify" the customer, or, in the more usual case, be in a better position to quantify the probability and timing of the sale. In this phase, all the acuity, training, and talents that sales engineers possess are brought into play. To assess the probability of success, sales engineers must answer these five key questions:

1. Do they really understand the customer's problem, so that they can offer a solution, since selling solutions is what they have to do?
2. Can they convince the customer that their solution is a good one, and if possible, a much better one than anyone else could offer?
3. After they complete their sales efforts, do they believe that their position is better than the competition's position? As good? Worse?
4. Have they determined whether the customer has a budget to purchase the equipment? Too often, sales engineers are hesitant to ask this key question, which a prospective customer would normally answer willingly.
5. Have they determined who the decision maker is? Have they talked to the decision maker? In many cases, the final decision is made at the executive level, but there is always someone whose influence is key to that executive decision. Sales engineers must find out who the influential person is and concentrate on selling to that person.

4.6.5 Quantifying Probability and Timing

There are as many forecasting methods as there are companies selling equipment. Some of these methods use a weighting factor that is the product of the probability percentage of success multiplied by the money value of the booking as the forecast bookings value. The argument here is that where there are many customers the statistical average of this type of forecasting gives a meaningful result. However, selling is a binary business. You either sell or you don't sell. If there are relatively few qualified customers, then these statistics can be very misleading. Suppose that there are five customers, each of them a prospective buyer of equipment that sells for $10 million. Let us further suppose that the sales engineer thinks the chance of success with any of the customers is slim, say 10%. Does the sales engineer truly believe that, with these 10–1 odds against selling to anyone, sales will total $5 million (10% × 5 × $10 million) worth of equipment? Nonsense! It is far more likely the sales engineer will sell nothing.

Still, insisting that sales engineers assign a probability of success percentage to each prospective booking can be a good discipline. Sales engineers have to be confident of success and, by nature, optimists. They might be so sure of success that even before they know whether the customer has a budget, they assume that they are "80% sure" of an order. Rules can inject some realism into the forecast process. For example, the rules might constrain sales engineers to assign two separate probabilities. The first is the probability that the customer will order from anyone, and the second is the probability that the sales engineer's company will be awarded the order. If it is not known for sure that a budget exists for the purchase, the maximum first probability could be limited to, say, 50%. If there is a total of three prospective bidders, and if at an early stage in the forecast process their relative standing is not known, the rules indicate equal probabilities for each. That is, the total probability of success is now 50% of 33.3%, or less than 17%. Yet, without these rules, overconfident sales engineers might have insisted on their 80% guess for the probability.

But what is done with these probability figures? For the purpose of forecasting orders, it might be best to divide the probabilities into three categories. In the first category, probability is below a predefined low threshold of, for example, 20%. If the forecast probability is that low, it might be best not to count on that order at all. Certainly, the sales engineer needs to follow the prospective order and strategize how to win it, but until the forecast probability is higher than the established threshold, it is best not to count on success here and to leave this prospective order value out of the sum of all prospective orders.

The second category could contain prospective orders for which probability is above a predefined high threshold of, for example, 75%. If the forecast probability is that high, the company might decide that the probability of an order is high enough that its value is completely included, in unweighted fashion, in the total forecast. Again, the sales engineer needs to follow the prospective order and strategize how to win it. Now, however, the sales engineer and the sales manager must concentrate their efforts on winning this order as a matter of high priority.

The third band could be an intermediate one, between these two probabilities. Here again it might be best not to count on any success. However, the objective of sales engineers for prospects in this category is to strategize what they need to do to bring this prospect into the higher category.

The category thresholds can be changed as the company acquires more experience in forecasting. The lower and higher threshold values can be changed as a result of actual success and failure rates.

Based on the categories that prospective customers fall in and the strategy that sales engineers decide to pursue, throughout the sales cycle they should continue to update and refine the information in the database. The database should contain entries of sales successes, as well as sales prospects. Periodic review of the database should indicate when existing customers should be contacted. Failure to maintain contact almost invariably facilitates entry of the competition.

4.7 EXISTING CUSTOMERS

What actions should sales engineers take for existing customers? At the very least, they must call often on the customers they are responsible for. If they believe otherwise, they have much to learn. Perhaps a brief but true anecdote concerning a company that failed to maintain close contact with a key customer illustrates the danger.

- An American electronics company well-known for its instrumentation for antenna measurements established itself as the leading supplier throughout the world. One of its foreign sales and service subsidiaries sold a large system for automatic measurement of antenna characteristics to the leading government laboratory in their country. The equipment worked well, and the customer was very satisfied with its performance.
- The most important characteristics of an antenna are related to its three-dimensional, far-field radiation pattern at various frequencies. The automatic measurement system determined these characteristics by measuring the intensity and phase of the radiation pattern at different spatial positions.
- As time passed and more and more measurements were required for highly directive phased-array antennas, laboratory personnel began to investigate using other instrumentation to measure intensity and phase. At the time, network analyzers manufactured by a leading supplier of instrumentation that were used for intensity and phase measurements of RF components were not as fast as those supplied with the automatic antenna measurement system. However, not long after, this supplier started to offer a much faster network analyzer and proposed its use for antenna measurements to the government laboratory personnel.
- A full year passed before funds needed for the purchase of new instrumentation were available. During this year, the company that supplied the original system developed new instrumentation that was even faster than the competitor's network analyzer. The sales engineer who should have been visiting the laboratory on a regular basis heard that measurement speed was important to the customer and only then decided to visit. To his chagrin, he was informed that approval had just been obtained to place the order with his competitor, and the approval cycle was too long and difficult to start anew. Needless to say, his competitor had kept close to the customer throughout this long period.
- The sales engineer believed that he was the victim of bad luck. He and his customers were very competent technically, and he knew that orders for such equipment took a long time to mature. He did not believe that continual contact with such customers was needed until he had something new to offer.

Had the sales engineer kept in contact with his customer by visiting him every month or so, he would have been aware of the problems. He undoubtedly could have kept the customer content by offering him an upgrade. But what could his reason be for such frequent visits? Simply stating that he thought he would make the visit because he was in the neighborhood would be a poor excuse. However, if his stated reason for each visit was to discuss any problems with the technical people, he would have been made welcome at any time.

Proper continuity in a sales effort entails keeping track of existing customers and ensuring that they are aware that a sales engineer is available to help them.

4.8 LICENSING AS A METHOD OF SELLING

Licensing a manufacturer in a customer's country as a way of penetrating the market has been already discussed. However, there is another aspect of licensing that should be addressed, especially with regard to selling to a developing country. Sales engineers must be aware of this aspect even when there is no customer request for licensing.

Offering to license a product for manufacture in a developing country can be very attractive for both the company and customer. The prospect of furthering their industrial capability by signing a license agreement for manufacture of some advanced technology product is welcomed in most countries. Sometimes, there is a request for proposal (RFP) for the supply of some product, and only when replies are received does the customer ask for a license agreement.

If sales engineers sense that an offer to license the product for manufacture could be of interest, and if the company is not opposed to the idea, then offering such a license might help sales efforts. An example from real experience illustrates this possibility.

- Some years ago, a well-known American company was trying to sell its commercial marine radars to a country in the Far East. The market was not very large, and a small measure of success was obtained. The sales engineer decided to investigate whether the navy of that country would purchase any of these commercial radars, which were much less expensive than military shipborne radars and could perform the required tasks. There was reluctance on the part of the navy officers to even consider purchase of other than MIL-specification equipment. However, when the sales engineer mentioned that he could probably arrange for local manufacture, which would assure local service, supply of spares, and when needed, more radars, the attitude quickly changed.
- The navy officers stated that they wished to pursue this arrangement. The sales engineer was then faced with two formidable tasks. The easier task was to find a competent local firm that was acceptable to the navy. The more difficult task was to convince his company that their trade secrets would be protected and that the increase in revenue from sales and royalties would more than compensate for any possible decrease in sales as a result of the license or loss of markets to the licensee.

- The sales engineer was convinced that the local company would take years to arrive at a position at which it could manufacture the complete radars. He believed that during that time he could sell kits of assemblies to the local manufacturer, to help it fulfill its orders from the navy. The difficult selling job was to get to the decision makers in his own company and convince them. He prepared his internal sales campaign well and succeeded.
- The result was that no competitor ever succeeded in selling similar radars to the navy of that country for about 10 years! Even better, the local company decided not to manufacture the radars and continued to purchase kits of subassemblies and parts for all those years. The sales engineer's decision to exploit the idea of licensing paid off very handsomely.

Another true example follows, with results that were much less satisfactory.

- Another well-known American company manufactured a line of mechanical positioners for antennas, complete with controllers and servos. The company was very successful in selling these products to a certain Mideastern country. However, the authorities in that country requested that the company grant a license to manufacture the positioners in their country.
- The sales engineer was afraid that, unless his company complied, his customer would successfully develop a local equivalent or obtain a license from a competitor. Regrettably, he was not able to convince his company to grant a license: the company manager was convinced that, as the world market leader, they could successfully resist any requirement for licensing and continue to sell in that country.
- The result was unexpected. The customer was not only successful in having a local company develop a similar line of products, but these products were plug-to-plug compatible with the American company's products. Furthermore, because the design was more modern, in some respects the local products were better and cheaper. Not only was that particular foreign market lost, but the local company went after the worldwide market very aggressively and was successful. The American company has since redesigned its own products and is fighting back, but it has lost an important share of the total market to this new competitor.

The lesson is clear. Licensing can be a good way to penetrate a foreign market, and there are dangers in refusing to grant licenses. Very often, the vision of what could occur is clear to sales engineers, but they might not be able to convince the key people in their organizations of that vision. Their selling skills might be more taxed in accomplishing this selling than in selling to the foreign customer!

4.9 GIFTS

The subject of gifts can be a very sensitive one, full of moral, political, and legal implications. In the discussion that follows, some questions that are posed are left unanswered, and readers must arrive at their own answers. Under this heading are included gifts that range from the simplest tokens offered to customers, such as a pencil with the company name and logo printed on it, to the costlier gifts, such as offers of free trips abroad or substantial bribes.

Everyone knows the sorts of gifts that are acceptable to a customer in one's own country and that are legally and morally permissible. But individuals brought up in different cultures do not necessarily share the same attitude about giving gifts. As an example, anyone who has had extensive dealings in India will have had the experience of admiring some object in an Indian's home or office. If they expressed that admiration, they might have been startled to find that their Indian host insisted on giving the object to them as a gift—a gesture that was far from what they intended when they complimented the object. Sales engineers must be sensitive to the culture of the country in which they hope to do business and be aware of cultural differences.

In Europe, no one would hesitate to invite a customer to dinner, but there are countries and customer categories (military ones, for example) for which this would not be acceptable. What does the culture of a country permit? Will offering a gift to a customer aid selling? If yes, what sort of gift is acceptable? If sales engineers are suddenly faced with a demand for a gift, how should they react?

In many countries, the exchange of gifts is considered common courtesy. Individuals who have had dealings in Japan can testify to their surprise and often delight at receiving some delicate gift from their customer. Should they have offered a gift? In Arab countries, simple gifts, such as pencils or lighters, are often given to customers with no complications and with friendliness. In all these situations, sales engineers should consult their foreign representatives for advice beforehand. The advice might be to offer a key member of the customer's personnel a free trip to the company factory. Sales engineers must be on their guard, however, to detect if the advice implies a substantial bribe.

Bribery is immoral by any Western standard and is illegal by most standards, yet it is widely practiced. Many respectable companies do not tolerate bribery and will penalize severely any employees involved in it. In the United States an important law, the Foreign Corrupt Practices Act, forbids companies and their employees or representatives from giving gifts to foreign government employees or functionaries for the purpose of influencing procurement. It imposes harsh penalties, including imprisonment of company directors.

Some argue that, in developing countries, government officials rely on gifts to supplement inadequate incomes. It is further argued that if one company refrains from bribery, another company that does employ bribery will get the business. There is much truth (but no justification) in these arguments, just as there is truth in the argument of some companies that if they refrain from selling lethal arms to countries, others will get the business.

There is a relatively recent example of arms sales involving bribery. The Swedish arms manufacturer Bofors obtained a 8.4 billion SEK artillery contract from India. An investigation by the Swedish National Audit Board revealed that Bofors had made payments of between 170 and 250 million SEK to its Indian agents, under suspicious circumstances. Even when pressed, Bofors declined to reveal details of this payment. However, the payment precipitated the resignation of India's defense minister, and talk of corruption was one of the reasons the late Rajiv Gandhi subsequently lost the election.

The two true examples described below involve gifts that are in the nature of bribes. Readers are left to decide for themselves how they would react and how they would advise their companies to react under like circumstances.

- In a North African country, the army was renovating a former military airfield that had fallen into disuse. An international conference of unaligned countries was going to take place in the country, and the army believed they could best ensure the safety of the eminent participants by landing aircraft in that airfield.
- As the conference drew close, the officer in charge of the airfield renovation suddenly realized that it would be wise to have a surveillance radar on site to help with air traffic control. Time was very short, and he asked several qualified companies if they had a suitable radar that could be delivered, installed, and operating within three months. Obviously, very few suppliers could meet these delivery requirements.
- A sales engineer from a European company heard about the requirements and could satisfy them with a surplus radar in inventory. He visited the officer in charge. Knowing that competition was limited, he made an offer at a fairly high price, with a substantial margin of profit for the company.
- The officer agreed to purchase the radar and to arrange for a letter-of-credit payment upon shipment; he said that he would send a military transport aircraft to pick up the radar. But he also explained (in private) that he wanted the price doubled and that 50% of the money was to be deposited in his personal bank account in Switzerland. Everyone would benefit (except for the poor taxpayer in that developing country). The sales engineer knew that, although there was not much competition, there was some. He wanted to make the sale and feared that by not complying with the officer he would lose it. Yet, he was very uneasy about the request. He had to react swiftly. What was he to do?

Another example follows, again involving a developing country. This example concerns an American company acting under the constraints of the Foreign Corrupt Practices Act. All facts cited are true, although references to the country and company are disguised.

- A developing country with extensive natural resources was seeking to modernize its communications. The country's minister of communications wished to implement TV reception in a number of towns, together with telephone communications. He wished to be able to originate TV programs from a number of these towns and to rebroadcast the programs using TV transmitters located in the towns. Geographic conditions made it very difficult to use coaxial cable or microwave links, which were considered too vulnerable to damage. Satellite earth stations connected to small telephone exchanges and to local TV transmitters seemed a good answer to the problem.
- The project was fairly large, worth tens of millions of U.S. dollars, and financing was required. The country was considered a good credit risk because of its extensive

natural resources, and it requested that any company proposing to sell it the needed equipment offer the necessary financing. Japanese, Italian, French, Spanish, and American companies were invited to bid.

- One American company was invited to bid as a result of the sales efforts of its Spanish subsidiary. Few Americans in its satellite communications division could converse in Spanish, a common language in the customer's country, and the division management thought that the probability of success was small. They were pleased to allow the Spanish subsidiary to do the selling, supporting it with the necessary technical and price information.
- A turnkey system was required, which included civil works, roadways, buildings, and the supply of prime power. The Spanish subsidiary obtained quotations from its foreign agent, whose organization was capable of accomplishing the work. This amounted to approximately 5% of the entire price. The agent himself was to receive 5%, a fairly large commission given the size of the order. The satellite communications division added the 10% total to the prices and prepared price, project management, and technical proposals to be translated into Spanish by its subsidiary. At this point, the financing proposal was not yet required, only a statement acknowledging that it could be arranged.
- The Spanish subsidiary submitted the proposals and visited the customer with the agent. It was quite apparent that the agent was on intimate terms with the customer. After some discussion, it also became apparent that the agent was familiar with contents of competitive proposals. The company was thanked and told that the government would let them know the results of their deliberations very soon. They were then told by their agent that the proposal was well received, but that the one from another competitor was more attractive as it included local civil works at about 10% of the total price, versus only about 5% for them. No mention was made of total prices from competition except to say that they were reasonably close to one another.
- At this point, the Spanish subsidiary asked the agent what could be done to increase the chances of obtaining the contract. The answer from the agent was that a new price offer for the civil works needed to be made, increasing it from 5% of the total price to 15%. The agent added that the total price for everything could be increased by this extra 10% and insisted that the increased total price would in no way decrease chances of success, but would assure it! It seemed rather perplexing to the sales people that this move would increase their chances of success, because, normally, a higher price should have the opposite effect. Despite this, the agent seemed so assured of victory and his contacts with the customer seemed so close that the price increase was made to the proposal.
- The customer then asked for a financing proposal, and financing for this project was obtained from the appropriate American government agency. As with all similar agencies, the money for such financing comes from the American taxpayer.
- Success crowned the sales efforts, and the contract was awarded to the American company. However, within a very few weeks following the award, upon investigation, the American company executives realized that the agent was so closely con-

nected with the customer that collusion between them could be presumed. Furthermore, it was eminently clear that the local civil works could be accomplished well within 5% of the contract price and that the 15% was at least 10% too high. There was the distinct risk that the Foreign Corrupt Practices Act would be violated and American taxpayers' money would be used illegally, both criminal violations that were subject to severe penalties. Yet the contract was very lucrative and, from all other points of view, extremely attractive. What were they to do?

Some people who possess limited experience in the marketing field believe that bribery is permissible in many cases and, indeed, is a way of life in some geographic areas. Some even believe that if an independent representative mediates between seller and buyer, so that the seller can disclaim all knowledge of what is involved, bribery can be used. Whether or not bribery can help in isolated cases, the overall issue of company integrity is too important and must not be compromised. This point cannot be stressed strongly enough: bribery is usually illegal and always unethical. It might be instructive to read an excerpt from the policies and procedures manual of a large American corporation.[2]

POLICY
Company (***) and its officers and employees shall conduct business in accordance with high ethical standards and the applicable law of the United States and other nations, where the company, its divisions, and subsidiaries engage in business. The company's business transactions shall be recorded properly and accurately on the company's books.

PROCEDURE
In furtherance of the policy stated above, all officers and employees of the company shall comply with the following:

A. No money or other thing of value shall be paid or given directly as a bribe, kickback, or other means of improper influence for the purpose of securing or retaining business.
B. Without limiting the generality of the above statement, all officers and employees of the company, its subsidiaries, and divisions shall comply fully with the U.S. Foreign Corrupt Practices Act of 1977, as amended (FCPA). The FCPA prohibits direct or indirect offers, payments, gifts, and promises to pay or give money or anything of value to a foreign official political party or candidate for political office for the purpose of influencing a government's decision to award business to any person or help anyone retain business. Violators might be fined and imprisoned. Managers might be held responsible for the acts of employees or outside sales representatives if the managers know of the acts or, under the circumstances, have reason to

2. Reprinted with permission from Scientific Atlanta, Inc.

know. No commissions or other payments will be paid to agents, consultants, distributors, or sales representatives with the understanding that any part of the payment will be used for a purpose prohibited by the FCPA. Agents, consultants, distributors, and sales representatives who assist the company in sales to foreign government agencies shall be required to agree in writing to comply with the FCPA.

Reasonable entertainment of commercial customers and business associates is permitted for proper business purposes. Entertainment of U.S. government employees is prohibited by law and by this policy. All entertainment shall be documented on expense reports and subject to supervisory review.

All receipts and expenditures of money and other assets by or on behalf of the company shall be recorded accurately on the books of the company and its subsidiaries and divisions. No false or inaccurate documents shall be created for the purpose of misleading company personnel, customers, or officials of any government agency.

Employees who authorize, select, or recommend products, supplies, or services to be purchased by the company shall not accept money or any other thing of significant value from any supplier or representative thereof. This policy shall be made known to suppliers. Gifts of items exceeding a market value of $50 will generally be viewed as in violation of this policy unless approved in writing by the recipient's supervisor or manager. Employees might accept the hospitality of suppliers at business meetings, unless so extravagant as to permit a reasonable inference that improper influence is intended.

Employees are required to report to their supervisors or managers any offers or gifts of items exceeding nominal value, even if less than $50 in value. The supervisors or managers shall decide whether the employee might accept the gift, or whether it should be rejected, returned, or otherwise disposed of. Avoidance of both the occasion and the appearance of improper influence are the guiding objectives on which the decision shall be based. An employee shall not be considered in violation of this policy if all the facts are disclosed to the employee's supervisor and the supervisor's approval of the employee's conduct is given.

Gifts exceeding $50 in fair value that cannot be rejected without embarrassment or harm to the company shall be delivered to the corporate treasury department within three days of receipt or three days after traveling recipient returns to his or her principle work location. The treasury department shall determine final disposition of the gift.

Employees shall disclose any substantial interest in any firm that conducts or seeks to conduct business with the company when the employee is in a position to influence any element of the business relationship. An employee will be deemed to have a substantial interest in a firm if the employee, a close relative, or any person living in the employee's home is an officer or director of the firm or owns 1% or more of the outstanding stock or other equity of the firm. Unless a division or corporate officer with management responsibility for the employee determines, after review of all relevant facts and circumstances, that the company's best interest will not be jeopardized by the employee's interest in the firm, the business relationship with the firm will be ended or the employee will be reassigned to prevent the possibility of improper influence.

4.10 TRAINING

Many companies ensure that their sales engineers are not only well trained technically and very familiar with the products they sell, but are also well trained in what are called sales techniques. There are specialist agencies in many parts of the world that offer courses in which sales engineers learn how to approach clients, use questioning techniques and listening skills, manage objections, ask for the order, and negotiate. At least one "excellent" company (IBM) uses its most skilled sales engineers as instructors, and these instructors are typically assigned to the task for two to three years. The instructors are then assigned elsewhere, and 75% of them become line managers.

Some companies give their sales engineers a broad base of training in all their products rather than detailed instruction on one product. This is typically done by companies that have achieved a leadership position in a market segment and that manufacture multiple products or categories of products, for example, general purpose electronic instrumentation. These organizations can call upon specialized help as needed, but their broad range of products can be sold by sales engineers who are not necessarily deeply knowledgeable about every item.

On the other hand, companies that are not market leaders often employ highly specialized sales engineers. Because of their intimate knowledge of the product they sell and the field it serves (for example, fast-Fourier transform instrumentation for vibration analysis), specialists can sell the product by helping customers solve technical problems. These products might be higher priced than the market leaders' products or even inferior in some specifications. Without the added value of specialized knowledge, the sales engineers probably couldn't win orders from the market leaders.

Many companies, including IBM, Hewlett-Packard, Coca-Cola, ICI Americas, and National Semiconductor emphasize strategic selling, and many of their sales engineers are trained by Miller Heiman & Associates, Inc. In their book *Strategic Selling*, Miller and Heiman stress the importance of strategizing the sale and explain that part of that process involves determining who the decision maker is [4]. They point out that there are really three decision makers: the ultimate "economic" decision maker; the "user" decision maker, who must be convinced as well; and the "technical" decision maker, who screens out competitors who do not meet technical requirements. (Sometimes, these three are one and the same person.) They also stress the importance of finding a "coach" in the customer's organization who will help the sales engineer.

There is always an individual or small group who make the ultimate decision to purchase or not purchase a product. The decision maker might rely on the recommendations of technical people but usually possesses enough technical knowledge to understand the problem that the product must resolve. This decision maker is the person to convince, and clarity and simplicity will count much more than technical depth. Technical training should enable sales engineers to perform this kind of selling, but need not be so profound as to enable them to discuss design in detail. It is equally important for sales engineers to be familiar enough with the customer's decision-making process to sense when someone in the loop might say no and know how to combat that no.

4.11 THE FOREIGN REPRESENTATIVE

Choosing the best channel of distribution is one of the keys to success in selling to a foreign market. Chapter 3 discusses the various channels of distribution in foreign countries and describes how organizations can select the appropriate channel. To review, companies sometimes establish wholly or partially owned subsidiaries in foreign countries from which they obtain a strong market share. Companies that do not make use of subsidiaries instead employ independent local (foreign) representatives.

Sales engineers normally have only limited time for visits to foreign countries and so local representatives are needed to provide continuity of contact. In addition to understanding local culture, the foreign representative should also be familiar with the culture of the sales engineer's country. The foreign representative will help the sales engineer bridge cultures and avoid inadvertent faux pas.

It is usually far better to choose foreign representatives who possess all the desirable attributes over candidates who are only well connected, even if the connection is excellent. No matter how good foreign representatives are, they will seldom be good enough to accomplish a sale without substantial help from a sales engineer.

4.12 SERVICE AND THE SERVICE ORGANIZATION

The most successful international companies place service first among their top priorities. The former and well-known vice president responsible for worldwide marketing for IBM, Buck Rodgers wrote a very persuasive book on marketing called *The IBM Way*. One of the chapters of his book is entitled "Service, service, service . . . and more service." Rodgers writes in this chapter that "IBM pioneered the idea that *selling* and *servicing* were inseparable in the marketing function, and although no dictionary would consider the two words to be synonymous, IBM does" [5]. All successful companies adopt this attitude toward service, and their service organizations reflect that fact.

The following list identifies some of the tasks that service departments are responsible for. The list is a formidable one, reflecting the importance of the service organization to the company and its customers.

- Predelivery inspection of products
- Site studies and installation surveys

- Installation of equipment and systems

- Maintenance and repair
- Warranty services
- Postwarranty repairs
- Calibration services
- Equipment upgrades and refurbishment

- Maintenance of an adequate spares inventory
- Technical bulletins to customers
- Organization of technical symposiums
- Technical assistance to customers

It might be obvious that service is of prime importance to a customer, especially a foreign customer who is remote from the company's factories. What is not so obvious is the fact that sales engineers should include consideration of service in their selling efforts. Sales engineers must assure themselves that the product they sell can be maintained and serviced properly. Their proposals must include this stipulation. If the company cannot offer the service needed to ensure customer satisfaction, the sales engineers must determine how to train their customer's or representative's technicians to service the product. They must also ensure that an adequate supply of spares is on hand, whether the spares are purchased or not. Clearly, it is better to convince customers of the importance of purchasing spares, not for profit but because lack of spares can sour relationships. Sales engineers who underestimate the importance of good service learn, to their regret, that success is difficult to achieve with dissatisfied customers. As soon as customers realize that they purchased equipment they cannot maintain properly, they will almost assuredly turn against the sales engineer and the company and look elsewhere.

There are many modern ways of servicing complex electronic or electromechanical equipment that can be implemented remotely. User friendly diagnostic hardware and software can be included with the product to help customers locate and isolate problems. In addition, diagnostic tools can be transmitted via modem connections to telephone lines.

Telephone calls from customers should be transferred quickly to knowledgeable service people. Customers who get fast and helpful answers to problems learn to trust a company's service capabilities. If telephone service personnel are fast, courteous, and helpful, customers will be confident that they are dealing with a reputable company with a high standard of quality. If they are kept waiting on the phone or simply do not receive assistance, they will conclude rapidly that the quality of service and perhaps the quality of the equipment are not high.

Selling service is normally a very profitable practice. Service revenue can be high and augment the less tangible revenue that comes from the future orders of satisfied customers. Professional sales engineers understand this and their selling efforts include selling both products and maintenance service.

Problems can arise with a customer's equipment that might affect the organization's production. Should a customer complain of a such a problem, the sale engineer must attend to the matter. The fault might lie with the customer or with equipment supplied by a third party, but, regardless of whose responsibility it is, failure to resolve the problem might result in irreparable damage to the reputation of the sales engineer and, consequently, the company. Timely corrective action can only devolve to the sales engineer's benefit. The following true example is typical of such problems.

- A servo positioner controller was sold to a well-known Italian company by the Italian subsidiary of an American company. That controller was to replace a previously supplied manual model. The input signals to the new controller came from a computer supplied by Hewlett-Packard, sold by its own Italian subsidiary.
- The new controller did not accept the computer-generated signals, although it was supposed to. The Italian customer blamed the Italian subsidiary that supplied the controller for its failure to rectify the problem quickly. The sales engineer in the subsidiary contacted the head office in the United States. The project engineer in the head office assured the sales engineer that the matter was under control and that the Hewlett-Packard program manager in Santa Rosa, California was aware of it. This manager had admitted that the software Hewlett-Packard supplied to its Italian subsidiary was outdated. He explained that new software was being sent to the subsidiary, which would install it. Meanwhile, the Italian Hewlett-Packard subsidiary disclaimed all knowledge of any problems, stating that its computer met all of the specifications.
- The problem quickly became acute and the purchaser stated that his production was stopped. He threatened to cease all future dealings with the American subsidiary and its company.

This is an example of a dissatisfied customer. What should the sales engineer do? Readers can ponder this problem and decide what they would do in the sales engineer's position.

How are sales engineers to know if their customers are satisfied? The only way to know is to check periodically and frequently. This checking instills confidence in customers, who will come to trust the sales engineers and be more likely to consult them about new requirements long before they consult the competition.

Checking is best accomplished by personal visits. Sales engineers who are very knowledgeable about their products are especially welcome because they might be able to resolve equipment problems during their visits. In fact, it is so easy for sales engineers to gain access to customers through this approach that it is surprising that more do not adopt it. If visits are too costly, at the very least sales engineers should make telephone calls to customers. They can use their customer databases to document reminders to make telephone calls or schedule visits.

4.13 EMPLOYEE CONSIDERATION, MOTIVATION, AND REWARDS

To be successful at selling, it helps an organization to have outgoing, optimistic sales engineers. It is commonly noted that some sales engineers experience wide swings in their emotions; they are over the moon when a booking is made and depressed when a booking is lost. The most successful, though, are stable people who are well adjusted to life, with self-confidence in their ability to succeed. Sales engineers need to believe that the product they and their companies are selling will solve their customers' problems.

Much attention has been paid to the problem of sales engineer incentives. These can certainly be financial, but managers who imagine that they can get any results they want by offering enough money will seldom be successful in the long run. There are other motivating factors that are at least as important. The following are keys to motivating sales engineers:

- They must feel that they are an important part of the company and, indeed, must be proud of the company. This is different from loyalty, which is automatically expected. The culture of a company should be conveyed to its sales force, including history and accomplishments. Above all, they must be treated with dignity and respect; otherwise, it will be impossible to encourage pride in belonging.
- They must receive recognition for anything they do well. This can be done in many ways, including such public acknowledgments as an honorary dinner, a thank-you note from a superior, or a gift to the engineer or the engineer's family.
- They must feel a sense of achievement and creativeness in their work. If they are simply a small part of a large team performing routine tasks instead of individuals to whom specific tangible objectives are assigned, it is doubtful they will ever feel truly creative.
- They should receive financial remuneration befitting their role. If the company can assign specific goals in terms of sales achieved versus budget for a given period, it is common practice to reward sales engineers with bonuses. Many companies are firm in their belief that some sort of commission bonus is a strong incentive to sales engineers, spurring them on to meet and exceed budgets.

In a book entitled *L'Impératif Humain* (see Appendix D), Manfred Mack stresses the fundamental importance of employee consideration. According employees the dignity they merit as human beings, listening to them, creating a real team, is something "excellent" companies have practiced for a long time. So many Japanese companies are noted for the single-minded purpose that is displayed by their employees that one wonders whether this is not one of the keys to their success. Of course, Japanese culture cannot be transplanted easily to other areas. Still, their awareness of the importance of employee consideration is striking. There is some indication, for example, that during times of recession, Japanese-owned manufacturing companies in Britain make far fewer employee redundancies (layoffs) than British manufacturing as a whole and choose redundancies only as a last resort.

The importance of employee consideration is so apparent that the subject is usually dismissed. And yet, the majority of companies are managed in a highly disciplined bureaucratic manner, often with fear injected as a means of managing and with little thought to this matter. Managers must understand that a highly motivated team of employees can easily out-perform another, and the results they achieve will show this. Human beings differ from one another and do not fit neatly into the rectangles drawn on an organization chart.

To obtain the best from everyone requires that managers understand employees' strengths and weaknesses, utilize those strengths, and either help individuals overcome weaknesses or use other resources as needed to accomplish their aims.

The list of motivating factors above included recognizing and rewarding achievement. An excerpt from Buck Rodgers' book, *The IBM Way,* might be instructive.

> Money isn't the only thing that motivates people. Almost anything that can bolster self-esteem can work. I don't mean that compliments or titles or certificates will satisfy a person who can't pay his bills—not for long, they won't—but they're a wonderful adjunct to a decent money package.
>
> Each time an IBM rep achieves his annual quota, he becomes a member of the Hundred Percent Club. He doesn't have to brag about his results; his membership in the club is well publicized throughout the company. Among his peers he's recognized as a high achiever.
>
> There's no doubt in my mind that a survey of new reps would show that their first goal, after being assigned a territory, is not to make "a lot of money" but to achieve membership in the Hundred Percent Club. A rep who has failed to make it for three years probably won't get the chance to go for it for a fourth.
>
> The top 10 percent of successful salespeople are elevated to the Golden Circle and their achievement is acknowledged throughout the entire organization, worldwide. They and their spouses are invited to a place such as Bermuda or Hawaii, and given full VIP treatment. Their celebrity status becomes known throughout the company and industry. At this meeting, it's not unusual to hear the spouse say "You better bring me back here next year."

Rodgers also writes,

> Another innovative program I recall was the Eagle Award, given to marketing reps who set new sales records in their divisions. The "best of the best" were thus honored—less than one hundred people who attain new highs in performance. Besides the attention and publicity accompanying so significant an award, the winners received a check for $5,000 and a beautiful trophy. [6]

IBM is probably one of the best examples of a company that consciously motivates its people in this way, but certainly not the only one.

4.13.1 The Inverted Pyramid

Jan Carlzon joined Scandinavian Airline System (SAS) some years ago as its CEO. He found a dispirited organization, with many unmotivated people and low morale. There were constant customer complaints about inadequate service. What Carlzon accomplished as CEO to turn SAS around into a highly successful company was remarkable, and he attributed much of this enormous improvement to a change in organization philosophy.

Orders and objectives permeate down from the top to the bottom, the level that has the most contact with the outside world of customers. Above this bottom layer, managers are sometimes so busy planning and managing that they seem to resent the interference in this process by customers! In the usual organization there is a pyramid, with the CEO at the apex, followed by top management, and successive management and employee strata under them. Pressures in such an organization can easily result in passivity and strict obedience to regulation on the part of those at the bottom of the pyramid. Failure to recognize that all employees must be accorded dignity and consideration can only exacerbate this situation.

Carlzon inverted the pyramidal structure, as shown in Figure 4.2. He insisted that those at the base, where customer contact was greatest, be made aware of their preeminent importance in the organization and that those "below" them (as the inverted pyramid narrowed) were not there to command, but to assist the larger group in fulfilling their roles. This attitude, Carlzon stated, must "go down" the pyramid to the CEO himself. His main job is to assure that he assists his "subordinates," above him in the inverted pyramid, in every way possible.

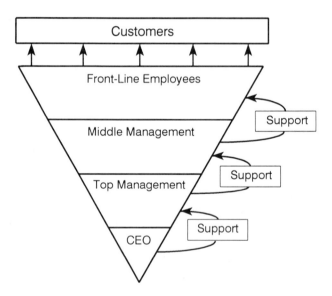

Figure 4.2 The inverted pyramid.

According to Carlzon's organizational structure, each person in an organization works for the customer, not for some superior. Of course, such an organization can only function if intrinsic human values replace the "command and obey" concept of the traditional pyramid structure. Organizations would do well to ponder deeply this inverted pyramid and realize the enormous benefits that can result when all the members of a closely knit team pull toward the same objective. Not only is it a pleasure to work for such an organization, but its efficiency can be so high that profit objectives are much easier to reach than otherwise.

Regrettably, many people enter the managerial levels of an organization without understanding all this. Possibly one of the reasons for the relative rarity of inverted pyramid organizations is the prevalence of managers who feel they must dominate their subordinates. Managers of marketing groups have a team under them that includes many employees in direct contact with customers. That team is best directed using concepts of support taken from the inverted pyramid.

4.13.2 Bonus Policy

If sales objectives are realistic and demanding, the results obtained should be judged against them. Many companies grant bonuses to their marketing managers for their "direct reports," as well as to their sales engineers. The magnitude of sales engineers' bonuses are a function of objective achievement and are often given monthly or quarterly in the form of commissions on bookings.

Some managers decide that a sales team should share the bonus (possibly with individual bonuses in proportion to both salary and booking achieved for the period). The logic behind this is that it tends to create a cooperative team spirit and that it might be too difficult to divide the territory and markets in neat and separable portions and assign them individually. Other managers assign clear objectives for a given territory or product line to individual sales engineers, who receive bonuses that depend strictly on their own results.

Bonus policies need to be simple, clearly stated, and unambiguous. When results can be measured quantitatively, as they often can be for sales engineers, the employees included in the plan should be able to calculate their own bonuses, to encourage them to achieve budgeted results. Bonuses should be given as soon after bookings as possible, or their value as incentives becomes diluted. The commission bonus is simple but, because many people (including the CEO) might have participated in obtaining the order, the bonus might be unwarranted. Still, it is best not to exclude certain types of booking from the bonus policy and a common way to avoid giving unwarranted "windfall" bonuses is to impose an upper limit. This can be high enough not to undermine motivation for the sales engineers.

Where results cannot all be measured quantitatively, many companies still reward their marketing managers and their direct reports with bonuses. These are invariably based on some sort of evaluation of results versus objectives. Some of these objectives might be qualitative, for example, a manager's objective might be to manage the sales group effectively so that its objectives are achieved. The judgment as to how well the manager meets these objectives is subjective. It is normal in these cases for the manager's superiors to pass judgment and assign the bonus amount.

Whether the objectives are measured qualitatively or quantitatively, they should all be measured against established and agreed-upon objectives. In the case of sales engineers, the objective might be as simple as the annual bookings volume for a given territory or the bookings for a quarter or a list of assigned products. For financial or technical service directors, the objectives are more complex and less quantitative but still needed.

Different companies have different criteria concerning the relative ratio of bonus amount to total income. Most companies seem to allot at least 10% and often as much as 50% of employees' total yearly compensation as the bonus they will receive if they meet their objectives. Many companies increase the bonus rate substantially if the objectives are surpassed.

To be meaningful, objectives must be achievable, even if they are tough to reach. They should be presented to the sales engineers, certainly not imposed on them. Furthermore, organizations should be able to determine to a high degree the benefits sales engineers should receive when others share the credit for bookings. Best, of course, would be an unambiguous statement of individual responsibility in yearly objectives.

Companies that do not have a bonus policy and wish to formulate and implement one can modify the sample policy given below. Sometimes, sales engineers' first reactions to bonus policies are to oppose them. They fear that their take-home pay will be reduced if they do not meet budgets. A considerable amount of discussion might be needed to persuade these sales engineers of the benefits, which include the possibility of increasing take-home pay substantially. If the bonus system is new, for the first year the target commission amount could be approximately equal to the normal yearly salary increase they would otherwise receive. The ratio of bonus to fixed amount can be increased yearly, until the desired ratio is reached.

4.13.3 An Example of a Bonus Policy

The following is an example of a bonus policy that is flexible enough to be applied even where individual sales engineers might have to share some bookings credit with other sales engineers. It is much simpler to apply if there are no "indirect" bookings, and all bookings can be uniquely and totally attributed to individual sales engineers.

Purpose

The purpose of this policy is to provide a financial incentive bonus to sales engineers, based upon their bookings performance compared to their bookings goal.

Direct and Indirect Bookings

Direct bookings are defined as bookings that are uniquely attributable to the sales engineers under this policy. Indirect bookings are bookings that are attributable partially to the sales engineers and partially to one or more additional sales engineers. The sum of all direct and indirect bookings for all sales engineers shall be equal to the total group bookings. (Note: group to be defined.)

Sales Engineers' Bookings

Sales engineers' bookings are defined as the sum of all direct bookings for product lines and customers assigned to them, plus an agreed-upon percentage of indirect bookings. That percentage shall be agreed upon by the sales manager, the sales engineers, and each of the other sales engineers to whom the booking is partially attributable. Should there be disagreement, then the sales manager's ruling shall be final. The sum of all indirect booking percentages for every single booking shall add to 100%.

Bookings Goal

The bookings goal is defined as the total sum of direct bookings and the agreed-upon percentage of indirect bookings that a sales engineer is expected to make during the fiscal year. The bookings goal shall be discussed and agreed upon by the sales engineers before the start of the fiscal year.

Target Bonus

The target bonus is that amount that a sales engineer would receive in the fiscal year (or lesser period if newly employed) if actual bookings are equal to the bookings goal. The target bonus and bookings goal will be used to calculate the commission rate for the sales engineer. The target bonus shall be discussed and agreed-upon by the sales engineers at or before the start of the company financial year.

Commission Rate

The ratio of target bonus to bookings goal will be the sales engineer's commission rate. This rate will be used for bonus determination until the sales engineer's cumulative bookings in the fiscal year reach the bookings goal. When the sales engineer's cumulative bookings exceed the bookings goal, the commission rate for the excess bookings will be double this rate.

Fiscal Period

Sales engineers' bonuses will be paid at the end of a fiscal period. This fiscal period will be every month, every three months, or every six months, as decided by the sales manager and communicated to the sales engineers before the start of the fiscal year.

Bonus Determination and Payment

Direct and indirect bookings credited to sales engineers will be determined at the end of every fiscal period. If the cumulative total of direct bookings plus percentage of indirect bookings does not exceed the bookings goal, the bonus for the fiscal period will be this total multiplied by the sales engineer's commission rate. As soon as the total exceeds the bookings goal, the sales engineer's bonus for that portion exceeding the bookings goal shall be that portion multiplied by twice the commission rate. Payment shall be effected as soon as possible after the fiscal period and no later than two weeks after its end.

Maximum Bonus

The maximum yearly bonus a sales engineer might receive under this policy shall not exceed twice the individual's yearly fixed salary.

Formal Notification

Each sales engineer included in this plan will receive formal notification to this effect, and notification will include:

- The fiscal period;
- A list of the assigned product lines and customers (or territory);
- The bookings goal;
- The target bonus and commission rate.

4.14 SUMMARY

This chapter presents a brief introduction to the entire selling process. Many aspects of this process are not touched upon, such as market research, niche markets, pricing, payment methods, currency exchange problems, and meeting market requirements for products. These aspects are commonly treated in standard marketing literature. In fact, marketing text books usually concentrate on consumer product marketing (and selling) while this book focuses on selling high-tech products in foreign markets. This focus continues in Chapter 5, which presents several relevant marketing cases.

REFERENCES

[1]   Harvey-Jones, John, *Making It Happen*, Harper Collins, 1989.
[2]   Sherlock, Paul, *Rethinking Business to Business Marketing*, New York: The Free Press, 1991, p. 21.
[3]   Morita, Akio, *Made in Japan*, Fontana, 1988.
[4]   *Strategic Selling*, Miller Heiman and Associates, Warner Books, 1985.
[5]   Rodgers, Buck, *The IBM Way*, Fontana, 1986, p. 185.
[6]   Rodgers, Buck, *The IBM Way*, Fontana, 1986, p. 218.

Chapter 5

Three Marketing Cases

Students often learn about real-life business situations and problems by studying and discussing cases of actual companies. The names of the companies and the people involved might be changed, but the situations are true. As in most real situations, it might be that not all the facts needed to formulate a logical plan of action are known. Part of the plan might be to determine all the facts, or a plan might be formulated on "best guesses." Furthermore, there is seldom a perfectly logical or unique solution to problems. It might even be necessary to formulate the essential problems. And when the problems are identified, there are usually several solutions, and it might be difficult to decide which one is best.

When students work with cases, typically they first try to formulate for themselves the critical issues and some possible plans of action. They might spend two hours on this activity and then meet with other students in small groups to discuss the case and formulate answers to the questions posed. Finally, all groups meet together for an open discussion to identify the critical issues, formulate answers to the questions posed, and propose action plans. Instructors try to elicit all points of view, assist individual students in expressing their opinions, and ask how those opinions were arrived at. The instructors *do not* provide the correct answers (there might not be any) or point the way to good choices. They act as catalysts, stimulators, and organizers—but not as providers of wisdom.

The object of studying cases is to sharpen students' abilities to *focus on the essentials* and, despite a maze of possibly irrelevant or even missing information, *formulate a plan of action* and *communicate that plan to others*. In particular, students are required to consider the following:

1. What do you believe are the most fundamental, critical, or urgent issues or problems before the company? Why do you think so?
2. What do you think should be done about these problems? Who should do this? When? Why do you think so?
3. How would you communicate your ideas to the top management of the company? Why would you choose that method?

5.1 CASE 1: ELEKTROLIPA MARKETING CHANNELS IN SCANDINAVIA

Electrolipa came into existence when a small division with 160 employees withdrew from Lipa, a major Yugoslavian manufacturing company: the core of Elektrolipa was a group of young experts with ambitious development plans.[1]

In close collaboration with the Janez Jernej institute, the experts of Elektrolipa designed an independent program of contactors used in industrial electric installations, in machinery, and miscellaneous equipment. The contactors were in compliance with the harmonized European standards, in cooperation with a West German customer. Elektrolipa has been granted the VDE certificate for these products. The West German customer is manufacturing switching equipment as well and it has purchased in the last two years over 170,000 contactors from Elektrolipa in the total value of approximately 1.9 mio DEM. The quality is good and end users are satisfied. The production capacity of Elektrolipa is approximately 150,000 contactors annually.

The former manager of the R&D department for electric component parts in Lipa, Luka Mejan, a PhD in English, held for years the post of vice-chairman in a well-known Danish institute. However, he has maintained contacts with his native country. He would like to come back if he could only obtain proper conditions for his professional activity. He has always been willing to help with his advice and connections, as much as possible.

Therefore he had a key role in the endeavors of Elektrolipa to obtain the strict Swedish SEMCO certificate for its new products. (If a product is granted this certificate, it is easy enough to apply successfully for other Scandinavian certificates, such as DEMCO, NEMCO, and FEMCO.) After being granted the SEMCO certificate, Elektrolipa found themselves quite unexpectedly in a position to enter the Scandinavian market. But how?

The management of Elektrolipa was very well aware that Lipa s.p., a strong and pretty large company, which emerged after the reorganization of Elektrolipa's former parent Lipa, was going to establish its own trading subsidiary in Stockholm. Even more: representation of Lipa Commerce, the marketing division of Lipa s.p., visited Elektrolipa and proposed it participate in establishing a marketing company, Lipa Scandia, with an initial capital of 450,000 SEK (1 ECU is approximately 7.5 SEK). This would entitle Elektrolipa to operate through this firm by paying only its own costs and to employ in it an own sales engineer (estimated annual cost for Elektrolipa would not exceed 350,000 SEK).

Almost at the same time, Mr. Luka Mejan, the friend of Elektrolipa from the Danish institute, became acquainted at one of the technical conferences with a successful business man, the owner of Dansk Trading, a small agency from Copenhagen. Dansk Trading would eventually be willing to sell the products of Elektrolipa for a moderate 5% commission as a sales agent.

---

1. This case was prepared by Dr. Mitja Tavcar, Vice President of Iskra Commerce and part-time Associate Professor in the Faculty of Economics and Business Administration, Maribor University, Yugoslavia. The case is based on several real business experiences in the international marketing network of Iskra, Ljubljana. (Copyright (c) 1989, Mitja Tavcar, Iskra Commerce, Ljubljana Yugoslavia, reference 590-012-1.) Reprinted with permission.

Elektrolipa management evaluated both proposals carefully. They were not very keen to participate in Lipa Scandia for it would be hard for them to spend 800,000 SEK or even more as the initial investment and for the first year of sales engineer's work—until substantial orders would have been concluded. This sum would equal almost 5,000 SEK (or about 700 ECU) per Elektrolipa employee. And above all, they had not forgotten their past difficulties in the large, rigid, and ineffectual Lipa parent company. Even supposing that the new Lipa s.p. were different, Elektrolipa's independence, gained with such efforts, could be seriously endangered.[2]

At that time, Jan Jensen, the owner of Dansk Trading visited Elektrolipa. He was well impressed by its production facilities and its products. He had long discussions with the manager and his young associates. It was evident that he knew his business and that he was keen to cooperate. After the second day, they reached an agreement and on the day after they completed the formalities by signing a short contract. For all its activities throughout Scandinavia, Dansk Trading would be entitled to 7.5% on the value of all Elektrolipa shipments. He in turn agreed that his firm would take over all marketing for Elektrolipa in Scandinavian countries in the next ten years.

This Elektrolipa management decision soon proved to be right. While Lipa Commerce was still cutting red tape to establish Lipa Scandia, Dansk Trading was already ordering samples and documentation, and had proposed several improvements, visited Elektrolipa with customers three times—and started to produce orders.

Already in the first year Elektrolipa exported 10,000 contactors (for approximately 300,000 DKK) to Denmark; in the second year, 50,000 contactors (1.5 mio DKK) to Denmark and 20,000 contactors to Sweden (600,000 SEK); in the third year, 60,000 contactors to Denmark (1.8 mio DKK), 80,000 contactors to Sweden (2.4 mio SEK) and 5,000 contactors to Finland (for 80,000 FIM). For the fourth year Elektrolipa expected the exports to Scandinavia to reach 250,000 contactors and it started therefore substantial investments in production.

However, the events turned out to be different. In the fourth and in the fifth year, the sales stagnated at approximately 150,000 contactors. Elektrolipa had large vacant capacities in production and was trying to find work for over 120 newly employed and semi-skilled workers. All pressures on Dansk Trading to increase sales to expected levels were in vain. Dansk Trading encountered them with plausible arguments: worse business trends, products becoming obsolete, mistrust of Scandinavians towards products of Yugoslavian origin, excessively high prices—and more in the same line.

In the meantime, Lipa Scandia was more and more successful. For the third year, its sales of similar products increased by 30–35 percent annually in almost identical market segments—above all in Sweden and Norway.

During his last visit to Denmark, the manager of Elektrolipa threatened to terminate the contract with Dansk Trading and to choose a more successful partner. He was bitterly surprised with a firm answer—that he should not do that in the next few years unless he

---

2. The numbers in this paragraph are slightly changed from the original case for consistency. 1 DEM is equal to approx. 3.5 SEK or 4.0 DKK or 2.2 FIM. 1 DKK = 0.9 SEK = 1.8 FIM.

wished to damage the interests of his company. He got the same advice from a lawyer for Elektrolipa who had in turn consulted the experts for international business law.

What happened? What went wrong? Whose fault was it?

5.2 ELEKTROLIPA CASE DISCUSSION

This case might be short, but much thought might be needed to answer the questions. Those that are posed at the end of the case are:

- What happened?
- What went wrong?
- Whose fault was it?

Analysis of what happened should begin with an examination of the profitability of Elektrolipa's business in the three Scandinavian countries. (It is interesting to note that no mention is made of Norway; it must be presumed that Dansk Trading did not sell Elektrolipa's contactors in this Scandinavian country.) The various currencies involved necessitate conversion to a common currency. One case write-up suggests the ECU; one ECU is approximately equal to one U.S. dollar. The conversions relate to the given time period.

Table 5.1
Currency Conversions

ECU	1.00 (U.S.)
DEM	2.14
SEK	7.50
DKK	8.57
FIM	4.71

Let us assume that Elektrolipa's sales in Germany resulted from their own direct marketing efforts, possibly from sending their own sales engineers to Germany. This is in contrast to their sales channel in Scandinavia. They might have chosen this direct sales channel because the language was easier or because the distances involved were much smaller. Let us assume further that the direct sales income statement for Germany approximates the statement shown in Table 5.2. For the purposes of the case, the profit and lost (P&L) enumerated in Table 5.2 can be applied to sales in Yugoslavia or in Germany.

Table 5.2 assumes that the R&D percentage is applied to sales in whatever country they occur. However, the marketing costs for selling to Scandinavia, where Dansk Trading

Table 5.2

P&L for Sales in Germany or Yugoslavia

Item	Percentage	ECU/Device
Sales	100.0	5.22
Cost of sales	50.0	2.61
Gross margin	50.0	2.61
Marketing	25.0	1.30
R&D	15.0	0.78
Profit before tax	10.0	0.52

is the agent, are only 7.5% of sales (plus internal Elektrolipa costs). The profit before tax (PBT) is no longer 10% of sales, but rather the result of the gross margin received by Elektrolipa, less its marketing and R&D costs.

Table 5.3 shows an assumed distribution of costs and margins for Germany, Denmark, Sweden, and Finland. The sales figures are the cumulative figures given in the case for each of these countries.

Table 5.3

P&L for Sales in Various Countries

Item	Germany Amount	%	Denmark Amount	%	Sweden Amount	%	Finland Amount	%	Total Amount	%
Quantity sold	170,000		120,000		100,000		5,000		395,000	
Sales in local currency	1,900,000		3,600,000		3,000,000		80,000		–	
Sales (ECU)	887,850	100	420,070	100	400,000	100	16,985	100	1,724,906	100
Unit price (ECU)	5.2226	–	3.5006	–	4.0000	–	3.3970	–	4.3668	–
Unit cost (ECU)	2.6113	–	2.6113	–	2.6113	–	2.6113	–	2.6113	–
Total cost (ECU)	443,921	50.0	313,356	74.6	261,130	65.3	13,057	76.9	1,031,464	59.8
Gross margin (ECU)	443,929	50.0	106,714	25.4	138,870	34.7	3,929	23.1	693,442	40.2
Marketing costs (ECU)	221,963	25.0	31,505	7.5	30,000	7.5	1,274	7.5	284,742	16.5
R&D costs (ECU)	133,178	15.0	63,011	15.0	60,000	15.0	2,548	15.0	258,736	15.0
PBT (ECU)	88,789	10.0	12,198	2.9	48,870	12.2	107	0.6	149,965	8.7

Given the ever-present threat of competition, the device price will probably affect the quantity sold. Note the device prices in Table 5.3. Do they seem to be reasonable? Why? How do you think they were determined?

- What do you notice about the PBT in each county?
- Is Elektrolipa getting the PBT it should in each country?
- Why do you think that the quantities sold per year in Scandinavia stagnated in the last year? Could something have been done about it?
- What could have been done by Elektrolipa before the agreement was concluded to ensure that the sales quota reached every year was reasonable? How does one determine what is reasonable?
- What are your estimates for the PBT in Scandinavian countries if Elektrolipa had agreed to join forces and sent a sales engineer to Lipa Scandia?
- Do you think that Elektrolipa should have expanded when it did? Why?
- What is your opinion about the arguments that Dansk Trading used to explain their failure to increase sales?
- What should be done in Scandinavia at this point?
- During the first three years, should Elektrolipa have tracked the agent's progress? If so, what should they have been questioning and tracking?

This case requires that students understand all the channels of distribution that could have been chosen and the sorts of clauses that should be included in any agreement. The students might wish to study the problem more extensively and propose a marketing strategy for export. Such a plan could even take into account, in determining costs, the experience curve for Elektrolipa. However, if it does that, the plan should also take into account inflation in Yugoslavia, to arrive at an estimate of how increased production experience affects the cost change per year.

Table 5.4 lists some approximate statistics for 1986–1988 that could have been used in this plan. The population estimates are in millions of people and the gross national product (GNP) is in millions of ECUs. These are not the only statistics a good market analysis should take into account, but they suffice for this superficial study.

Table 5.4
Statistics for a Preliminary Plan

Item	D	I	GB	F	S	N	DK	SF
Total population	61.0	57.3	56.8	55.4	8.4	4.1	5.1	4.9
Employee population	25.0	20.9	24.2	21.3	4.3	2.1	2.6	2.6
Employees in manufacturing	8.0	4.7	5.5	5.0	1.0	0.4	0.5	0.6
Gross national product	898	596	570	660	122	69	79	69

Although the figures in Table 5.4 are approximate, they can be used to formulate a preliminary marketing plan. A preliminary plan could help management decide what data they needed to construct an accurate plan and to estimate the sales to be obtained from a particular market. Tracking actual sales could also aid distribution decisions.

5.3   CASE 2: INTERACTIVE COMPUTER SYSTEMS (I.C.S.)

In September 1980, Mr. Peter Mark, Marketing Manager of Interactive Computer Systems Corporation was faced with a perplexing conflict between his company's U.S.A. group and the European subsidiaries.[3] The U.S.A. sales group had begun to sell a display controller that had been developed in Europe. The product had been selling in Europe for several years and sales were relatively strong. Now however, several major European customers had begun to purchase the product through their U.S.A. offices and ship it back to Europe. The Europeans were complaining that the U.S. pricing was undercutting theirs and that they were losing sales volume that was rightfully theirs. Both the U.S. and European groups claimed that their pricing practices followed corporate guidelines and met the profit objectives set for them.

Interactive Computer Systems Corporation

Interactive Computer Systems Corporation (ICS), headquartered in Stamford, Connecticut, was a large multinational manufacturer of computer systems and equipment. The company made a range of computer systems and was best known for its small or "minicomputers." ICS was considered one of the industry leaders in that segment of the computer industry which included such companies as Data General, Digital Equipment, Prime Computer, Modcomp, and Hewlett-Packard.

The company was primarily a U.S. based corporation with the majority of its engineering and manufacturing facilities located in the eastern United States. In addition, ICS had manufacturing facilities in Canada, Singapore, West Germany, Brazil, and a joint venture in South Korea.

Sales were conducted throughout most of the non-Communist world by means of a number of sales subsidiaries, with sales offices located in Canada, Mexico, Brazil, Argentina, Chile, Japan, Australia, and several European countries. Elsewhere, sales were conducted through a network of independent agents and distributors.

---

3.   This case was prepared by Mark Ulrich under Jean-Pierre Jeannet, Associate Professor of Marketing, Babson College, Wellesley, Massachusetts, U.S.A., and Visiting Professor at IMEDE Management Development Institute, Lausanne, Switzerland. The material is based on an actual situation and is intended as a basis for class discussion rather than to illustrate either effective or ineffective handling of a business situation. Copyright 1981 IMEDE (Institute pour L'Etude des Méthods de Direction de L'Entreprise), Lausanne, Switzerland, reference M-289, JPJ 17-81. Reprinted with permission. Names and data in this case are disguised. All prices are shown in U.S. $.

Product Line

The ICS line of products was centered around a family of 16-bit minicomputer systems. "Minicomputer" was the popular term for small- to medium-sized computer systems that were used in a wide variety of applications, including industrial control, telecommunications systems, laboratory applications, and small business systems. The term "16-bit" refers to the size of the computer "word" or unit of data. These systems were different from the large computer systems of IBM, Univac, and Honeywell, which had word sizes of 32–36 bits.

In addition to computer central processing units (CPU) and memory units, ICS produced a line of peripheral devices required for making complete computer systems. These included devices such as magnetic tape units, disk storage units, line printers, card readers, video and hard copy terminals, display units, and laboratory and industrial instrumentation interface units. These various peripherals were used as appropriate and combined with the final computer systems to meet the specific customer's requirements. ICS produced most of these products in-house but some, such as line printers and card readers, were purchased to ICS specifications from companies specializing in those products, such as Data Products and Documentation.

ICS manufactured several CPUs that were positioned in price and performance to form a product family. They all were similar in design, accepted (executed) the same computer instructions, and ran on the same operating system (master control programs). The difference was in speed, complexity, and cost. The purchaser was able to select the model which economically met the performance requirements of the intended application.

This family of CPUs, together with the wide range of available peripheral devices, formed a family of computer systems offering a considerable range of price and performance but with compatible characteristics and programming.

Communications Interfaces

A communications interface was a peripheral device used for transmitting data to or from the computer system. This could either be:

- A terminal on which a user could enter data, for example on a typewriterlike "keyboard," and have the data displayed, typically on either a video screen or a "hard copy" produced by a typewriterlike printer.
- For other computers, either of the same type or from a different manufacturer.

These connections were made by direct wire, if the distance involved was short (50–100 feet). In cases where the distance was longer, the connection was made via telephone lines or special high speed "data lines," which were specially treated telephone lines.

The communications interface operated under control of the program running in the computer to take data, either as presented to it by the program or itself coming directly from the computer's memory (depending on the specific interface), and to send the data out on the "communication line," transformed as a string of digital pulses. When the computer received data, the interface worked in the reverse manner. If telephone or data lines were used, connection was made via a special adapter called a modulator-demodulator, or "modem," suitable for transmission on a telephone line. Modems followed industry standards and were available from a large number of modem vendors.

The pieces of data being sent (or received) were usually referred to as "characters" since they most often consisted of alphanumerics (letters and numbers) or special characters, such as punctuation or brackets. There existed several common systems for constructing the digital pulse sequence representing the characters, ranging from 5 to 8 bits in length (a bit was a single digit in the binary number system of 0 and 1). The most common was "8-bit ASCII" as specified by the American Standard Code for Information Interchange.

In addition to being organized as strings of characters, the data could be sent to another computer or a more sophisticated terminal, often organized into a message, or "packet," using one of a variety of protocols. A protocol was simply a definition of the orderly rule or format by which data could be exchanged. The protocol aided this data transfer process by including in the message a header with a message of identification, length count, and sometimes source and destination codes or other information, depending on the protocol used. In addition, more information could be included to aid in the detection and sometimes correction of errors in the data received.

A number of protocols have been tested, each with its own relative advantages and proponents. Some of the more common protocols were:

BSC or Bi Sync	IBM, dated
HDLC	CCITT (European Standards
SDLC	Organization)
2780	IBM, similar to HDLC
3271	IBM, remote batch station protocol
X.25	IBM, display terminal protocol
	CCITT (packet switch networks
	protocol, gaining wide acceptance)

Model 431 Communications Interface

The specific product in question was the model 431 communications interface, a 4-line programmable multiplexer.

The 431 consisted of one electronic circuit module, which plugged into the I/O (input/output) "bus" of the computer. (A bus was an electrical cable or wiring on which data signals flowed in some organized manner.) It provided the interface for four separate communications lines, which were connected by means of specially designed connectors on the module. Such multiline interfaces were typically called multiplexers after the manner in which they worked internally. They offered the advantages of more efficient space utilization and lower per-line costs, compared with the normal alternative of a separate single-line interface per line. Depending on the computer vendor, multiplexers come in various sizes, such as 2, 4, 6, 8, 16, 32, and 64 lines.

ICS already had 4, 8, and 16-line multiplexers in its line of high volume standard products. The specific advantage of the 431 was its programmable nature. It could be loaded with software to handle any of several different protocols directly in the interface, using its own microprocessor on the module. It also performed error checking and moved data directly to or from the main computer memory. Since these functions had previously all been performed by a program running on the computer, the 431 relieved the computer of this load and freed it up to do other work. The result was a net improvement in system speed and performance.

The model 431 was designed in 1977 at ICS's small European engineering facility assigned to its German subsidiary, Interactive Computers GmbH, in Frankfurt and was manufactured there for shipment worldwide to those ICS subsidiaries who were selling the 431. Sales had initially started in Europe and then spread to other areas. Sales volumes are given in Table 5.5.

Table 5.5
Model 431 Sales Volume (Units) for Selected Countries

Country	1977	1978	1979	1980 (fcst)
Germany	30	100	110	100
U.K.	5	40	60	70
France	10	20	50	40
Canada	–	–	5	5
Switzerland	3	20	30	15
Australia	–	–	10	30
U.S.	–	2	80	200

Intersubsidiary Transactions

With the exception of the Korean joint venture, all of ICS's subsidiaries were wholly owned, and products moved freely between them. ICS had set up its procedures and accounting systems in line with the fact that it was basically a U.S.-based company manufacturing a uniform line of products for sales worldwide through various sales subsidiaries. For the major product lines, the only differences by countries were line voltages and some minor adaptations to comply with local government regulations.

Although the subsidiaries in the various countries were essentially sales offices established to sell products in those countries, they were separately incorporated entities and wholly owned subsidiaries, operating under the laws of that particular country. Careful accounting of all transactions between the parent company and the subsidiaries had to be maintained for the purpose of import duties and local taxes.

When a customer ordered a computer system, the order was processed in the subsidiary and then transmitted back to the parent company (ICS) in the U.S. to have the system built. The order paperwork listed the specific hardware items (CPU, memory size, tape and disk units, etc.) wanted by the customer, and each system was built specifically to order. The component pieces were built by ICS in volume to meet the requirements of these specific customer system orders. Like most companies, ICS expended a great amount of effort attempting to accurately forecast the mix of products it would need to meet customer orders.

When the customer's system, or any product, was shipped to the subsidiary, the subsidiary "bought" it from the parent at an intercompany discounted price or "transfer price" of list minus 20%. The level of subsidiary transfer price discount was established with two factors in mind:

- It was the primary mechanism by which Interactive repatriated profits to the U.S. parent corporation.
- The 20% subsidiary margin was designed to give the subsidiaries positive cash flow to meet their local expenses, such as salaries, facilities, benefits, travel, and supplies.

Import duties were paid on the discounted (list – 20%) transfer price value according to the customs regulations of the importing country. Some typical import duties for computer equipment are shown in Table 5.6.

Table 5.6
Import Duties for Computer Equipment for Selected Countries

Importing Country	Duty
U.S.	5.1%
Canada	8.8%
Japan	9.8%
Australia	2.0%
Within the European Economic Community*	0.0%
Outside of the European Economic Community†	6.7%

* There is no duty between countries comprising the European Economic Community (EEC), or Common Market. At the time of the case, the EEC included the U.K., France, Italy, Germany, Belgium, the Netherlands, Ireland, Denmark, and Luxembourg. (Today, Greece, Portugal, and Spain are also members.)
† EEC members imposed a uniform duty on imported computer equipment.

Most countries are quite strict on import and export and customs duties and required consistency in all transactions. Therefore, all shipments were made at the same discounted sales price, including shipments among subsidiaries and shipments back to the United States.

Pricing

ICS set prices worldwide based on U.S. price lists which were referred to as master price lists, or MPLs. Prices in each country were based on the MPL plus an uplift factor to cover the increased cost of doing business in those countries. Some of these extra costs were:

- Freight and duty: in those countries where it was included in the price (in some countries duties were paid separately by the customer).
- Extended warranty: in some countries, the customer warranty periods were longer than in the U.S., e.g., one year versus 90 days.
- Cost of subsidiary operations and sales costs: to the extent that they exceed the normal selling costs in the U.S.
- Cost of currency hedging: in order to publish a price list in local currency, ICS bought U.S. dollars in the money futures market.

Uplift factors were periodically reviewed and adjusted if needed to reflect changes in the relative cost of doing business in each country. Typical uplift factors for some selected countries are shown in Table 5.7.

Table 5.7
Typical Country Uplift Factors

Country	Uplift Factor
U.K.	8%
Germany	15%
France	12%
Switzerland	17%
Sweden	15%
Australia	12%
Brazil	20%
Canada	5%

Each subsidiary published its own list price in local currency. The list was generated quarterly by use of a computer program which took a tape of all the MPL entries and applied the uplift and a fixed currency exchange rate that had been set for the fiscal year.

This price list was used by all salespeople in the subsidiary as the official listing of products offered and their prices.

Special Products

In addition to its standard line of products, which were sold worldwide in volume, ICS had a number of lower-volume, or specialized, products. The model 431 communications interface was considered one of these. Specialized products were typically not on the MPL and prices were set locally by each subsidiary wherever they were sold. They were either quoted especially on a request-for-quote basis or added to a special product list price supplement produced by each country. This was a common procedure in the computer industry. IBM, for example, had several products "available on a RPQ basis" (request product quotation) only.

To support sale of the specialized products, ICS had a separate team of specialists, with one or more specialists in each subsidiary. They were responsible for the pricing of their products and had a high degree of independence in setting prices in each subsidiary. The specialist or team in each subsidiary was responsible for all aspects of the sales of their assigned products and essentially ran a business within a business.

For the purpose of internal reporting to management, the specialists were measured on achieving a profit before tax, or PBT, of 15%, which was the ICS goal. The results were shown on internal reports that were separate from the legal books for the subsidiary. The purpose of the internal reports was to give ICS management more information on the profitability of its various product lines. These reports took the form of a series of profit and loss statements of operation by line of products, with overhead and indirect costs allocated on a percentage-of-revenue basis. For these internal P&L reports, the cost of the goods was the actual cost of manufacture (internal cost) plus related direct costs, instead of the discounted price paid by subsidiaries and shown on their official statements of operation.

431 Sales in Europe

The model 431 communications interface was designed in 1977 by the European engineering group in Frankfurt as a follow-on to some special engineering contracts for European customers. It was introduced in the European market in 1978, where it had grown in popularity.

The 431 was produced in Frankfurt only on a low-volume production line. The manufacturing and other direct costs amounted to U.S. $1,500 per unit. Because there are no fixed tariffs within the EEC and shipping costs were covered by allocated fixed costs, there were no other direct costs. The allocated fixed costs in Europe were running at 47% of revenue. Thus, a contribution margin of 62% was required to achieve a 15% PBT. Based on these costs, a list price of U.S. $3,900 had been set within the EEC. The resulting P&L is shown in Table 5.8.

Table 5.8
Model 431 European P&L

P&L Factors	P&L Results
European list price ($U.S.)	3,900
Manufacturing and other direct costs	1,500
Contribution margin	2,400
Contribution margin %	62%
Allocated fixed costs (47%)	1,833
PBT	567
PBT %	15%

Because of the popularity of this product, it had been listed on the special products price list in most European countries. Within the EEC, the price had been set at the same level with any variation only due to local currency conversions. In European countries outside the EEC, the price was increased to cover import duties.

At the above price, the 431 had gained market acceptance and had grown in popularity, especially in Germany, the U.K, and France. Its customers included several large European-based multinational companies who were of major importance to ICS in Europe. These customers designed specific system configurations and added programming to perform specified applications and shipped the systems to other countries, either to their own subsidiaries for internal use (e.g., a factory) or to customers abroad.

431 Sales in U.S.A.

The 431 was brought to the attention of the U.S. sales group in two different ways. In sales contacts with the U.S. operations of some European customers, ICS was told of the 431 and asked to submit price and availability schedules for local purchase in the U.S.A. U.S. customers expressed irritation at being told that the model was not available in the U.S.

Secondly, the U.S. sales force heard of the 431 from their European counterparts at sales meetings at which the Europeans explained how the 431 had been important in gaining large accounts.

As a result of this pressure from customers and the sales force, the U.S. special products specialists obtained several units for evaluation and in 1979 made the 431 available for sale in the U.S.

Originally, the U.S. specialists set the price equal to the European price of $3,900. However, it became obvious that the market in the U.S. was more advanced and more competitive, with customers expecting more performance at that price. As a result, the price had to be reexamined.

The 431 was obtained from Frankfurt at the internal cost of $1,500. Transportation costs were estimated at $200. In the U.S.A. accounting system, import duties and transportation are not charged directly and were absorbed by general overhead. This came about because ICS was primarily an exporter from the U.S. with very little importing taking place. Consequently, it was felt that import costs were negligible. Thus, the only direct cost was the $1,500 internal cost. Overhead and fixed expenses in the U.S. averaged 35%.

The result, as shown in Table 5.9, was a revised price of $3,000 with a contribution margin of 50% and a PBT of 15%—the ICS goal. Following this analysis, the U.S. price was reduced to $3,000. The 431 was not listed on the main U.S.A. price list but was quoted only on a RPQ basis. Subsequently, this price had also been listed on the special products list supplements that were prepared by the U.S. product specialists and handed out to the sales force in each district.

Table 5.9
Model 431 U.S. P&L

P&L Factors	P&L Results
U.S. list price	3,000
Manufacturing and other direct costs	1,500
Contribution margin	1,500
Contribution margin %	50%
Allocated fixed costs (35%)	1,050
PBT	450
PBT %	15%

Current Situation

The repricing of the 431 to $3,000 was instrumental in boosting U.S. sales. The sales volume continued to grow and some large customers were captured. These customers included existing ICS customers who previously used other, lower performance, communications interfaces, or had bought somewhat equivalent devices from other companies that made "plug-compatible" products for use with ICS computers. Also, a good volume of sales was being obtained from the U.S. operations of European multinationals who were already familiar with the product. ICS's U.S. group, who had first viewed the European designed product with suspicion, was now more confident about it.

But the Europeans were not entirely happy with the situation. Recently, they have started complaining to ICS management that the U.S. pricing of the 431 was undercutting the European price. This was causing pressure on the European subsidiaries to reduce their price for the 431 below the $3,900 they needed to meet their profitability goals. Pressure was coming from customers who knew the U.S. price and from European sales people who, as a result of travel to the U.S. or discussion with U.S. colleagues, knew the U.S. price and what the uplifted European price "was supposed to be."

The price difference had also been noticed by several of ICS's larger European multinational customers. They started buying the 431 through their U.S. offices and reexporting it, both back to Europe and to other countries.

So far, three customers had done this, two German firms and one French customer. Several additional customers were showing definite signs of "shopping around."

This loss of customers to the U.S. was particularly painful to the Europeans. They had invested considerable amounts of effort into cultivating these customers.

In addition, the customers still expected to receive technical and presales support from their local ICS office (i.e., European) as well as warranty and service support, regardless of where they placed the purchase order. Attempts to discuss this with the customers or persuade them to purchase in Europe had not been successful. Typical reactions had been "that's ICS's problem" (U.K. customer) and "but are you not one company?" (German customer).

In brief, the ICS European subsidiaries were complaining that they were "being denied the profitable results of their own work" by the unfair pricing practices of the U.S. parent company.

In the eyes of the U.S. team, however, they were pricing in accordance with corporate guidelines to achieve a 15% PBT. They also maintained that the market did not allow them to price the 431 any higher. Furthermore, they felt that they were simply exercising their right to set their own country prices to maximize profits within their specific country market.

The U.S. group was so pleased with the market acceptance of the 431 in the U.S. that they wanted to begin an aggressive promotion. As an important part of this, they were now planning to list the 431 on the official ICS U.S. price list. This was viewed a key to higher sales since, especially in the U.S., products tended to be sold from the regular price list and the sales force tended to lose or ignore special price list supplements.

At this point, both the European and U.S. specialists were upset with each other. Both sides maintained that they were following the rules but that the actions of "the other side" were harming their success and profitability.

It had been a long day and it was time to go home. As he turned his car out into the traffic on High Ridge Road, Mr. Mark was still feeling confused and wondering what should be done.

5.4 ICS CASE DISCUSSION

The author of this case devoted much attention to describing the organization of ICS, the products ICS made and sold, and relations between ICS companies in different countries. He provided this background to promote an understanding of the conflict, even though it might seem, in retrospect, that the information is not all necessary to understanding the problem or proposing solutions. But in real life there is always much more information one needs to understand key issues of a particular problem. And yet, without an appreciation of the whole picture, an observer might find it difficult to separate what is pertinent to the problem from what is extraneous.

No doubt each ICS company has its own parochial view of the problem. Yet there must be a solution that is optimal for the company as a whole. To determine how to reach such a solution, how to propose it, and who to propose it to, students must first consider a number of important issues. Questions they must answer include:

- How should price be determined in each country?
- Overhead and fixed expenses for the 431 communications interface are stated to be 47% of revenue for ICS GmbH but only 35% for ICS in the United States. What is the reason for this difference ?
- In Table 5.5, the forecast for European countries for 1980 is decreasing, yet the forecast for the U.S. is increasing. To what do you attribute these differing trends?
- Using the data and facts given, would your 1980 forecast for European and American sales volume be different if the pricing were revised?
- Using your own 1980 forecasts for different countries based on your own revised pricing, how would you maximize the total company PBT?
- What do you think should be done about this conflict? Who should be convinced to do it? How would you convince them?

In seeking a solution, students should try to avoid basing opinions on what they feel are the right and wrong actions of the case, since it is unlikely that such arguments will prove to be very convincing. In the final analysis, the company bottom line, in this case its PBT, is what counts. Students should ponder how the optimum PBT can be achieved in the future. What happened in the past is useful only to the extent that it leads to a better understanding of what should be done.

5.5 CASE 3: TELESAT

In early August 1987 Ms. Linda Rankin, Vice President of Telecommunications Services, Mr. Peter Norman, Director of Market Planning, and Mr. Richard Jestin, Director of Anik Systems, sat in the Ottawa office of Telesat discussing the new service that Telesat planned to launch in September 1987.[4] The management team of Telesat was in the process of finalizing the marketing plan for the introduction of an innovative satellite commu-

---

4. This case was prepared by Helen Steers, Research Assistant, and Professor Adrian B. Ryans as a basis for class discussion rather than to illustrate either effective or ineffective handling of an administrative situation. Marketing information, research methodology, pricing strategies and nonpublic data have been disguised in order to protect the confidentiality of competitive information. Copyright 1899. School of Business Administration, The University of Western Ontario. Reprinted with permission.

nication service for voice, data, and image (VDI) customers. The new VSAT (Very Small Aperture Terminal) service represented a major new thrust for Telesat. As Linda Rankin remarked: "VSAT is the real future of satellite-based communications. It represents the future of Telesat. We have to become a retailer of satellite telecommunication services, not just a wholesaler, if we are to survive and grow."

The introduction of the VSAT service had become a matter of greater urgency in May 1987 when Cancom, one of Telesat's Canadian competitors, had announced that it was going to be offering a similar VSAT service in Canada. At the press conference Cancom indicated it hoped to begin demonstration trials in November 1987, with the first commercial service being available in January 1988.

Company Background and History

Telesat was the world's first operator of a domestic, geostationary satellite communications system. The company did not construct satellites or earth station equipment itself, but rather it set the specifications for and bought equipment from aerospace manufacturers, such as Spar Aerospace, Hughes Aircraft, and GE Astro-Space Division, and then operated the satellite and provided the services carried on the satellite.

The company was established by an Act of Parliament in September 1969, with a mandate to provide all types of telecommunications and broadcast distribution services via satellite throughout Canada. Fifty percent of Telesat's shares were owned by the Government of Canada, twenty-five percent were held by Bell Canada, and the remainder were held by twelve other common carriers across Canada, primarily the major telephone companies. Telesat was not a Crown Corporation, nor did it receive government assistance; its financing was dependent on revenue generated from operations and commercial borrowing. In 1986, Telesat had net earnings of $13.6 million on operating revenues of $105.3 million. Summaries of Telesat's financial statements are given in Tables 5.10 and 5.11.

Organization

About 500 employees worked at Telesat's headquarters, which were located in Ottawa, Ontario. The company's main earth station facility at Allan Park, near Toronto, employed another 50 people. Regional operations centers were maintained in Calgary, Harrietsfield (Nova Scotia,) and Iqaluit (Northwest Territories).

Ms. Linda Rankin was responsible for the Telecommunications Services Department. Within her group, Mr. Brian Olsen directed the Broadcast Services Division, Mr. Larry Boisvert directed the Network Services Division, Mr. Peter Norman headed the Market Planning Division, and Mr. Richard Jestin directed the Anik Systems Division. Market Planning was responsible for developing new services and determining their viability. The Anik Systems Division took over new VDI services once they had been developed. Network Services, which employed over 200 people located in all parts of Canada, was responsible for installing equipment and servicing Telesat customers across Canada. A partial organization chart for Telesat is shown in Figure 5.1 (page 125).

Table 5.10
Consolidated Statement of Earnings and Retained Earnings (1982–1986)

Earnings	1986	1985	1984	1983	1982
Operating revenues	105,305	101,233	109,170	88,082	53,822
Operating expenses					
• Depreciation	48,844	47,014	44,099	42,144	26,529
• Operations & administration	44,046	39,211	32,078	27,692	21,605
Total operating expenses	92,890	86,225	76,177	69,836	38,134
Earnings from operations	12,415	15,008	32,993	18,246	15,688
Other expenses (net)	2,226	11,461	17,866	20,437	−1,877
Earnings before Telecom Canada					
settlement and income taxes	10,189	3,547	15,127	−2,121	17,565
Telecom Canada settlement	20,000	19,397	18,820	28,033	5,185
Earnings before income taxes	30,189	22,944	33,947	30,454*	22,750
Income taxes	16,626	12,202	17,049	14,964	6,040
Net earnings	13,563	10,742	16,898	15,490	16,710

* Telesat Canada received an extraordinary payment of $4.612 million in 1983 from a customer as compensation for moving a satellite to meet the customer's needs. This move significantly shortened the useful life of the satellite. The customer made a one-time payment to compensate Telesat for its opportunity cost.

Anik Systems Division

In 1987, four groups reported to Richard Jestin, the Director of Anik Systems (see Figure 5.2, page 126). The VDI sales organization was organized by geography and by type of business, resulting in a quasimatrix reporting structure. The Ottawa branch office was under the jurisdiction of the Government Sales Manager and the bulk of sales in this area were typically made to government customers. Salespeople dealing with nongovernment customers reported to the Government Sales Manager but also had a dotted line responsibility to the Industrial Sales Manager, who managed the Toronto and Calgary branch offices. Similarly, salespeople with government customers in Toronto reported to the Industrial Sales Manager and had an indirect reporting relationship with the Government Sales Manager in Ottawa.

The engineering and sales group formed a closely knit team, making joint presentations to the customer. The technical parameters, configuration, and design for a service were explained to the client by the engineer in the presence of the account executive. Both the engineers and the salespeople had a broad understanding of many products, although salespeople were sometimes further specialized by end-user industry. The Calgary office largely focused its efforts on the oil industry and other resource-based industries.

Table 5.11
Consolidated Statements of Financial Position as at December 31, 1986
with Comparison Figures for 1985

Earnings	1986	1985
Property		
• Satellites in service	258,157	252,714
• Satellites held for future service	68,101	132,883
• Earth stations and other	177,829	165,800
	504,087	551,397
Accumulated depreciation	203,801	217,339
	300,286	334,058
Construction in progress	41,559	10,171
	341,845	344,229
Other assets	29,260	10,422
Investment in associated company	600	—
Cash	2,099	—
Total	$373,804	$354,651
Shareholders' equity and liabilities		
Shareholders' equity		
• Capital stock	60,000	60,000
• Retained earnings	100,302	89,739
	160,302	149,739
Debt financing	82,876	92,580
Deferred income taxes	100,933	85,176
Other liabilities	29,693	26,729
Bank overdraft	—	427
Total	$373,804	$354,651

The Telecommunications Market in Canada

Terrestrial and satellite telecommunications services in Canada were demanded by two broadly different classes of customers—companies operating in the broadcasting industry and users of VDI services.

Television and Radio Broadcasting

The broadcasting industry was divided into four segments: the national, regional, and local program distributors and networks (e.g., CBC, CTV); broadcasters offering new pay and specialty services (First Choice/Superchannel, The Sports Network (TSN)); government (TVOntario, Radio Quebec); and "Direct-To-Home" (DTH) service providers, such as

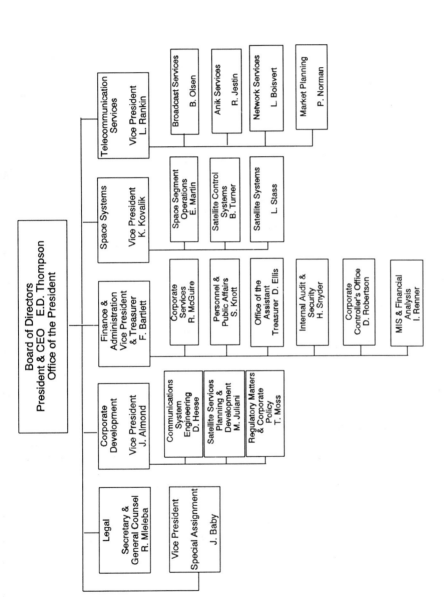

Figure 5.1 Partial organization chart.

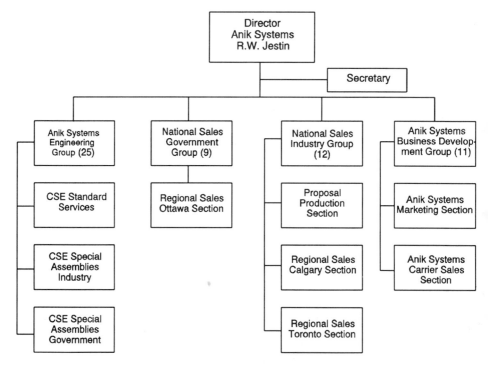

Note: Numbers in parentheses indicate
          number of persons in each group.

Figure 5.2 Anik systems division organization.

shop-at-home networks. Since satellite systems provided cost-effective, flexible coverage on a wide-area basis, Telesat had captured 100% of the national television broadcasting market in competition with terrestrial systems. Even in the regional broadcasting business, with customers such as TV Ontario, Telesat had approximately a 50% share of the market. This resulted in Telesat having an overall market share of 71% of the $65 million/year Canadian broadcasting industry market in 1986. The market was expected to expand by about 11–12% compounded over the next five years. Telesat earned another $3.6 million/year from occasional-use television broadcasting, e.g., news networks, special events, and private entertainment networks. This segment of the market was expected to grow to $5.5 million/year by 1991.

Voice, Data, and Image Services

In 1987 there were two national telecommunications systems, Telecom Canada and CNCP Telecommunications, providing voice, data, and image (VDI) transmission services across

Canada. Telecom Canada was an association comprised of the major Canadian telephone companies plus Telesat, the domestic satellite carrier. CNCP was a partnership of the telecommunications divisions of the major railways. CNCP Telecommunications provided a range of private-line business services similar to that of Telecom Canada. Usually CNCP's services were priced slightly lower, and some customers would use both Telecom Canada and CNCP Telecommunications in order to have access to a back-up system. In addition, all telephone companies provided VDI services within their own territories.

Telesat's estimated 1987 revenue from the sale of satellite services to Telecom Canada was $36.7 million. It was anticipated that this market would decline by 10–11% compounded over the next five years as long-distance telephone traffic migrated from satellites to land-line transmission, particularly the fiber-optic networks that were playing an increasing role in Canada and elsewhere.

The Connecting Agreements

On 31 December 1976 the original Connecting Agreement was executed between Telesat and the nine telephone company members of Telecom Canada. The companies agreed to interconnect their respective services to form a combined terrestrial and satellite trans-Canada telecommunications network. While Telesat was responsible for the communication satellite design, the overall system design and associated capital costs were subject to the concurrence of all Telecom Canada members.

Under the terms of the Connecting Agreement, Telesat was barred from selling its services directly to VDI end users, and its customer base was limited to the Regulated Canadian Telecommunications Common Carriers (the telephone companies). In return for accepting this limitation, Telesat was guaranteed a fixed after-tax rate of return by annual transfer payment for the provision of satellite services. In the mid-1980s Telesat had substantial overcapacity in its satellite facilities.

Concerned about its future viability, given the limitations on its business mandate, Telesat renegotiated the Connecting Agreement with the member companies of Telecom Canada in 1985. The revised terms allowed Telesat the opportunity to market all its satellite service offerings directly to any customer. In return, Telesat accepted that the transfer payments would be capped at a maximum of $20 million in each of the years 1985, 1986, and 1987 and would terminate after 1987. The terrestrial members of Telecom Canada committed to lease at least eight of Telesat's ninety-six Ku-band channels until 31 December 1998. Effectively, the modifications allowed Telesat to become a retailer of VDI services in addition to its function as a "carrier's carrier," or wholesaler.

Regulation of Telesat

Telesat's activities were regulated by the Canadian Radio-Television and Telecommunications Commission (CRTC). The CRTC's regulation of common carriers, such as Telesat, CNCP, Bell Canada, and the federally regulated telephone companies, was designed to ensure that all users were charged equal prices for equivalent services and that telecommunications carriers did not take unfair advantage of their market position in dealing with subscribers, other carriers, or competitors.

In the mid-1980s the CRTC had regulated Telesat's rates so that it earned between 13% and 15% on its equity base. Recognizing the increasing competition Telesat's satellite services faced from terrestrial services, private owners and resellers, the CRTC had recently removed the upper limit on Telesat's rate of return, but it continued to require a minimum return of 13% on each service. However, space segment services continued to be regulated under the historical ROE criteria. This reflected the "compensatory test" requirement that each competitive service had to compensate Telesat adequately, so that Telesat could not use profits from space segment services to cross subsidize competitive earth segment services or vice versa.

Satellite Technology

The Telesat satellite communications system included active satellites in geostationary orbits, tracking, telemetry and command facilities, a satellite control center, network operations centers, teleports, and over one hundred earth stations of various types. The earth stations could be linked by terrestrial systems to telephone exchanges, TV and radio transmitters, and private business networks. Transportable earth stations were employed for short-term uses, such as the broadcasting of sports events. Figure 5.3 illustrates Telesat's communications system and the interfaces with customers.

The Anik Satellites

By 1987, Telesat owned and operated five Anik satellites. One Anik D satellite was used primarily for television broadcasters in the C-band (6/4 GHz frequency range), and a second Anik D provided voice and data services in the C-band. Two Anik C satellites were used for Ku-band (14/12 GHz frequency range) services for broadcasters and VDI customers respectively. A third Anik C satellite was stored in space and could be brought into use when needed.

The higher frequency Ku-band radio waves were shorter than C-band radio waves and could therefore be detected by a proportionately smaller antenna. Another advantage of using the Ku-band was that its frequencies were less subject to interference, because the Ku-band was reserved solely for satellite use. The C-band was also used by terrestrial microwave systems. However, critics of Ku-band systems pointed out that extremely heavy rain had been known to interfere with the shorter radio waves.

Two new satellites, Anik E1 and E2, were scheduled for launch in 1990. These satellites were designed to provide Canada-wide communications and complete U.S. coverage for cross-border applications, with each satellite carrying twenty-four C-band and thirty Ku-band channels. It was intended that Telesat's older satellites would eventually be retired as the new spacecraft came upstream.

Industry experts expected that fewer satellites would be launched in the immediate future. The explosion of the space shuttle Challenger along with a string of rocket failures,

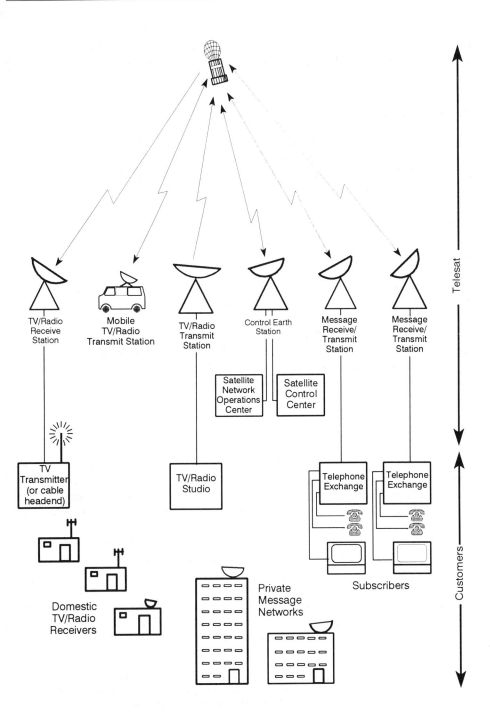

Figure 5.3 Telesat communications system.

had left the satellite companies with fewer means of getting their satellites launched. The launch failure problems also resulted in higher insurance rates, which increased the price of adding satellite capacity.

Satellite Coverage Patterns

The Anik C (Ku-band) satellites were equipped with two repeaters, each with a capacity of thirty-two radio frequency (RF) channels. Each channel could handle about 10 megabits per second (mbps) or 10,000 kilobits per second (Kbps).[5] One repeater served the Western two regions while the other repeater served the Eastern two regions. The Anik D (C-band) satellites had a similar antenna system to that of the Anik C satellites, except that full Canadian coverage was provided.

Teleports

A teleport was a central ground satellite communication facility owned and operated by Telesat that included all the ground equipment needed to provide full satellite communications service. In effect, it allowed a number of Telesat customers that might not find it economical to have their own ground facilities to share facilities. The teleport was linked to the customers' own computer or telecommunications system by a "local loop," which was typically a terrestrial line leased from the local telephone company. Telesat had opened teleports in Montreal and Toronto during 1987 and was constructing additional teleports in Calgary, Edmonton, and Vancouver.

Voice Interconnection

The amended 1985 Connecting Agreement gave Telesat the right to negotiate the interconnection of Telesat's services with facilities of the terrestrial member carriers of Telecom Canada, in order to provide private line end-to-end satellite services to end users.

Interconnection was only an issue for voice communications. There were two types of interconnection. Type 1 interconnection was the connection of a voice circuit, owned or leased by Telesat, to a telephone company local central office switching system, through a circuit owned by the telephone company. Type 2 interconnection was the connection of a circuit, owned or leased by Telesat, to a customer's equipment (normally a PBX) comprising the customer's private network, which was in turn connected to a telephone company switching system. Type 1 and Type 2 connections are shown schematically in Figure 5.4.

Bell Canada and B.C. Telephone allowed Telesat both forms of interconnection, but some of the other Telecom Canada companies only allowed Telesat Type 2 interconnec-

---

5. In order to visualize how much capacity this represented, it is useful to note that a high quality voice circuit historically requires 64 Kbps. However, advanced multiplexing techniques allowed two or more conversations to be carried on such a circuit by 1988. Approximately four pages of text per second could also be transmitted over a 64-Kbps circuit.

Type 1 voice interconnection

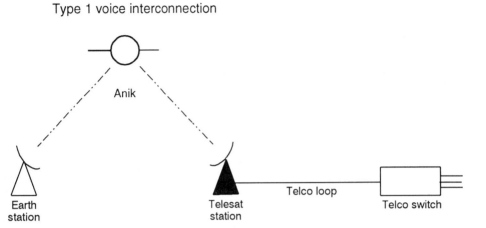

Type 2 voice interconnection

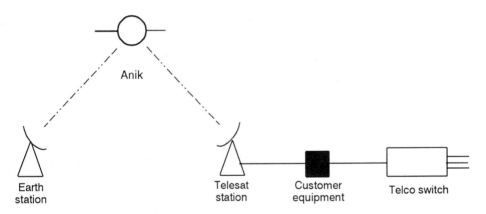

Figure 5.4 Type 1 and Type 2 voice interconnections.

tion. Two carriers, Manitoba Tel and Saskatchewan Telecommunications, still denied Telesat any interconnection to their facilities. While all the telephone companies had agreed to interconnection when they signed the 1985 Amendments to the Connecting Agreement, it was clearly in their short-term interest to delay interconnection. Interconnection was absolutely vital if Telesat was to have nationwide access to the Canadian telecommunications market.

The Retail Voice, Data, and Image Market

Prior to 1985, Telesat had not focused much attention on the retail VDI telecommunications market, in comparison with its wholesale business to the telephone companies. The company in 1986 had only a minute share of the retail VDI market, estimated to be worth $6 billion a year in Canada.

However, as the telephone companies completed their fiber-optic networks, it became clear that a major market segment for Telesat, private-line business traffic, was under threat from land transmission systems. Fiber-optics technology, which used beams of light to transmit information, carried telephone traffic more efficiently than satellite technology and avoided the delays experienced in satellite transmission. Telesat had to search for new business to replace the vulnerable voice traffic.

Private data networks, which enabled companies to transmit computer data by satellite to widely scattered locations, were an example of an emerging application of satellite technology. Private business television and other new video services provided further opportunities for growth as the wholesale telephone business declined. Telesat recognized that in order to compete effectively in the VDI segment it would have to become a market-driven retailer of complete telecommunications services to the business community, providing voice, data network, and video services rather than technology alone.

When the renegotiated Connecting Agreement was signed in 1985, Telesat made the decision to develop and introduce a standard product line for the VDI market. As of mid-1987 the services of this type that were available from Telesat were:

1. *Point-to-point "special assembly" services.* Telesat aimed to serve large businesses (greater than 500 employees) with long distance or remote locations in Canada or cross-border with very high voice and data transmission requirements by providing customized services with leased earth station facilities. For example, the head office of the Canadian subsidiary of an oil company might have a need to transmit large amounts of data to the corporate head office in Houston, Texas. Telesat anticipated revenues of $2.2 million in 1987 from this market, but it was facing increasing telephone company competition on popular telecommunications routes where the telephone companies were increasingly using fiber-optics technology. Revenues were expected to be $3.2 million in 1991.

2. *Multipoint "special assembly" services.* These customized services were targeted at large businesses with multiple remote locations in Canada and cross-border. Although satellite's distance-insensitive pricing advantage put Telesat in a strong competitive position compared to the telephone companies, its inability to provide voice connection into the regular public switched network in all parts of Canada reduced its attractiveness to many customers. Again, the service faced strong competition from terrestrial competitors and the potential competition of

other satellite-based competitors. Revenue from this business were expected to be $5.4 million in 1987, and Telesat expected that this would rise to $13 million by 1991.

3. *Anikom*^{TM}*100.*[6] Anikom 100 was targeted at medium to large, one-way, point-to-multipoint data broadcast customers. For example, a company might use such a service to send reports from its head office to all its plants and offices in Canada. The 1987 revenue from these services was expected to be $0.4 million, and little growth was expected.

4. *Anikom 500.* Anikom 500 was targeted at medium to large national organizations with significant VDI traffic between geographically dispersed locations. It provided two-way, point-to-point digital transmission at Kbps rates of 56 to 512. For example, a customer with large offices in Toronto and Calgary and heavy telephone traffic between them might use Anikom 500 to link the company's PBXs in the two cities. With 512 Kbps of capacity, this would provide the company with the equivalent of about 16 voice circuits between the two cities. A 56-Kbps Anikom 500 service cost approximately $5,000 per month. The service used dedicated earth stations located on the customer's premises. The Anikom 500 service had been announced in May 1987 and by early August Telesat had attracted its first three customers. Revenues were forecasted to reach $7.1 million in 1991.

5. *Anikom 1000.* Anikom 1000 was functionally similar to Anikom 500 but was designed to accommodate higher volumes of two-way, point-to-point VDI traffic between geographically dispersed locations. It provided digital transmission at either 772 Kbps or 1544 Kbps rates. A 772-Kbps Anikom 1000 service, which was required for a high-quality video conferencing service, cost over $30,000 per month. Growth in video conferencing and other VDI services was expected to increase Telesat's revenue from Anikom 1000 from a forecasted $1.4 million in 1987 to $8.7 million in 1991.

Anikom 100, Anikom 500, and Anikom 1000 were all standard services, with tariffs filed with the CRTC. The cost to a particular customer was calculated by adding up the applicable tariffs, including special assemblies tariffs for the service components.

VDI Customers

Both the newer tariff services (Anikom 100, Anikom 500, and Anikom 1000) and the special-assembly network services (Point-to-Point, Multipoint) were targeted at larger business organizations, typically the Canadian "Financial Post 500" companies, which had high-volume dispersed and remote communications requirements. Although Telesat was

---

6. Anikom^{TM} is a registered trademark of Telesat.

clearly utilizing satellite's strengths in targeting this market, there were some potential problems in taking this approach. The Financial Post 500 group provided Telesat's terrestrial competitors with the majority of their revenues in VDI services. In targeting a small number of large business customers, high competitive risk was involved, since the loss of even one customer could mean significant loss of revenue and market share for Telecom Canada and the telephone companies involved.

The New Anikom VSAT Service

It was with this background that Linda Rankin, Richard Jestin, and Peter Norman sat back to consider the marketing opportunities open to Telesat with the launch of its new service, provisionally named Anikom 200, based on the Very Small Aperture Terminal (VSAT) technology.

VSAT Technology

A VSAT network had three distinct components: a shared hub or teleport with a large central earth station, a satellite, and a number of remote satellite dishes or terminals. At the shared hub, a transmitter could send signals to the satellite, which would then relay the signal (whether voice, data, or image) to the remote terminals operated by the customer or Telesat. Similarly, signals could be sent from the remote terminals to the central hub, or even transmitted to other remote dishes via the central hub. Telesat owned and operated the hub, offering shared services and considerable network control and management to its customers. Telesat estimated that the cost of each hub would be $5 million. The initial hub would be located close to downtown Toronto.

Since VSAT technology had developed to the point where terminals could function as both receivers and transmitters, two-way interactive communications services could be offered between any combination of the multiple locations served from the hub. The terminals themselves were compact antennas, from 1.8 to 2.4 meters in diameter. VSATs were easier to install on customer premises and less likely to infringe urban planning regulations than conventional satellite dishes, which could measure 4.5 meters or more in diameter. Apart from this, the key advantage of smaller earth stations was cost: VSATs were about one-third the cost of conventional dishes. The price of a typical VSAT earth station had dropped dramatically over the past three years to the point where a fully equipped two-way VSAT terminal could be purchased for less than $25,000 in large quantities.

VSAT promised to be the single most important innovation in telecommunications technology in the next decade of Telesat's history. VSAT had the potential to make certain satellite telecommunications services less costly than the equivalent terrestrial systems because satellite transmission costs were distance insensitive. Companies could afford to equip large numbers of remote locations, even if the traffic volume was not particularly heavy. In fact, the economies of a VSAT network improved with the number of remote terminals, since the use of the hub or teleport was a fixed cost that did not vary with the number of terminals connected to it.

Anikom 200

The proposed Anikom 200 VSAT service was a complete transmit/receive earth station, supporting data, video, and voice communications. A possible Anikom 200 VSAT configuration is shown in Figure 5.5. At the remote customer site an indoor electronics unit was connected to the customer's terminating equipment (e.g., printers, personal computers, private telephone exchanges, or mainframe computers) and also to an outdoor unit and a lightweight antenna. Anikom 200 accommodated interactive and batch data applications, video and voice, and, unlike the equivalent terrestrial networks (Dataroute[TM], Datapac[TM] [7], and long distance analog private lines), was not constrained by geographic location or network availability.

The Potential Market for the VSAT Service

Possible applications of VSAT technology abounded wherever there was a need to share information and to transmit voice, data and/or images to and from multiple remote locations operated by an organization. A major advantage of a VSAT network was that any combination of voice, data, and image traffic could be sent over the same network simultaneously. A company could, for example, use a network that was primarily used for the transmission of data between plants and offices as a private television network. The television network could be used to announce new products, for training, or for a variety of other purposes. Multiple potential uses of VSAT promised to be an important customer benefit that could be employed as part of the selling strategy.

Market Research

In order to develop estimates of the market potential for VSAT, Telesat had conducted a market survey in March 1986. The survey had been restricted to companies with 100 or more employees. Telesat's management estimated that these companies generated more than 80% of Telecom Canada's data services revenue.

The core sample was a representative sample of 500 Canadian companies with 100 or more employees and multiple locations. This core sample, which by its nature included mostly small- and medium-sized companies, was supplemented by the Financial Post 500 companies to ensure that all Canada's largest companies were included in the survey. Telesat followed up this broad survey with meetings with and presentations to 30 companies in a number of different end-user industries. In these meetings the VSAT product concept was presented and data was gathered on each company's telecommunication network. Given the data on the company's telecommunications network and potential applications at the company, Telesat was able to give the company some rough estimates of the likely cost of a VSAT network to them. This allowed the interviewees to give more informed

---

7. Dataroute[TM] and Datapac[TM] are registered trademarks of Telecom Canada.

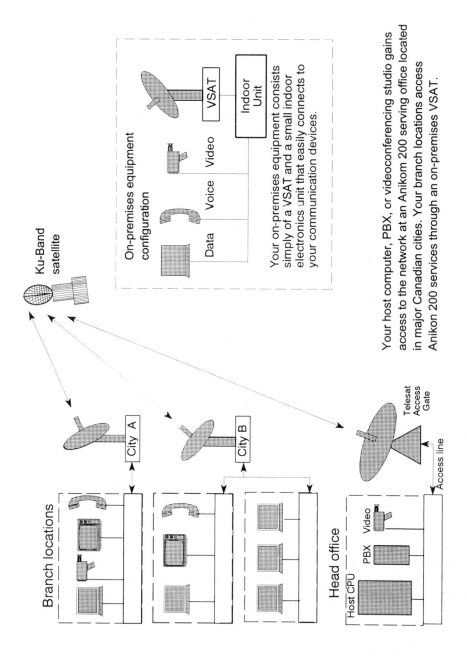

On-premises equipment configuration

Your on-premises equipment consists simply of a VSAT and a small indoor electronics unit that easily connects to your communication devices.

Your host computer, PBX, or videoconferencing studio gains access to the network at an Anikom 200 serving office located in major Canadian cities. Your branch locations access Anikom 200 services through an on-premises VSAT.

Figure 5.5 Possible Anikom 200 network organization.

reactions to the VSAT product concept. From these interviews Telesat obtained feedback on technical service requirements, service demand, timing of purchase, likely order quantities, and customer concerns.

Telesat managers also had discussions with U.S. firms offering or proposing to offer VSAT services. This gave Telesat additional information on potential customer reaction to particular service/price packages by industry segment and some indications of product acceptance by specific industry segment in the United States. The results of this extensive market research are summarized in Tables 5.12, 5.13, and 5.14 for each of the major potential end-use markets for VSAT technology in Canada. In its preliminary evaluation of the research results Telesat management felt that the retail/wholesale and service industry segments were the most interested in an Anikom 200 type service, since they saw the service as providing a major opportunity to reduce operating costs and to enhance competitive position. The next most interested segments appeared to be manufacturing, transportation, resources, and government. The final segment in terms of likelihood of using VSAT was the financial segment, which was dominated by the large Canadian banks. This segment was expected to be an early adopter of VSAT technology in the U.S. but not in Canada, since most observers believe the Canadian market to be significantly less competitive.

From the formal and informal market research a wide range of potential applications of the Anikom VSAT service were identified, including:

- Distributing data between head office and branch locations;
- Administering airline, hotel, and car rental reservation systems;
- Conducting interactive point-of-sale transactions;
- Controlling inventory;
- Collecting and distributing data from drill sites;
- Monitoring and controlling pipeline flows;
- Providing compan-wide training sessions;
- Performing interactive finance, insurance, and banking transactions.

Competition

Telesat faced two major types of competition with its proposed VSAT service: other satellite-based VSAT competitors, and terrestrial competitors providing functionally similar services using terrestrial telecommunications networks.

Satellite-based VSAT competition. Telesat's only direct Canadian competitor was the VSAT service offered by Cancom's (Canadian Satellite Communication Inc.) Satlink Business Services Division. Cancom had been in operation since 1982 and had accumulated losses of $25 million by 1986. Although it lost about $1 million on revenues of $21 million in 1986, its first profitable quarter was the last quarter of that fiscal year. Most of its revenues were accounted for by a division that had as its mandate the provision of television and radio signals to areas of Canada too remote or underpopulated to receive such

Table 5.12
Possible Segments with VSAT Applications

	Retail/Wholesale	*Manufacturing*	*Services*
Size	1513 companies with 0–499 employees, 267 companies with over 500 employees	2299 companies with 100–499 employees, 593 companies with over 500 employees	2164 companies with 100–499 employees, 743 companies with over 500 employees
Characteristics	Highly competitive industry with department stores, specialty chains, and shop-at-home services. Spend the largest portion of their budgets on communication line charges. In the U.S. 36% of companies plan to have private networks by 1988.	High proportion of budget on communication line charges. Often large national or multinational, with multiple divisions involved in manufacturing, distribution, sales and service, multiple branches in Canada, and one or more plants remote from the head office (some with plants in the U.S.). In the U.S. 36% plan to use private networks.	Two major segments: 1. Companies offering telecommunications services, database services, (e.g., financial information services), custom programs accessed via telecommunications, resellers of communications facilities, access to specialized computers (e.g., supercomputers); 2. Companies using telecommunications: hotels/ hospitality for reservations applications and video applications (in-room entertainment and conferences); health services for access to health databases and exchange of patient inform ation. Limited market in 1987, but expected to grow quickly.
Possible applications	1. Credit verification 2. Point-of-sale transaction processing 3. Inventory management and control 4. Administrative: accounting/finance, personnel 5. Electronic funds transfer 6. Broadcast video teleconferencing for training and promotion 7. Network management system	1. Sales order entry 2. Transactions processing: orders, bills, invoices 3. Inventory management and control 4. Electronic mail 5. Financial functions and administration 6. Broadcast video for training in manufacturing, marketing, and distribution 7. Future needs for electronic data interchange between manufacturers and their suppliers	1. Interactive reservation systems 2. Database inquiry/response 3. Customized interactive transactions (e.g., point-of-sale or credit verification system) 4. Batch file transfer 5. Financial functions and administration 6. Network management systems, to allow communication companies to manage systems and bill customers 7. Video conferencing and inroom television (hotels/ hospitality only)

Table 5.12
(continued)

	Retail/Wholesale	Manufacturing	Services
Data networks	1. Large department stores: star or multiple star data networks*, usually IBM; high traffic volumes, line speeds of 2.4–9.6 Kbps on main circuits; greater than 100 potential VSAT sites each; frequent network changes (new stores, communication upgrades). 2. Smaller retail chains, franchise operations, and wholesalers: less aggressive at automating networks; IBM, NCR, and Burroughs equipment.	Diverse. Use several common data communication protocols. Line speeds of 1.2–9.6 Kbps.	Networks are generally based on IBM protocol, but about 20% use other protocols. Data volumes are medium. Line speeds of 1.2–9.6 Kbps.

* A star network involves several locations communicating with one central location but not directly with each other. A multiple star network includes multiple stars, with the central location in each of the stars being interconnected.

signals by conventional means. This division provided radio and television signals to small cable companies and even directly to individual households with satellite dishes.

Since Telesat was the single-source supplier of satellite communications capacity in Canada, Cancom purchased satellite capacity from Telesat at the published tariffs that had been approved by the CRTC. Thus Cancom was a value-added reseller of Telesat's satellite capacity, with which it combined other facilities and services to market a complete VSAT package to its customers. While Telesat had to charge itself the same tariffed rates as any other purchaser of satellite capacity to prevent cross-subsidizations that could be injurious to competition, Telesat management believed that it still had an overall cost advantage over Cancom for two reasons. First, Telesat's greater operating experience would allow it to operate its network more efficiently. Second, Telesat was willing to wait a longer period of time to recover its capital costs than was Cancom, thus effectively reducing its monthly costs of providing service to its customers. In addition to these cost advantages Telesat management felt that they would be able to provide better service to national customers with VSAT locations scattered across the country than could Cancom.

In 1987, the government policy was that all cross-border services originating in the United States had to use Telesat owned and operated ground stations in Canada. With the

Table 5.13
Possible Market Segments with VSAT Applications

	Resource	Transportation, Communications, and Public Utilities	Government Agencies, Departments, & Crown Corporations
Size	168 companies with 100–499 employees, 77 companies with over 500 employees	445 companies with 100–499 employees, 148 companies with over 500 employees	330 companies with 100–499 employees, 139 companies with over 500 employees
Characteristics	Companies in oil, gas and mining. Have many remote locations poorly served by the terrestrial network. Majority located in Western Canada.	90% of segment in transportation. 40% of segment in communications (Telesat's competition). 6% of segment in public utilities. Transportation industry is mature and highly competitive, concerned about cost control and using new technology to gain a competitive edge. Public utilities are those with pipelines or electrical distribution networks.	Possibly largest potential user. Two- to three-year selling cycle with contract usually awarded to lowest cost supplier that meets specification. Segment seems to be risk averse and seems to prefer tariffed communications services. Three subsegments: 1. "must communicate" government departments, reach into far North but low traffic volumes; 2. large mesh networks serving southern corridor of Canada, terrestrial networks seem to meet their needs; 3. star networks, often national networks with low to high-volume traffic.
Possible applications	1. Monitoring of remote wells and pipelines 2. Data transmission between remote sites and company offices 3. Voice communications, particularly for mainte- nance personnel visiting remote unmanned sites	1. Reservations (need automatic dialout to the public network if VSAT system fails) 2. Credit verification 3. Transaction processing 4. Inventory management and control 5. Electronic mail 6. Financial functions and administration 7. Some need for subtoll quality voice	1. Voice communications 2. Database inquiry/response 3. Videoconferencing (limited opportunity since data and video often involve different decision makers)

Table 5.13
(continued)

Resource	Transportation, Communications, and Public Utilities	Government Agencies, Departments, & Crown Corporations
Data networks	A lot of the data collection comes from wellhead and pipelines and they currently use low speed VHF digital radio, which has low network cost. Make extensive use of unique or custom protocols, although a trend to standard protocols, particularly if it results in cost savings. Changes in regulatory environment will result in increased data volumes that VHF radio won't be able to handle. Line speeds of 1.2–9.4 Kbps.	Use common data communication protocols. Line speeds of 2.4–9.4 Kbps.	Diverse communication products and protocol. Trying to standardize on X.25 protocol. Line speeds of 1.2–19.2 Kbps.

real possibility of a Free Trade agreement with the United States, there was the potential for one of several companies offering shared hub VSAT services in the United States to move into Canada. However, any American competitor attempting to compete using its shared hub in the United States would face the increased cost its Canadian customers would bear of connecting the customer's host computer in Toronto, Montreal, or another Canadian city to the American company's hub in the United States. The cost of using terrestrial facilities to make such a connection would probably make the cost of using the American VSAT system noncompetitive. Under Free Trade it might be possible for a U.S. competitor to set up a shared hub in Canada. Since this would probably not be permitted for several years, Telesat and Canadian competitors like Cancom had a considerable lead time in which to get established in the market.

Terrestrial competition. Initially Telesat's VSAT service would compete directly with the leased analog and digital line services in point-to-point and point-to-multipoint configurations provided by Telecom Canada, CNCP Telecommunications, and other telephone companies. The digital leased line service provided by Telecom Canada was called Dataroute. A schematic figure showing a Dataroute application and the comparable VSAT application is contained in Figure 5.6. In both cases the network access points (the Dataroute Serving Area (DRSA) in the case of Dataroute and the satellite dish in the case

Table 5.14
Possible Market Segments with VSAT Applications

Financial Services

Size	669 companies with 100–499 employees, 339 companies with over 500 employees
Characteristics	Primary businesses: finance (33%), insurance (13%) and real estate (53%). High interest in optimizing network performance and minimizing communications costs. Finance concerned about high risk of satellite-based data communications. Use of multiple star networks makes them less suitable for VSAT.* But VSAT would provide interactive data communications to remote branches. Insurance and real estate have many batch applications (remote to host) for database access. Could provide a competitive advantage.
Possible Applications	1. Online teller 2. Loan and mortgage processing 3. Access to insurance policy master files 4. Branch claims processing 5. Access to databases on commercial real estate sites and rental details 6. Access to actuary interface/support 7. Dial-in VSATs for occasional database updates 8. Electronic mail 9. Financial functions and administration 10. Video conferencing for insurance and real estate for training and marketing seminars
Data Networks	Most banks use exclusively IBM systems and protocols. Others use IBM and/or other vendors with X.25 and other protocols. Line speeds of 1.2–19.2 Kbps.

* A star network involves several locations communicating with one central location but not directly with each other. A multiple star network includes multiple stars, with the central location in each of the stars being interconnected.

of VSAT) could be linked to one or more terminals. For example, an oil company could link all the point-of-sale credit card readers in its service stations in the Halifax area to one VSAT. The VSAT could then be linked by satellite to a computer in Calgary for credit verification/authorization.

The VSAT service was also potentially a competitor to Telecom Canada's Datapac service in high-volume applications with dedicated access connections. Datapac was a packet switching network, where data was accumulated in "packets" and the packets were then sent over the Datapac network to a particular "address." For example, a bank's computer in Calgary might communicate intensively, but only periodically, with a head office computer in Toronto using Datapac where the volume and intensity of usage did not justify a leased line. In essence a number of other customers could be sending packages down the same telecommunications line one after the other. The total number of digital data service connections by leased line (Dataroute type services), packet switched (Datapac type services), and circuit switched services were forecasted to grow dramatically in Can-

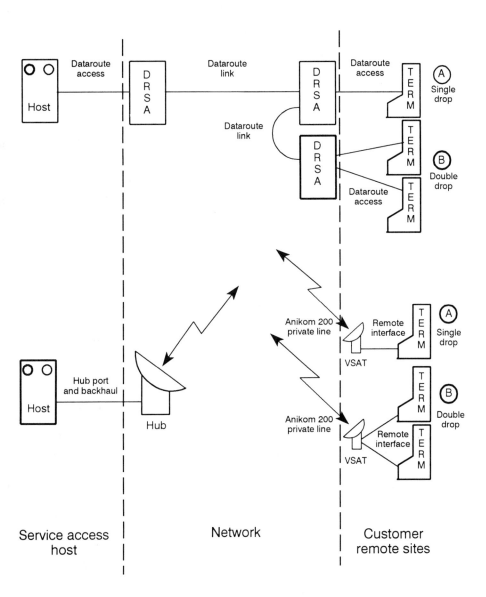

Figure 5.6 Schematic diagrams, Dataroute and VSAT networks.

ada between 1988 and 1991, as more companies established or increased their usage of telecommunication networks (see Table 5.15).

Dataroute and Datapac had quite different pricing structures. The cost of a Dataroute communications network was a flat monthly charge that was dependent on the number of

Table 5.15
Forecasted Market Size for Selected Telecommunications Services in Canada

Total Connections per Service	1988	Forecast 1989	1990	1991
Leased line	28,000	30,000	35,000	40,000
Packet switched	60,000	80,000	110,000	150,000
Circuit switched	8,000	9,000	10,000	11,000
Total	96,000	119,000	155,000	201,000

Source: Telesat estimates.

access points, the speed of the links (measured in Kbps) and distances in each leg of the network. The Datapac price, on the other hand, was comprised of an access charge plus a charge for each package sent, which reflected the volume of data in the package, the distance the package was sent, and the data communication protocol employed.

A number of the other similarities and differences among Dataroute, Datapac, and the proposed Telesat VSAT service are shown in Table 5.16. Telesat's VSAT system promised to offer customers a number of advantages over Dataroute or Datapac. It would be a national service available to all locations in Canada, provided through a single service provider and a single technology. Dataroute and Datapac were available in most business centers in Canada, but they were not available in smaller communities or in remote locations. This forced customers with facilities in such places to make use of lower quality analog lines to connect these locations to the Dataroute or Datapac network. A customer's network growth and changes could be readily accommodated and these changes would not be disruptive to the customer's business. Voice, data, and image could be transmitted simultaneously without cross impact, whereas Dataroute and Datapac allowed for the transmission of data only.

A potential future threat to the VSAT service was the Integrated Services Digital network (ISDN), which was a planned, all-digital network with new features and capabilities. ISDN was an evolving worldwide standard for communicating VDI information from ISDN terminals through telecommunication networks to other ISDN terminals. In 1987 ISDN trials were underway in many countries. A possible threat was that ISDN networks installed to carry voice between different locations might be able to carry data at a lower incremental cost than either separate data lines or separate networks (such as VSAT). Since there was not even preliminary data on ISDN pricing in Canada, it was difficult to assess the degree of threat that it posed. ISDN was not expected to be widely available until mid to late 1990s.

Table 5.16
Competitive Comparison

	Anikom 200	*Dataroute*	*Datapac*
Geographical coverage	Any location in Canada	Dataroute-served markets (most business markets). Nonbusiness locations served by analog private lines	Datapac-served areas (most business markets). Off-network locations served by analog private lines.
Transmission capacity	Up to 56 Kbps	Up to 56 Kbps	Up to 9.6 Kbps
Fastest response time	2 seconds	1 second	1.5 seconds
Ease of making network changes	Not disruptive	Disruptive to reconfigure	Not disruptive
Protocols	Supports popular protocols	Supports all protocols	Supports popular protocols
Features	Data, image, and voice simultaneously. International to U.S. customer network. Management reports and console.	Data, international to U.S. customer network. Management reports.	International to 75 countries. Customer network. Management reports.
Basis for pricing	To be determined	Access charge plus fixed monthly rate based on speeds, distances, synchronous or asynchronous data, and 24-hour versus business-day use.	Access charge plus usage-sensitive monthly charge that depends on locations and data communications protocol employed.

Pricing the VSAT Service

One of the major decisions facing Telesat management was how to price the VSAT service at introduction and how the pricing structure might evolve over time. There were a number of elements to the cost structure that would ultimately have to be reflected in the pricing. These included:

1. *Satellite dishes.* For technical reasons all users of the Telesat VSAT system would have to adopt the same satellite dish technology that would be compatible with the shared hub. Thus all satellite dishes would have to be bought from the same supplier. Telesat was considering giving customers two options:

   a. Purchase directly from Telesat.
   b. Lease from a third party, who would purchase from Telesat.

By using Telesat's purchasing power for the potential VSAT market in Canada, Telesat expected to be able to negotiate a price with the chosen supplier that would be as low or lower than the price charged by the manufacturer to any other customer in North America. On the basis of a 5-year lease, the monthly lease price for a large volume customer was expected to be about $630 per terminal (based on a price close to Telesat's cost of $25,000 per dish). One issue was to what extent purchase price and monthly leasing cost should vary with the volume of VSATs purchased or leased by a customer.

2. *Administrative fee.* The cost of managing and controlling the VSAT network for a particular user was expected to vary directly with the number of VSAT terminals the customer had. The monthly cost was expected to be about $30 per terminal.
3. *Operations and maintenance.* Whether purchased from Telesat, provided by the customer, or acquired through a third party, the operation and maintenance cost for each VSAT terminal in major metropolitan areas was expected to cost about $100 per month. This cost would be higher for terminals located in remote areas or remote from Telesat service facilities.
4. *Local loop.* All customers would need to connect their host facility to the Telesat hub. This would require the lease of a digital telecommunications circuit from their local telephone operating company. The cost of such a circuit would depend on the capacity of the circuit and the distance between the host computer and the hub. For example, a 56-Kbps-capacity line for a distance of 25 kilometers would cost about $370 per month.
5. *Hub/satellite capacity.* The most crucial aspect of the pricing decision was how to charge the customer for the use of the hub and the satellite capacity. There were three major options:

   a. Do an analysis of a customer's particular network requirements and develop a charge based on the exact combination of facilities and capacities used. This seemed to be the approach that Cancom and the Houston International Teleport, a United States VSAT company, were using. This charge would have to be reassessed each time the customer changed its network.
   b. Base the price on the amount of VDI traffic the customer sent over the VSAT network. Although a usage-based system was attractive on some dimensions, the actual VSAT management system on the market in 1987 did not have the capability to measure the usage. However, such a capability would become available in a few years.
   c. Base the price on the network capacity that the customer needed. For example, a large customer might want to purchase 56 Kbps of capacity. This would allow the customer at any point in time to be transmitting up to 56 Kbps of voice, data, or image between the host and remote locations or between two remote locations.

Assuming that the hub/satellite capacity was priced on the basis of option c, a Telesat manager performed an economic analysis from the point of view of a customer comparing a VSAT system with Telecom Canada's Dataroute service. Part of this economic analysis is reported in Table 5.17 and Figure 5.7. The analysis suggested that a VSAT-based network would become economically very attractive relative to a Dataroute-based network as the number of remote locations in the network increased.

In some respects the most attractive pricing structure for VSAT would be a totally "bundled" service price, where the VSAT hardware and all other facilities would be transparent to the customer. In this case, a customer would simply order a circuit and specify the locations and performance requirements for each of the locations to be served. Telesat would maintain ownership of the VSATs and would provide whatever facilities were needed to deliver the required services. This would represent a much greater investment on Telesat's part (at lease 7 to 10 times greater). While the Telesat management team had rejected this as an initial pricing strategy, they recognized that they might want to consider it in the future.

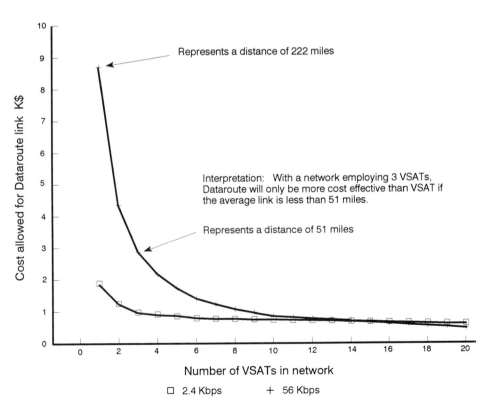

Figure 5.7 Extrapolation from Table 5.17 data.

Table 5.17
Simplified Economic Analysis of Telesat's VSAT versus Telecom Canada's Dataroute

Anikom 200

		Shared Common Costs				Costs Related to VSAT Location				Total	Access Charge		Shared Cost	
A. Number of VSATs on Network	Speed (Kbps)	B. Local Loop*	C. Anikom 200 Hub/Satellite Price†	D. Total (B)+(C)	E. Cost per VSAT (D)/(A)	F. Lease of VSAT	G. Operation and Maintenance (Zone 1)	H. Access Charge	I. Total Cost (F)+(G)+(H)	J. Cost per Drop (E)+(I)	K. Shared Cost††	L. Drop Specific (K)/(A)	M. Cost Allowed for Link (J)−(L)	N. Number of Miles Allowed for Link
1	2.4	370	1100	1470	1470	630	100	30	760	2230	350	350	1884◊	888
1	4.8	370	1567	1937	1937	630	100	30	760	2697	400	400	2297	657
1	9.6	370	1883	2253	2253	630	100	30	760	3013	500	500	2513	463
1	19.2	370	3450	3820	3820	630	100	30	760	4580	900	900	3680	252
1	56	370	9083	9453	9453	630	100	30	760	10213	1500	1500	8713	222
2	2.4	370	1100	1470	735	630	100	30	760	1495	525	263	1233	475
2	4.8	370	1567	1937	968	630	100	30	760	1728	600	300	1428	283
2	9.6	370	1883	2253	1127	630	100	30	760	1887	750	375	1512	146
2	19.2	370	3450	3820	1910	630	100	30	760	2670	1350	675	1995	85
2	56	370	9083	9453	4727	630	100	30	760	5487	2250	1125	4362	76
3	2.4	370	1100	1470	490	630	100	30	760	1250	700	233	1017	350
3	4.8	370	1567	1937	646	630	100	30	760	1406	800	267	1139	166
3	9.6	370	1883	2253	751	630	100	30	760	1511	1000	333	1178	102
3	19.2	370	3450	3820	1273	630	100	30	760	2033	1800	600	1433	61
3	56	370	9083	9453	3151	630	100	30	760	3911	3000	1000	2911	51

Notes:

* Cost of leasing a local loop between Telesat hub and company's host computer facility. All costs are monthly.

† Possible Anikom 200 price that would cover anticipated shared hub and satellite costs.

†† Cost of accessing Dataroute with one remote location, two accesses (one ate host computer and one at remote site) would be required.

◊ To break even, the customer could to spend $1,880 on the Dataroute link between the host site and the remote, a distance of approximately 888 miles.

Since initially the only VSAT hub would be located in Toronto, Telesat management was considering having several VSAT serving offices located across Canada. These serving offices would be linked to the Toronto hub by leased terrestrial loops. The customer could be required to pay the cost of linking to the closest serving office and Telesat could either charge the customer for its share of the costs of the terrestrial link between the serving office and Toronto or build the cost of the link into its overall VSAT pricing. A 56-Kbps leased line between the Toronto hub and Calgary would cost about $20,000 per month. When the VSAT usage in a city or region reached a certain level, Telesat would open additional VSAT hubs. One VSAT hub would be able to serve over 3,000 VSAT terminals, although it might run out of transmission capacity before this many terminals were linked to the hub.

The Nature of the VSAT Business

Telesat management recognized that there were a number of significant differences between the proposed VSAT business and Telesat's more traditional services. Even a service like Anikom 500 often only involved two or three customer locations. A major VSAT sale could well involve hundreds of VSAT locations. Managing such a business would require that Telesat have an effective system to keep track of the equipment at each customer location, both the VSATs and the "port" cards that were required to support each application, such as credit verification, inventory control, and television broadcasting. Accurate, current information on each customer's VSAT network would be essential for accurate billing. In addition, an extensive service infrastructure would be needed to respond to customer service problems, maintain the customer's hardware and software, and upgrade or change a customer's network. Each account would need to be effectively managed, to help identify new VSAT applications and to ensure that Telesat obtained the full VSAT revenue growth potential from each account. One manager had noted that the cost structure for VSAT was very different from their traditional businesses, since the revenue per customer location served would be much lower. This was one indicator that VSAT represented a significant redefinition of Telesat's business.

The Situation in August 1987

Linda Rankin, Richard Jestin, and Peter Norman had a number of other major decisions to make in finalizing the marketing plan for Anikom 200. Since the range of potential customers was large, the choice of target segments was going to be crucial. Should one segment be targeted initially, or should they pursue several or all segments simultaneously? The positioning of the VSAT service in the marketplace was also crucial. The marketing communication strategy, particularly the personal selling program, would also be essential if Telesat were to achieve significant market penetration with the VSAT service.

Telesat expected to have the technical capability to begin commercial trials in March 1988, and to begin commercial service in June 1988. An obvious opportunity to announce the VSAT service was at a major telecommunications forum, the Canadian Business Telecommunications Alliance (CBTA) Conference. This conference was just over one month away. The marketing plan for Anikom 200 had to be finalized quickly.

Table 5.18
Glossary of Telecommunications Terms

Term	Definition
Channel	A single path for transmitting radio signals in one or two directions. The paths might be separated from other similar paths by frequency or time division. In the Telesat system a channel is also used to describe a band of frequencies (e.g., Anik A3 Channel 1).
Data communications protocol	Procedures that two computers or one computer and a terminal use in order to achieve an error free data communication connection. These communications protocols include error checking and correction procedures.
Geostationary orbit	An orbit 22,600 miles above the surface of the earth at the Equator such that from earth the satellite appears to remain in the same position in the sky.
Repeater/transponder	A unit on the satellite that receives signals from earth on one radio frequency, amplifies them, and simultaneously retransmits them back to earth on another frequency.
Satellite coverage pattern	The "footprint" on earth where the satellite "downlink" power is focused, so that reception of the satellite's signal is possible within the footprint area.
Terrestrial	Any earth-based (nonsatellite) means of sending signals, such as twisted-pair cable, fiber-optic cable, or microwave transmission.

5.6 TELESAT CASE DISCUSSION

We have progressed from a very short case, Elektrolipa, to a rather long one, Telesat. Telesat was set up by the Canadian government in 1969 to provide all types of telecommunications and broadcast distribution services via satellite throughout Canada. There are technical, financial, and marketing issues involved in this case. First, the technical issues include:

- What are the relative advantages of satellite and terrestrial communications?
- Telesat seems to have captured a dominant share of the broadcasting business. Exactly what is this business? Why should Telesat be so successful in this market segment?
- What exactly is a VSAT system, and what purpose can it serve?
- Under what conditions, if any, does a VSAT system offer advantages over a terrestrial point-to-point system?

With regard to the financial issues, apparently Telesat decided that unless it entered into a new market segment, its future business would decrease. The television and radio broadcasting business was forecasted to increase by 11–12% over the next five years. However, this would be counterbalanced by sales of voice-data-image (VDI) services being lost to Telecom Canada, the association of the major Canadian telephone carrier companies. This business was forecasted to decrease by 10–11% over the next five years, as long-distance telephone traffic migrated from satellites to land lines, and particularly to fiber-optic networks. If we assume that average expenses increase by 7% per year, the financial picture could look like the one portrayed in Table 5.19. The bottom line is that the ROE would decrease with time even if Telecom continued to subsidize Telesat with $20 million per year.

The projection of future decreasing profits led Telesat to ask for the right to market VDI services to end users without going through the telephone companies (Telecom). The price Telesat had to pay to receive this right was relinquishment of the subsidies it received from the telephone companies. Telesat decided to compensate for the reduced VDI sales to Telecom by marketing VSAT systems directly to the end users of VDI services. Two key financial questions were:

- What sales could be expected for VSAT services, as a function of time?
- What extra expenses would be needed to support the sales? Note that such expenses would precede the sales, because people had to be hired and trained, advertising and direct mailing campaigns had to be organized, and all this had to happen well before actual sales were made.

The financial model of Table 5.19 is compiled from data given in the text (Tables 5.10 and 5.11), together with some assumptions stated in the notes. Figures are in thousands of U.S. dollars ($K). Students should study the model and comment on its validity. They should also be able to suggest figures for revenue and expenses that would yield an acceptable ROE. The key question is whether the financial model is realistic in view of the market size and growth and the competition. Note that extra costs to market the VSAT system will have to be sustained long before sales are made.

A number of key marketing issues must be considered, including the following:

- For a particular number of VSAT terminals and data rate, Table 5.17 shows the maximum number of miles of connection between subscribers below which a terrestrial system (Dataroute) is more economical. Does this suggest a marketing approach?
- In view of the market size and competition, what customer segments should Telesat target initially?
- Some increase in marketing personnel can be visualized for the extra sales work in approaching end customers directly. What sort of people should be hired, and in what organization of Telesat should they fit?

Table 5.19
A Possible Financial Model

	1986	1987	1988	1989	1990	1991	#
Revenues:							
Broadcast industry	65,005	72,152	80,089	88,899	98,678	109,532	1
Specials	3,600	3,919	4,265	4,643	5,054	5,500	2
VDI to telecom	36,700	32,663	29,070	25,872	23,026	20,493	3
VDI direct	0	0	0	0	0	0	4
Total	105,305	108,734	113,424	119,414	126,758	135,525	
Expenses:							
Depreciation	48,844	52,263	55,921	59,836	64,025	68,506	5
Operation and administration	44,046	47,129	50,428	53,959	57,735	61,777	6
VDI direct marketing	0	0	0	0	0	0	7
Other expenses	2,226	2,382	2,549	2,727	2,918	3,122	8
Total	95,116	101,774	108,898	116,521	124,678	133,405	
Gross earnings	10,189	6,960	4,526	2,893	2,080	2,120	
From telecom	20,000	20,000	0	0	0	0	9
PBT	30,189	26,960	4,526	2,893	2,080	2,120	
Tax	16,604	14,828	2,489	1,591	1,144	1,166	10
PAT	13,585	12,132	2,037	1,302	936	954	
Investment:							
Capital	60,000	60,000	60,000	60,000	60,000	60,000	
Retained earnings	100,302	109,434	108,471	106,773	104,709	102,663	11
Equity	160,302	169,434	168,471	166,773	164,709	162,663	
ROE	8.5%	7.2%	1.2%	0.8%	0.6%	0.6%	

Notes:
1. Broadcast revenues forecasted to increase 11% per year.
2. Specials forecasted to increase to $5.5 million in 1991.
3. VDI to Telecom Canada forecasted to decrease 11% per year.
4. VDI to end customer not yet forecasted.
5. Depreciation forecasted to increase 7% per year.
6. Operations and administration forecasted to increase 7% per year.
7. Extra marketing and other costs for VDI to customers not yet forecasted.
8. Other expenses forecasted to increase 7%.
9. Telecom Canada settlements after 1987.
10. Tax calculated at 55% of PBT.
11. Earnings forecasted to accumulate at profit after tax (PAT), less $3 million per year, which is assumed to be given as a dividend to shareholders.

Chapter 6

Conclusion

Chapter 1 examines the following issues and their strategic implications:

- The experience curve and the assumption that higher margins increase market leaders' chances of maintaining their leads;
- The so-called ecological view, which amounts to stick to what you know;
- The importance of selecting a niche market segment that offers an opportunity for market leadership;
- The product life cycle, the importance of constantly reviewing products, mature products as a source of cash, and phasing out declining products;
- Product portfolios that contain a balanced mix of products;
- The importance of planning any marketing program;
- Top management's crucial role in marketing;
- The importance of international and global marketing.

Chapter 2 is devoted to a review of product impact on market strategy (PIMS). It presents some of the quantitative conclusions of a statistical study of thousands of businesses and suggests how these conclusions support the strategic implications identified in Chapter 1. In particular, Chapter 2 examined

- The correlation between market share and ROI;
- The impact of quality on ROI, noting especially that high quality increases ROI not only because it aids in the achievement of a good market share (with consequent economies of scale) but also because high-quality products command higher prices;
- The negative correlation between high investment and marketing expenses and ROI;
- How PIMS analysis can assist in a determination of whether the ROI from a product is above or below par for look-alike industries;
- How PIMS can assist internationalization.

Chapter 3 examines the special problems related to selecting suitable channels of distribution in foreign markets. The discussion stresses the importance of employing good foreign representatives and suggests ways of finding and keeping them.

Chapter 4 discusses some approaches to selling high-tech products and services in foreign markets and illustrates these approaches with a number of real-life examples. The approaches might seem to be merely common sense; nonetheless, if sales representatives don't exhibit this common sense, they will flounder in foreign markets.

The three cases presented in Chapter 5 were chosen because of their relevance to topics discussed in previous chapters.

Four appendices provide supplementary information. Appendix A, "Sources for Marketing Information," offers information about foreign markets and representatives. Appendix B contains a typical representative agreement, which includes many clauses that have been refined as a result of years of resolving problems involving agents and distributors. Appendix C, "An Introduction to Finance for Marketers," barely skims the surface of the topic it attempts to present. If nothing else, it does define the financial terms marketers must understand. Appendix D is hardly an exhaustive list of relevant literature. Many of the books are highly recommended to anyone who wishes to further pursue related topics.

Appendix A

Sources for Marketing Information

A.1 SELECTED LIST OF TRADE DIRECTORY PUBLISHERS

Trade directories contain information about commercial organizations in various countries. They are useful for marketers who want to gain an appreciation of the industrial makeup of a country, for market research, and in the hunt for suitable foreign representatives.

Kompass publishes trade directories that cover some 45 countries worldwide. A Kompass listing appears in the telephone directories of most major cities, along with information about where to purchase publications. Information can also be obtained from the following address:

Kompass International Management Corporation
Rutistrasse 38
Gockhausen, Zurich CH-8044
Switzerland

Another widely used set of trade directories is published by Dun & Bradstreet. The company publishes approximately 100 publications, covering about 40 countries in Europe, the Middle East, Asia, and North and South America. Here again, information about where to purchase publications is often available in telephone directory listings for Dun & Bradstreet or from the following address:

Dun & Bradstreet Limited
Holmers Farm Way
High Wycombe
Bucks HP12 4UL
England

EUROPAGES are contained in some 10 volumes, which cover 25 European countries (including Eastern Europe), and are published in Dutch, English, French, German,

Italian, and Spanish. There are agencies in over 15 European countries, and general information about these publications can be obtained from:

EUREDIT S. A.
Central Office
9, Avenue de Friedland
75008 Paris, France

Table A.1 is a partial listing of the other publishers of trade directories.

A.2 INTERNATIONAL ORGANIZATIONS

The *Europa Year Book* is a very comprehensive source of data on international organizations and countries of the world. The book is published annually by Europa Publications Limited, 18 Bedford Square, London WC1B 3JN, England. It provides detailed descriptions of international organizations, followed by detailed descriptions of countries (arranged alphabetically). Over 270 pages are devoted to international organizations. These include various United Nations (UN) organizations; UN regional commissions; various UN bodies, such as the UN Conference on Trade and Development (UNCTAD); various specialized UN agencies, such as the General Agreement on Tariffs and Trade (GATT), International Bank for Reconstruction and Development (IBRD), the International Finance Corporation (IFC), and the International Telecommunications Union (ITU). Some of these organizations are discussed in this appendix.

Information in the *Europa Year Book* about countries is also detailed. Introductory surveys cover location, climate, language, religion, flag, and capital. Also covered are recent history, government, economic affairs, social welfare, and education. The book goes on to present and evaluate many country statistics. Statistics are provided for these areas:

Area and population	Education
Agriculture	Communications media
Fishing	External Trade
Mining	Transportation
Industry	Tourism
Finance	

Some of the key organizations of interest in international marketing investigations are listed below. A much more detailed description is contained in the *Europa Year Book*.

UN Conference on Trade and Development. The UNCTAD promotes international trade, particularly in developing countries. Several publications are available from UNCTAD, including an annual *Handbook of International Trade and Development Statistics*.

Table A.1
International Publishers of Trade Directories

Africa
Braby's Commercial Directory of South,
  East, and Central Africa,
A. C. Braby (Pty) Ltd.
P. O. Box 1426, Pinetown
South Africa

Australia
Universal Business Directory
316 St. Kilda Road
St. Kilda, Victoria
Australia

Brazil
Delta Directory,
Albeisa do Brazil Editores Ltdda
Rua 24 de Maio, 276
8° Andar, Cj. 84,
CEP 01041 San Paulo, Brazil

Bulgaria
Bulgarian Chamber of Commerce
Department of International Relations
11a Stanboliski,
Sofia 1040, Bulgaria

Canada
Canadian Manufacturing Association
Canadian Trade Index
1 Young Street
Toronto, Ontario MSE 1J9
Canada

Finland
Finnish Foreign Trade Directory
MERGIN' Oy Ltd.
P.O. Box 129
00129 Helsinki, Finland

Germany
Directory of German Industries
Seibt Verlag GmbH
Leopoldstrasse 208
D-8000 Munich 40
Germany

Gulf States
Falcon Directory Publications WLL
3rd Floor, Bahrain Tower
P. O. Box 2738, Manama
Bahrain

Arab Communicators
P. O. Box 551
Manama, Bahrain

Hong Kong
Current Publications Ltd.
1501 Enterprise Building
228 Queens Road Central
Hong Kong

Hungary
Industrial Almanac Hungary
Almanac Publishing Ltd.
Budapest Szenpharomsag
Ter #6 1014 Hungary

Ireland
Thom's Directory Ltd.
38 Merrion Square
Dublin 2, Ireland

Japan
Japan Yellow Pages Ltd.
ST Building, Iidabashi 4-chome
Chiyoda-Ku, Tokyo 102, Japan

Korea
Korean Chamber of Commerce & Industry
45 Namdaemunno 4-GA
Chung-Gu
Seoul, Korea

Taiwan
Taiwan Yellow Pages Corp.
2nd Floor, Chouwoo House
57 Tun Hua Rd. Sec 1
Taipei, Taiwan, R.O.C.
(P.O. Box 81-02,
Taipei, Taiwan, R.O.C.)

The address of UNCTAD is Palais des Nations, 1211 Geneva 10, Switzerland. The telephone number is 41-22-346011.

UN Development Program. The UNDP was established to help developing countries increase the wealth-producing capabilities of their human and natural resources. It is the world's largest source of technical assistance grants for developing countries. The address is One United Nations Plaza, New York, NY 10017, U.S.A. The telephone number is 1-212-906- 5000.

General Agreement on Tariffs and Trade. The GATT was established in 1948 with the aim of liberalizing world trade. In 1987, the group contained 95 contracting parties (countries, really, although some parties are as small geographically as Hong Kong). GATT is of interest to marketing people chiefly as a source of information on trade barriers. The organization publishes a number of documents, available in English, French, and Spanish. The address is Centre William Rappard, 154 rue de Lausanne, Geneva 21, Switzerland. The telephone number is 41-22-395111.

International Bank for Research and Development. The IBRD, better known as the World Bank, assists the economic development of member nations by making loans when private capital is not available to finance productive investments. The address is 1818 H Street, NW, Washington, DC 20433, U.S.A. The telephone number is 1-202-477-1234.

International Finance Corporation. Although the IFC is a separate legal entity from the World Bank, its directors are the executive directors of the World Bank, and the two are affiliated. It was founded to encourage the growth of productive private enterprise in its member countries, particularly in the less developed areas. Its address and telephone numbers are the same as for the IBRD.

International Monetary Fund. The IMF was established at the same time as the World Bank to promote international monetary cooperation, facilitate the expansion and balanced growth of international trade, and promote stability in foreign exchange. It publishes many reports and compilations of finance and trade statistics. The address is 700 19th Street, NW, Washington, DC 20431, U.S.A. The telephone number is 1-202-477-7000.

International Telecommunications Union. The ITU is the agency of the UN that encourages world cooperation in the use of telecommunications, to promote technical development and harmonize national policies. Among other matters, the ITU establishes world telegraph, telephone, and radio regulations, including satellite communications. It holds World Administrative Radio Conferences (WARC) on occasion to revise radio regulations. ITU activities include the International Frequency Registration Board (IFRB), the Comité Consultatif International de Télégraphie e Téléphonie (CCITT), and the Comité Consultatif International de Radio (CCIR). ITU publishes a wealth of technical manuals, including *Telecommunications Journal.* The ITU address is Place des Nations, 1211 Geneva, Switzerland. The telephone number is 41-22-995-1111.

UN Industrial Development Organization. The UNIDO promotes industrial development in developing countries. Apart from the technical assistance UNIDO provides on request to developing countries through governments, industries or other bodies, it maintains investment promotion offices in Cologne, Milan, Paris, Seoul, Tokyo, Vienna, Warsaw, Washington, and Zurich to publicize investment opportunities and provide information to investors. The UNIDO address is P.O. Box 300, 1400 Vienna, Austria. The telephone number is 43-1-26-310.

International Chamber of Commerce. The ICC is a very important organization, founded in 1919, that promotes free trade and private enterprise, provides practical services, and represents business interests at governmental and intergovernmental levels. The ICC has many commissions, including one on marketing, and includes bodies for settlement of international disputes. It issues a quarterly magazine, *ICC Business World,* as well as a handbook and numerous publications on general and technical subjects.

Incoterms 1990 is an ICC publication that deals with the buyer and seller relationship as it concerns freight, customs duty, insurance, passage of ownership, mode of transportation, and so on. Many terms, such as CIF, FOB, C&F, Exworks, are defined in *Incoterms.* The subject of the publication is of the greatest importance to all involved in negotiating and executing sales contracts. The ICC address is 38 Cours Albert 1er, 75008 Paris, France. The telephone number is 33-1-45-62-34-56.

A.3 THE PIMS DATABASE

Chapter 2 describes the profit impact of marketing strategy (PIMS) databases. Of especial interest for international marketing are the start-up business reports the PIMS database generates. These reports rely on data and assumptions to evaluate proposed entry into a particular market. The reports are derived from the cumulative experience of many start-up businesses that faced analogous situations.

A.4 OTHER MARKETING DATABASES

A number of companies and specialized trade periodicals offer mailing lists of customers, often on computer diskette. Purchasers can use these lists, which are typically specific to market segment and product type, in planning mail campaigns.

P.C. Globe offers a particularly handy and simple fast reference database for IBM and Macintosh computers. The database programs are called PCGlobe and MacGlobe.

P.C. Globe, Inc.
4435 South Rural Road
Building 5, Suite 333
Tempe, AZ 85282
U.S.A.
Tel: 1-(602) 894-6866
Fax: 1-(602) 968-7166

Two CD-ROM products offer extensive databases of industrial, company, and country statistics. These catalogs of information are updated annually and available from the companies listed below.

CD-ROMS in Print: *An International Guide to CD-ROM, CD-I, CDTV & Electronic Book Products*, compiled by Norman Desmarais, Meckler Publishing Company, 11 Ferry Lane W., Westport, CT 06880, U.S.A., ISBN 0891-8198/ ISBN 0-88736-780-1.

The CD-ROM Directory. TFPL Publishing, # 702, 1301 Twentieth St. N.W., Washington, DC 20036, U.S.A., ISBN 1-870889-30-4.

A.5 STANDARDS

The British Standards Institute (BSI), in the United Kingdom, provides a range of services to exporters. It is also the liaison between the United Kingdom and the European Economic Community (EEC) Commission for Common Market Standards. The BSI's technical help to exporters (THE) provides advice on foreign requirements, including national laws, particularly in relation to safety and environmental protection, technical standards, and certification processes. The institute maintains an extensive library of standards and regulations for over 160 countries, as well as many English translations. The address is British Standards Institution, Technical Help to Exporters, Linford Wood, Milton Keynes MK14 6LE, England. There are similar organizations in all Western European countries.

A.6 SUMMARY

The sources of marketing information listed in this appendix are useful for companies planning marketing or searching for foreign representatives. These sources can provide a wealth of information on trade, service, and industrial organizations in different countries, as well as useful statistical data. Industrial groups, chambers of commerce, and embassies are also likely sources of information.

Appendix B

A Typical Foreign Representative Agreement

This sample agreement combines an agreement recommended by a U.S. legal authority and one that has been used for many years by a well-known U.S. corporation. Non-U.S. firms can use this agreement. It does, however, include a clause that relates specifically to the U.S. Foreign Corrupt Practices Act.

This sample is an agreement for exclusive representation by either an agent or a distributor, although it is slanted toward an agent. Parties can make it a nonexclusive agreement by substituting "nonexclusive" for "exclusive" in the first paragraph, numbering that paragraph 1.1, and adding this clause:

1.2 Representative rights granted by Supplier under this Agreement shall be nonexclusive. Supplier may appoint such additional sales representatives, or may use such other means as it sees fit, to distribute and sell the Products in the Territory.

The commission payable to the representative is specified in an annex to the agreement. In this annex, extraordinary orders (of high monetary value) are specifically referred to, as are mutually agreed-upon commissions, split commissions, exclusions, and payment terms.

It is common for prospective representatives to consult their lawyers when given an agreement, and for them to propose changes, which the user is warned to resist unless authorized by a lawyer acting on the company's behalf.

Readers who wish to delve more deeply into this subject are referred to the book:

Guide for the Drawing Up of Contracts: Commercial Agency
Publication No. 410
ICC Publishing S.A.
38 Cours Albert 1er
75008 Paris, France
Tel: 49-53-28-28

There is a similar publication, No. 441, entitled *Guide to Drafting Distributorship Agreements*. Most ICC publications are available in many languages. Publication No. 410 is available in English and French.

SALES REPRESENTATIVE AGREEMENT

This Sales Representative Agreement is made as of [*date*], by and between [*supplier*], a corporation organized under the laws of [*country*], having an office at [*address*] and [*representative*], a (corporation) organized under the laws of [*country*], having an office at [*address*].

1 Appointment

Supplier hereby appoints representative as exclusive sales representative for the products listed in Annex I, "Products," in the Territory described below, and Representative accepts such appointment on the terms and conditions of this Agreement.[1]

2 Territory

The representation rights granted pursuant to this Agreement shall be for the territory of [*territory*].[2]

3 Term of Agreement

3.1 This Agreement shall begin on the date when it has been executed by both parties and, unless sooner terminated as hereinafter provided, shall remain in effect until [*date*]. It shall not be automatically renewed; an extension of the relationship between the parties beyond such date will require mutual signing of a new agreement.

3.2 After the date specified in clause 3.1, Supplier shall have no obligation towards Representative beyond the payment of commissions on the sale of Products ordered by customers within the Territory and accepted by Supplier prior to that date, and Representative hereby agrees to assert no claim beyond that.

3.3 Upon termination of the Agreement by the Supplier pursuant to the 90 day termination clause 10.4 herein, but not for any of the other causes as stipulated in clause 10.1 (breach of provisions), clause 10.2 (bankruptcy, insolvency, nationali-

---

1. See the introduction at the beginning of this appendix if the agreement is to be nonexclusive

2. The territory should be specified in detail. Use of such vague geographic labels as, for example, Middle East, invites subsequent trouble. For agreements in the EEC, the term "principal marketing territory" is suggested, because parallel import rights must be preserved.

zation), or clause 10.3 (change of ownership), Supplier shall pay to Representative a lump sum as described in clause 3.3.1 below. Representative agrees that such payment shall reimburse it in full for any damage or loss it may suffer as a result of such termination. Representative agrees that no payment is due to it from Supplier if the 90 day termination is initiated by Representative.

3.3.1 The lump sum shall be an amount equal to two percent (2%) of the average annual value of orders accepted by Supplier from customers in the Territory of all Products covered by this Agreement, over the three years immediately preceding the date of the 90 day notice of termination. No payment shall be made unless the Agreement has been in effect for at least one full year. If the Agreement has been in effect for less than 36 months, then the average annual value of orders shall be calculated from the actual number of months the agreement was in effect, and the lump sum shall be 2% applied to this annual average.

4 Commissions and Discounts

4.1 Supplier shall pay Representative a commission as specified in Annex II, "Commissions." Such commission shall be Representative's sole compensation for its activities hereunder.

4.2 Orders placed by customers outside the Territory and shipped into the Territory will not cause a commission to accrue to Representative unless (i) Representative, in cooperation with Supplier sales unit outside the Territory, has been involved in negotiating the sale, and (ii) such unit has specifically requested the assistance of Representative, and (iii) Supplier has expressly agreed that under the circumstances Representative should be compensated to some extent. In such a case, the commission shall be agreed upon on a case-by-case basis prior to conclusion of the sale.

4.3 Commissions due Representative hereunder shall be paid to Representative not later than the last day of the first month following receipt by Supplier of full payment from the customer. If the order from the customer specified payments to the Supplier in several installments, then the total commission amount shall be determined in accordance with Annex II, and the amount of each commission payment to Representative will be in the same ratio to the total commission amount as each customer payment is to the total customer order amount. Commissions accrued to Representative hereunder shall be subject to debit for any credit issued by Supplier to the customer for returns or allowances on past sales. Commissions shall be paid to Representative by means of a bank draft mailed to Representative's above-stated address. All objections to statements of accounts rendered by Supplier are waived by Representative unless written notice is given within thirty (30) days after receipt of the respective statement.

4.4 Unless otherwise agreed between the parties, Representative shall be solely liable for its expenses incurred pursuant to this Agreement and shall not be reimbursed for such expenses by Supplier.

4.5 It is expressly agreed and understood that notwithstanding anything in this Agreement to the contrary, no amounts otherwise payable to Representative under this Agreement shall be due and payable if and to the extent such are prohibited, restricted, or limited by the laws or regulations within the Territory.

4.6 It is the intent that the primary method of serving customers in the Territory will be by direct sales to customers by Supplier as described. It is acknowledged that from time to time customer requirements or other conditions may result in acceptance by Representative of orders for its own account for resale to customers. When, by mutual agreement between the Representative and Supplier a direct sale by Representative to a customer is more appropriate, Supplier will sell the Products to Representative, subject to credit and sales terms established by Supplier, at its established export prices or quoted prices, less a discount numerically equal to the commission shown in Annex II. In the event of such direct sales by Representative to customers in the Territory, all responsibility to the customer will be assumed by Representative, except Supplier's standard product warranty will be extended to the customer, to be administered by Representative as explained under clause 5.2 below.

5 Representative Status and Responsibility

5.1 Representative agrees to devote its best efforts in the development, promotion, and sale of the Products in the Territory, and will cooperate with Supplier in any advertising or promotion programs with respect to the Products undertaken by Supplier.

5.2 Representative agrees to provide technical liaison and assistance to customers for warranty service of the Products sold in the Territory. Representative shall provide this service at no cost to Supplier or the customers, except for actual warranty repair of the Products performed by Representative at the request of Supplier, which repair services shall be invoiced to and paid by Supplier at mutually agreed upon labor rates.

5.3 Representative is an independent contractor and is not an agent, employee, or legal representative of Supplier. Representative is not authorized to do business in Supplier's name, or to obligate Supplier in any way. Representative will provide and maintain such facilities and qualified personnel as will enable it to render a high standard of service in the sale of Products to Supplier's customers.

5.4 Representative agrees during the term of this Agreement not to represent for sale any goods which are competitive with the Products.[3]

5.5 The annual amount of orders of the Products from customers in the Territory will serve as a principal standard for evaluating Representative's promotional and

---

3. This might not be enforceable in nonexclusive agreements.

sales efforts.[4] The minimum amount to be so ordered annually during the term of this Agreement is shown in Annex I, and failure of such orders to reach any such amounts will constitute just cause for termination of this Agreement by Supplier.

5.6   Representative will make no representation or warranties with respect to the Products on behalf of Supplier except as expressly authorized in writing by Supplier.

5.7   Representative shall at all times comply with the laws and regulations within the Territory in connection with its sales of the Products and other activities under this Agreement including any registration requirement.

5.8   Representative represents and agrees that it has not offered, given, promised to give or authorized giving, directly or indirectly, any money or anything else of value to any government official, political party, political official, or candidate for political office in connection with its activities hereunder.[5]

5.9   Representative will defend, indemnify, and hold harmless Supplier from any claims, suits, or liabilities arising out of any acts or omissions of Representative, its employees, and agents, including any breach by Representative of any of its obligations under this Agreement.

5.10 Should Supplier disclose to Representative data or information that is designated as confidential, Representative shall accord such data or information strict confidentiality and shall not disclose it unless expressly permitted by Supplier or the data or information otherwise becomes public through no fault of the Representative.

6 Assistance and Reports

6.1   Supplier will furnish Representative with such technical bulletins and sales data relative to the Products as Supplier considers appropriate from time to time. Supplier will also cooperate in reasonable ways to assist Representative in effectively promoting the sale of the Products. Supplier will train Representative technical sales and technical service personnel at Supplier's plants, at times and for periods to be mutually agreed. Unless other expense arrangements are agreed, representative will pay all travel and other expense, except the cost of training material, which shall be paid by Supplier.

6.2   Representative agrees to furnish sales forecasts, market surveys, reports of competitive conditions and any other data reasonably requested by Supplier that may be pertinent to proper development of the market.

---

4. The annual amount requirement may be the single most important enforcement aspect for the supplier, who will want assurance of the representative's performance. If such a clause is not really applicable, for example, if procurement for orders takes several years to mature, an alternative is the use of "target" amounts or other measurements to establish sales goals without the threat of termination.

5. Some firms use tighter clauses to protect against infringement of the U.S.A. Foreign Corrupt Practices Act.

7 Orders

7.1 Orders will be binding upon Supplier only when accepted and approved in writing by an authorized representative of Supplier, providing all governmental export control conditions are met both in Supplier's country and Representative's Territory, and customers shall be duly informed of this condition by Representative. Supplier will have the right to accept or reject any order, or to accept part of an order and reject the balance.

7.2 Unless expressly agreed otherwise in writing, all orders shall be filled on an Ex Works (EXW Incoterms) Supplier factory basis and will be subject to Supplier's standard terms and conditions in effect as of the date of shipment.

7.3 Supplier warrants the Products in accordance with its standard terms and conditions of sale, which may be modified by Supplier from time to time, and makes no other warranty, express or implied.

8 Account Collection

Unless Representative purchases Products for his own account, as provided under clause 4.6 above, Supplier shall have sole responsibility and control over collection of funds due from customers in the Territory, and shall have full discretion with respect to the collection, adjustment, or compromise of any or all accounts. Supplier shall not be liable to Representative for any loss of commission or other claim due to adjustment or compromise of a customer's account.

9 Trademarks and Names

Representative shall not use any of Supplier's trademarks, trade names, corporate slogans, goodwill or product designation in any advertising copy, promotional material, signs, or other written or printed material except as specifically authorized in writing by Supplier in advance.

10 Termination

10.1 Either party may terminate this Agreement if the other party breaches any of the provisions of this Agreement and fails to remedy such breach within 30 days after receipt of written notice of such breach.

10.2 If either party enters into or is placed in bankruptcy or receivership, is nationalized, becomes insolvent, or makes an assignment for the benefit of its creditors, the other party may immediately terminate this Agreement by written notice.

10.3 Supplier may terminate this Agreement immediately upon a change in the owner-ship or management of Representative that Supplier, in its sole discretion, deems advisable to its interest.

10.4 Either party may terminate this Agreement with or without cause, by giving ninety (90) days notice of termination to the other party.[6]

10.5 Neither termination nor expiration shall relieve either party from the obligation to discharge in full all obligations accrued or due prior to the date thereof.

10.6 Within thirty (30) days after the effective date of termination or expiration of this Agreement, Representative shall return to Supplier all price lists, catalogs, operat-ing and service manuals, advertising literature, and display material relating to the Products as well as other material containing confidential information received from Supplier, shall remove all reference to Supplier from Representative's letter-head, business forms, advertising literature, and place of business and shall not thereafter use any name or trademark suggesting that Representative has any rela-tionship with Supplier.

10.7 Neither party, by reason of the termination or expiration of this Agreement shall be liable to the other because of the loss of anticipated sales, commissions, or prospective profits or because of expenditures or investments related to the per-formance of this Agreement or the goodwill of the parties. All sums owed by either party to the other shall become due and payable immediately upon termina-tion or expiration.

11 Excuses for Nonperformance

No liability shall result from the delay in performance or nonperformance beyond the reasonable control of the party affected, including but not limited to Acts of God, fire, flood, war, embargo, accident, labor trouble, or shortage of material, equipment or transport, any government law, regulations, direction, or request of any legally constituted Court ruling in Supplier's country or the Territory.

12 Assignment

Representative shall not assign this Agreement or any right or obligation under this Agreement, and any purported assignment shall be void and ineffective.

13 Applicable Law and Dispute Settlement

---

6. In relationships with large, well-known representatives, this clause might be unnecessary. It might even be modified for a newly appointed representative by specifying that termination under this clause can only be ef-fected after the first six or twelve months of the starting date. The clause may be very controversial, as to the representative, it might appear to invalidate the term of the agreement, rendering it to one of 90 days, termina-ble at will. For the supplier it might represent the most important leverage available over a representative whose record is not acceptable to him.

13.1 The construction, performance and completion of this Agreement shall be governed by the laws of [*country*].

13.2 In the event of any dispute arising out of or relating to this Agreement, the parties undertake to make every effort to reach an amicable settlement of their differences. Failing such settlement, the dispute shall be referred to arbitration and settled by arbitration under the Rules of Conciliation and Arbitration of the International Chamber of Commerce by three arbitrators appointed in accordance with the said Rules. The decision of the arbitration shall be binding and conclusive upon each party and may be enforced in any court of competent jurisdiction. The arbitration shall be conducted in English and the arbitrators shall apply the substantive law of jurisdiction in clause 13.1 above. The site of arbitration shall be in Geneva, Switzerland. The costs and expenses of any such arbitration shall be borne as determined by the arbitrators.

14 Notice

Any notice required or permitted herein may be hand delivered, telexed, cabled, faxed, or mailed, properly addressed to the party to be notified at the address shown above or at the last known address given by such party to the other, and shall be deemed delivered when transmitted by any of the above means.

15 General Conditions

15.1 This Agreement shall be signed in duplicate but shall not be binding on the Supplier until a copy, signed by the Representative is received and signed by Supplier at its offices in [*location*].

15.2 This Agreement is entered into in the English language and supersedes all existing agreements between Supplier and Representative on the subject matter hereof, and all such prior agreements are hereby terminated by mutual consent by the parties.

By: [Representative]   By: [Supplier]
Title: Title:
Date: Date:

SALES REPRESENTATIVE AGREEMENT
ANNEX I: PRODUCTS

By: [Representative]   By: [Supplier]
Title: Title:
Date: Date:

Products included in this Agreement and any specifically excluded are listed in this Annex I, as follows:[7]

---

7. This annex should contain the list of products the representative can sell. If applicable, the list can also give export prices, but if it does, it should also specify the date and term of validity of those export prices. It should also include details relating to an agreed annual amount of orders expected in the Territory, as mentioned in Clause 5.5.

SALES REPRESENTATIVE AGREEMENT
ANNEX II: COMMISSIONS

The commission to be accrued by Supplier for Representative is calculated on any single order from a customer in the Territory as follows[8]:

For the portion of any order up to $25,000. . . . . 15%
For the portion of any order > $25,000 and < $100,000. . . . . . 10%
For the portion of any order > $100,000 and < $500,000. . . . . 5%
For the portion of any order > $500,000. . . . . 3%

Extraordinary Orders

For the purpose of this Agreement, an "Extraordinary Order" is defined as any order for the Supplier's products that is in excess of $300,000. Supplier may determine at its own discretion the commission amount for any Extraordinary Order, and its decision will be communicated to the Representative prior to final price submission to the customer. In no event will this amount be lower than that which is calculated by the above rules, for an order of $300,000 (i.e., $21,250).

Mutually Agreed Commissions

Notwithstanding anything to the contrary in this Agreement, including its Annexes, Supplier and Representative may agree on a case by case basis for different commission rates than those specified above, provided always that no legal restrictions, either of Supplier's country or the Territory, are contravened.

By: [Representative]   By: [Supplier]
Title: Title:
Date: Date:

---

8. These commission rates are suggestions, and the supplier's customary rates can be substituted. Note that there is a maximum commission, defined by an "extraordinary order." An extraordinary order is an order of over $300,000 (U.S.). Although the commission rate is specified for even higher orders, under the terms specified the supplier can elect to limit the commission to that for an extraordinary order. For convenience, the bands are shown in U.S. dollars but should be in the supplier's currency.

Appendix C

An Introduction to Finance for Marketers

A number of people embark on a technical marketing career with a strong technical base but, alas, with a scanty knowledge of the financial aspects of their business. For employees who wish to advance into management roles in marketing this knowledge is essential.

Business is both the science and the art of decision making. It promotes the most effective utilization of resources to achieve a goal or goals. From a financial standpoint, individuals must be concerned with generating funds, investing funds, and operating the business to maximize the return on funds invested. Simply stated, the object is to invest the minimum amount of funds in an endeavor, the proper operation of which will, over time, return the investment plus a profit for the owners.

The income statement and the balance sheet, which are summary financial statements, are used to evaluate how successful a business has been. The income statement shows the revenues generated by the operation of the business, what costs were incurred in generating the revenues, and any revenue, or profit, left. It might cover a period as short as one month, but is generally published for outside consumption on a quarterly or yearly basis. The balance sheet, on the other hand, is a snapshot of the financial condition of the business at a particular time. For that time, it shows investment (assets), obligations the business has incurred (liabilities), and the total book value of the business to the shareholders (equity).

A third financial statement is widely used by both potential investors and management. It is often called a cash-flow, or source and application of funds, statement. This appendix uses the term *funds flow*. The funds flow statement is (1) a means of analyzing the past and (2) a means of projecting the future.

This appendix discusses these three financial statements, as well as some general business principles. The approach is not one of an accountant, but rather the simplified approach of a marketer.

C.1 THE INCOME STATEMENT

Table C.1 shows a typical (simplified) income statement, also called a profit and loss (P&L) statement. The arbitrary units will be $K (thousands).

Table C.1
A Typical P&L Statement

Item	Amount ($K)	Total ($K)
Orders received		13,000
Backlog		2,500
Sales		12,000
Cost of sales		
Cost of materials	3,500	
Material handling cost	600	
Labor cost	1,500	
Factory overhead	500	
Total cost of sales		6,100
Gross margin		5,900
Marketing and selling expenses	2,500	
R&D	1,000	
Depreciation of other fixed assets	300	
Other costs (including reserves)	250	
Total direct overhead		4,050
Contribution		1,850
General and administration		500
Operating profit		1,350
Interest		200
PBT		1,150
Tax (assumed at 35%)		402
PAT		748

It is usual for a company to require that each of its strategic business units (SBUs) keep a separate P&L statement, so that its profitability can be determined. The sum total of the P&L for each SBU of the company is equal to the total company P&L.

The items on a typical year-end P&L statement fall into five distinct cost groupings: total cost of sales, total direct overhead, general and administrative, interest, and tax. The following sections discuss some of those account items.

C.1.1 Orders, Backlog, and Sales

Not all companies report orders received in a period, or orders received but not yet converted into sales (backlog), but for a market-driven company, these figures are of paramount importance.

The prime objective of the salespeople is to obtain orders for the product line. An order is a commitment from a customer to purchase a product. Such a commitment is usually firm and, barring unforeseen circumstances, the product is delivered to the customer, along with an invoice. The order is deemed to have been obtained when a firm commitment (usually written) is received from the customer, and an order acknowledgment is sent. The sale is deemed to have occurred when goods are delivered and the customer is invoiced.

For any one month, or quarter, or year, there is a total number of orders, as well as a total number of sales. The orders that have not been invoiced at the start of the period, plus the orders received during the period, minus the sales during the period, represent the total orders for which sales have still to be made. This total is called *backlog*.

Table C.1 shows $13,000K of orders for the year and $12,000K of sales. The backlog therefore increased during the year by $1,000K; because the backlog at the end of the year was $2,500K, it must have been $1,500K at the start of the year. The total backlog of $2,500K is the monetary equivalent of $2\frac{1}{2}$ months of sales at the rate shown.

If the average backlog appears to be shrinking, orders must be increasing more slowly than sales. In the future, the company will be forced to decrease production, which should not run at a greater rate than orders, unless forecasted orders, along with sound reasoning and supporting statistics, indicate that the production rate should be increased. The backlog of a company, especially one whose production cycle is fairly long (as is often the case with high-tech products), is of fundamental importance in production planning and, indeed, in the management of the company. The ratio of orders to sales is sometimes called the "book-to-bill ratio" and is used as a key measure of a company's health. A growing company normally has a book-to-bill ratio greater than one.

C.1.2 Cost of Sales

Table C.1 records expenditures totaling $6,100K for factory costs associated with the product line. These factory costs are material, at $3,500K; material handling, at $600K; labor, at $1,500K; and overhead, at $500K. They give us a total cost of sales of $6,100.

C.1.3 Gross Margin

The *gross margin* is the difference between the sales ($12,000K) and the cost of sales ($6,100K), or $5,900K. Depending on competition and perceived value, a company should aim for the highest possible gross margin at all stages in the life cycle of a product. A stable-state gross margin for a high-volume product in a high-tech industry could be on the order of 35%, while the gross margin for a low-volume product, which might have incurred high research and development costs, needs to be perhaps 50% or higher.

To determine the profit before tax (PBT), direct and indirect overhead and interest costs are subtracted from the gross margin.

C.1.4 Direct Overhead Costs

Direct overhead costs are costs that can be directly associated with the product line. These include marketing costs, research and development (R&D costs), depreciation of other fixed assets, and any other costs or special reserves that might be set aside for some anticipated contingency.

SBU managers should be able to control these costs. The difference between the total of these costs and the gross margin is called the contribution. Often, SBU managers are judged on the contribution their SBUs make to the expenses and profits of the company.

Marketing costs. Marketing costs include all direct and indirect costs of the marketing organization. Salaries, fringe benefits, travel expenses, trade show costs, advertising literature, and many other items are included here. There are indirect marketing costs as well, such as light, heat, rent, cleaning, telephone, and fax. In the example, these total $2,500K.

R&D. All engineering costs associated with developing products for the SBU are collected under this heading. Direct costs include salaries, fringe benefits, and so on. Indirect costs include all engineering overheads. In this example, R&D totals $1,000K.

Depreciation of other fixed assets. Insofar as possible, the accounting department allocates other fixed assets to the various SBUs. When specific plant and machinery or test equipment is used by an SBU, the allocation is simple. Other times, it is somewhat arbitrary. All of these assets depreciate with time, most of them over five to ten years. That depreciation ($300K in the table) is a cost factor and must be included under the direct overhead costs.

Other costs (including reserves). Despite extensive credit checking of prospective customers, customers still might refuse to pay some or all invoices. If a company must "write off" a debt, it loses an amount equal to the write-off. Rather than showing such a loss in one month, companies often set aside (in the accounting books) a reserve against bad debts. Such a reserve can be used for other purposes as well, for instance, to offset the costs of a forced reduction in employees. Apart from reserves, other costs include miscellaneous overhead expenses not attributable to the company management infrastructure. Other costs (in this case, $250K) are included under the heading of direct overhead because, theoretically, this cost factor is controlled by the SBU manager. Subtracting the direct overhead costs from the gross margin leaves the contribution made by the SBU to the company.

C.1.5 Indirect Overhead Costs

In this example, indirect overhead costs are collectively called general and administrative (G&A) expenses. These central costs (generated by corporate headquarters, the legal department, the accounting and personnel departments, corporate advertising, general research, and so on) are incurred in the management of any company and are often allocated to individual SBUs on an arbitrary basis. Allocation might be based on such criteria as headcount or sales. (There are many techniques for allocating overhead, which is beyond the scope of this book.) After the indirect overhead is subtracted from the SBU contribution, we are left with what some companies call *operating profit*.

C.1.6 Interest

Financial costs (interest to lending institutions) are usually paid centrally and allocated to SBUs on the basis of average capital employed by each SBU. In this case, the interest amounts to $200K. The capital employed by SBUs is considered again in the discussion of the balance sheet.

C.1.7 Profit Before Tax, Tax, and Profit After Tax

The *profit before tax* (PBT) is the difference between the operating profit and the interest cost. Corporate tax varies from country to country in the range of 25–50% (35% in this example). *Net earnings* is often used to denote the profit after tax (PAT). In this example, net earnings are $748K, or 6.2% of sales.

    The PAT, or net earnings, is the "return" in the term *return on equity* (ROE). The company's balance sheet indicates the amount of equity.

C.2 THE BALANCE SHEET

A balance sheet provides a snapshot of a company's financial status at a particular time. It shows the company assets, liabilities, and shareholders' equity. The total of a company's assets is equal to its liabilities plus the shareholder's equity. (In many balance sheets the shareholder's equity is included in the total liabilities.)

    The following discussion examines the various accounting aspects of a simplified balance sheet for the same company whose one SBU was represented by the P&L statement above (See Table C.2). The SBU balance sheet in a company with several SBUs (or divisions) might be somewhat artificial, if borrowings, interest, and tax payments are handled at a central location.

C.2.1 Total and Current Assets

Total assets include the following:

- Cash.
- Accounts receivable (that is, unpaid invoices) less any reserve for bad debt.
- Inventories.

- Fixed assets, such as property, plant, and equipment, less accumulated depreciation. This category covers all machinery, tooling, and test equipment as well as any real estate.
- Other assets (normally individually listed), such as company investments and pre-paid expenses.

Current assets are assets that can be converted into cash immediately or within a relatively short time (usually one year). All assets listed above, with the exception of fixed assets and some others, are in this category.

Long-term fixed assets and some other assets depreciate with time. The balance sheet shows the total of fixed assets less an accumulated amount for such depreciation. (However, the balance sheet evaluation of assets does not necessarily reflect the true present value of the assets. For example, real estate might be worth far more or less than the balance sheet value.)

The value of cash and accounts receivable can be determined accurately on the balance sheet. But this is not true for inventories and fixed assets, which are usually valued at cost less depreciation but might not reflect the true market value. The *true market value* is the amount for which these assets can be sold in the normal course of business.

C.2.2 Total and Current Liabilities

Total liabilities include the following, each of which is self-explanatory, except perhaps, accrued liabilities:

- Prepayments from customers (owed to customers until goods are delivered);
- Accounts payable (owed to suppliers for company purchases);
- Short-term borrowings;
- Accrued liabilities;
- Long-term borrowings (from banks and other institutions).

Accrued liabilities are any liabilities for which invoices have not yet been received. These might include social security taxes, retirement and redundancy benefits, bonus payments, and combined communication and power costs.

Current liabilities correspond to current assets. These are liabilities that are usually payable within a year. In this case, current liabilities include all the company's liabilities except long-term borrowings.

C.2.3 Equity and Return on Equity

The difference between the total assets and the total liabilities of a company represents the equity "owned" by the shareholders. It is often referred to as the company's *net worth*. The most important financial objective of the board of directors of a company is to ensure that equity grows steadily and that return on equity is optimized. (Note that, in many text books, total liabilities is defined as including equity.)

Equity includes the original and subsequent capitalization, as well as any retained accumulated profits. The ROE is the ratio of the PAT to the equity of the company. In this example, the PAT is $748K and the equity is $5,100K, making the ROE 14.7%.

C.2.4 A Typical Balance Sheet

Table C.2 is a companion balance sheet for the P&L statement in Table C.1. Just as in the P&L statement, the arbitrary currency amounts here are in $K (thousands). The discussion following the table correlates some of the items in the two statements.

Table C.2
A Typical Balance Sheet

Assets	Amount ($K)	Liabilities	Amount ($K)
Cash	700	Customer prepayments	1,150
Accounts receivable	5,200	Accounts payable	400
Inventories	2,200	Short-term borrowings	1,800
		Accrued liabilities	250
Current assets	8,100	Current liabilities	3,600
Fixed assets less depreciation	1,100	Long-term borrowings	500
		Total liabilities	4,100
		Shareholders' equity	5,100
Total assets	9,200	Total liabilities and equity	9,200

C.2.5 Investment and Return on Investment

The total *investment* is the amount banks (and other lending institutions) loaned the company on a long-term basis ($500K) plus the shareholders' equity ($5,100K). This total, $5,600K, then, is the investment in the company. Another way to calculate investment is to subtract current liabilities from total assets.

Cash must be distinguished from investment. For example, a customer that arranges a prepayment on a sale is not investing in the company. On the other hand, shareholders and the long-term lending organizations are most definitely investing.

The "return" in ROE has already been identified as the PAT. The "return" in ROI is normally (but not universally) the operating profit. The *operating profit* is the return to the company before interest and taxes. In Table C.1 the operating profit is shown as $1,350K and in Table C.2 the investment is $5,600K. The ROI, then, is 24.1%. In a well-run company, the ROI should be substantially more than the interest paid to the banks.

C.2.6 Asset Management and Return on Assets

One might imagine that the higher the value of a company's assets the better. Even the term "asset" denotes something positive. However, with a little reflection, it should be clear that assets should be as *low* as possible, consistent with the demands of the business. If the managers of the company examined in Tables C.1 and C.2 could reduce their accounts receivable and inventory by only 30% (say by $2,300K), they could repay all borrowings and reduce interest payments to zero. On the income statement, PAT would increase from $690K to $810K. Furthermore, the total assets would decrease from $9,200K to $6,900K.

In many companies, managers stress the importance of return on assets (ROA) rather than ROI or ROE, because these assets fall more directly under the control of many SBU managers. As with ROI, in ROA the "return" is normally the operating profit. In the example, ROA is ($1,350K)/($9,200K), or 14.7%.

C.3 THE FUNDS-FLOW STATEMENT

Funds-flow statements essentially deal with changes in the balance sheet and the income statement over a specified period. Generally, funds are thought of as cash. If a business is conducted strictly on a cash basis, as many small firms are, this interchangeable use of terms is appropriate. However, while a business operation normally involves many cash transactions over time, not all funds are obtained or committed by cash changing hands. A business might extend credit to a customer or obtain credit from a supplier. While the actual cash can be exchanged in the future, credit terms involve management decisions concerning cash commitment, as will be discussed later. Funds are received and dispersed through an organization via financing, investment, or operations.

- *Financing.* New financing (equity, short- or long-term debt) is a source of funds; dividends or repayment of debt is a use of funds.
- *Investment.* Investment in assets is a true use of funds; disposal of assets is a source of funds.
- *Operations.* Profitable operation results in the creation of new funds; loss in operations is a use of funds. Accounting write-offs do not affect funds flow, although they do affect profitability.

There is no prescribed format for a funds-flow statement. The nature of the particular business and the purpose for which the statement is being prepared determine, to a large extent, the form and format. The rules for determining sources and uses of funds, listed in Table C.3, are broken down into increases and decreases on the balance sheet and income statement. The professional marketer will find the concept of fund-flow projection and analysis particularly important when evaluating alternative strategies.

Table C.3
Rules of Funds-Flow Analysis

Sources of Funds	Uses of Funds
Decrease in assets	Increase in assets
Increase in liabilities	Decrease in liabilities
Increase in equity	Decrease in equity
Profit from operations*	Loss from operations*

* Before accounting write-offs.

It is not enough to evaluate the relative profitability of strategy A versus strategy B. From a profitability standpoint, strategy A, introducing a new product line, might appear to be more attractive than strategy B, expanding or upgrading an existing product line. Increased revenues and healthy gross margins from the new product line might indicate a substantial increase in the overall profitability of the business. But a funds-flow analysis might reveal that strategy A will demand increased investment in assets, such as in new facilities and finished and in-process inventory, and incur operating losses during the start-up phase. The magnitude of the needed investment might exceed the ability of the company to provide increased assets through operations, despite the projected increase in profitability. Thus, new financing would be needed, either through increased equity investment or additional debt. This increase in equity or liability might not be feasible or it might be extremely risky, making a decision to pursue strategy A more complicated than the projected-income statement suggests.

Funds-flow projections also help ongoing businesses anticipate and manage change over time. This is particularly true for seasonal or cyclical businesses, in which wide differences in revenues, profits, and receivables can result in a cash surplus at one time and a cash deficit at another. Businesses involved in long-term projects find funds-flow projections and analyses a necessity for effective management. Funds-flow projection forces complete analysis of both the financial and timing-based ramifications of making a decision and is essential to effective and efficient management.

Table C.4 lists a number of common funds-flow statement items. The actual items on an individual statement are determined by the nature of the business and the type of analysis being performed.

Financial departments are usually very willing to provide assistance in developing the proper format for a funds-flow statement; such participation is valuable to their overall financial function. Marketing executives who involve financial departments indicate that they understand that their responsibilities extend beyond generating orders.

Table C.4
Sources and Uses of Funds

Sources of Funds	Uses of Funds
Increased equity investment	Payment of dividends
Increased short-term debt	Repayment of debt
Increased long-term debt	New plant
Decreased working capital	New equipment
Gain in asset disposal	Paid interest
Decreased inventory	Increased accounts receivable
Decreased accounts receivable	Decreased accounts payable
Increased accounts payable	Increased inventory
Decreased deferred expenses	Increased prepaid expenses
Profit from operations*	Increased working capital
	Loss from operations*

* Before inventory write-offs and depreciation.

C.4 SOME OVERALL BUSINESS CONSIDERATIONS

As noted, the company whose year-end P&L statement and balance sheet were examined in the sections above is profitable but possibly not as profitable as it should be. Still, the profitability of many companies is cyclical; this company might have been more profitable in former years. Delving further into financial aspects of this business might provide more information.

Does this company have a sound business or is it in danger of declining? Can the ROE be improved by better management? A complete answer to these questions involves examination of several years of financial statements, as well as a critical assessment of future prospects, objectives, and strategy. An examination of several balance sheets can indicate, for example, whether the company is expanding and whether it has a good cash position or is embarking on a downward spiral of more borrowing, resulting in higher interest, lower profits, and even more borrowing. (At some point, banks might refuse to loan any more, and the company might have to declare bankruptcy.) The marketing department must play a vital role in helping determine the future prospects, objectives, and strategy of the company.

C.4.1 The Break-Even Chart

The preceding discussion of the income statement considered the total sum of labor costs, material costs, overhead, and expenses. Another useful analysis distinguishes *fixed costs* and *variable costs*.

At a given level of production, it is possible to segregate from the total costs that do not vary with sales. Those costs include expenses (marketing and R&D) and overhead

(G&A, for example). If the level of production were to change to the extent that fixed costs changed (for example, more or less supervision or sales representatives), then even those so-called fixed costs become variable. However, for the purposes of this break-even analysis, all those costs are considered to be fixed costs.

A first approximation suggests that, at a capacity utilization rate at which overhead and expenses are constant, material, labor costs, and factory overhead are the only costs that are directly proportional to sales. Even this proportionality is only approximate, because, for example, some overhead costs (such as electricity) are also proportional to sales, and factory overhead and labor costs are not. Figure C.1 shows fixed and variable costs, as well as sales, as functions of production.

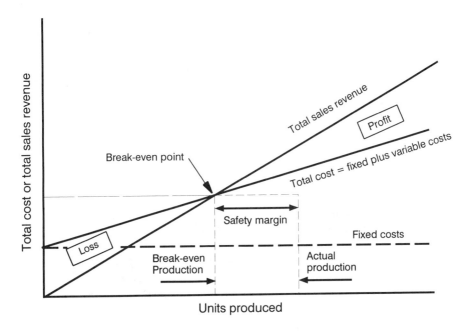

Figure C.1 The break-even chart.

In this chart—applicable to, say, one product of an SBU—*sales revenue* and *costs* are shown as functions of the output in *units produced*. The sales revenue is a linear function of units produced. The total costs, equal to the sum of fixed and variable costs, is also shown as a straight line, but displaced from zero in the Y-axis. There is a break-even point at which sales revenue and total costs are equal. Hopefully, the production rate is such that the product is making money and there is a suitable margin of safety between the actual and break-even production rates. The difference between total revenues and total costs is the PBT. Note that the PBT is positive (i.e., the company is profitable) above the break-even point but negative below it. Note also that if the slopes of the total cost and sales revenue do not differ very much, a small increase in the sales revenue slope (brought about by, for example, a unit price increase) can have a significant positive influence on profit.

This analysis can also be applied to the sum of all products of the SBU, or to the sum of SBUs that comprise the company. Instead of the x-axis of the graph being units produced, it can be sales, in which case (if the scales were the same), the sales revenue line would be at a 45° angle.

The distinction between fixed and variable costs is easily understood. However, in practice it might not be too easy to place a specific cost into one or the other category. One way to avoid approximation is to plot the total cost as a function of units produced. There will probably be discontinuities in the resultant straight line, but with linear regression analysis it should be possible to determine parameters for fixed and variable costs. However, even this refinement might be unnecessary for a quick break-even analysis.

One way to use break-even analysis in evaluating pricing and profitability dynamics is to compare the charts for each product in an SBU. Production can be forecasted for any product and a break-even analysis can be applied and tracked over time. Analysis can project the effect of a price change on sales—the slope of the sales revenue curve will change with price change—and a break-even chart can be made.

Break-even analysis is one of the valuable tools managers can use to understand the dynamics of decision making and select the right choice from among the possibilities.

C.4.2 The Current Ratio

As previously stated, the value of inventory and other fixed assets is not as readily determined as the value of other assets (cash, accounts receivable, and reserves). Thus, because it is equal to total assets less total liabilities, the value of shareholders' equity is also not readily determined.

In general, a healthy industrial company should be in a position to repay all of its current liabilities from its current assets. The ratio of current assets to current liabilities, which is called the *current ratio*, should therefore be greater than 1. An acid test of the ability of a company to repay its current liabilities from its current assets is to exclude the value of inventory and determine the "quick ratio." The quick ratio should also be greater than 1. These ratios vary from industry to industry. Table C.3 shows some typical values taken from relatively recent balance sheets of several large companies.

In the example in Table C.3, the current ratio is (8100/3600) or 2.25. The quick ratio is (8100 − 2200)/3600, or 1.64.

C.4.3 Working Capital

Working capital is the difference between current assets and current liabilities. In the example, this amounts to $8,100K − $3,600K, or $4,500K. For a single SBU, the working capital is the difference between the SBU's current assets and liabilities *before* any borrowing, because these are centralized by the company as a whole. Interest can be allocated against the SBU based on the ratio of its capital to that sum for all SBUs.

Table C.3
Some Current and Quick Ratios

Company	Current Ratio	Quick Ratio
Raytheon	1.4	1.0
Hewlett-Packard	2.5	1.9
Scientific Atlanta	3.6	2.6
Alcatel (Spain)	1.6	1.0

A company might be trading profitably, but if its sales increase it will have to obtain more working capital to finance this expansion. Its accounts receivable will increase, and its inventory is likely to increase. If it cannot obtain the extra capital needed, it might be in serious trouble and might become insolvent or be forced to restrict its own growth. Apart from retained profits from its PAT, the extra capital could be obtained by doing a combination of the following:

- Decrease accounts receivable;
- Decrease inventory;
- Obtain more customer prepayments;
- Delay payments to creditors;
- Increase equity;
- Increase borrowing.

Financial experts constantly stress the importance of collecting accounts receivable early and reducing inventory but there are limits. Increasing customer prepayments is another way of obtaining the extra capital. A company should always take full advantage of the credit terms offered by suppliers, but good business practice dictates that it should not take more. In any case, delaying payments to creditors is risky; they might start to limit the credit they extend to the company. In the extreme case, creditors might even refuse to do business with companies that do not pay on time. Increasing equity might not be feasible because the shareholders might not have more money to invest in the company or might be reluctant to increase their investment. What remains is increasing bank borrowings and paying the consequent higher interest.

Suppose the company under discussion doubles its sales. As a first approximation, assume that the accounts receivable and the inventory double, thereby raising the current assets by $7,400K, and that customer prepayments, accounts payable, and accrued liabilities double as well, increasing the liabilities by $1,800K. This growth increases net working capital by $5,600K, which has to be financed somehow. Ignore any cash benefit from the increased sales. Increasing short-term borrowing from the present $1,800K to $7,400K is a possibility, but will the banks be willing to loan the extra money needed?

The interest will increase much faster than the operating profit, so that PAT as a percentage of sales is less, as is ROI. The current ratio will decrease from 2.25 to 1.55, not a good sign to the bank. Worse, the quick ratio will decrease from 1.64 to 1.11, barely enough to pay back all creditors, again not a good sign. The banks might wonder how sound the inventory is or whether it is overvalued. If they decide not to increase the loans to the company, it might be in real trouble. The answer to the dilemma must be to control the growth in accounts receivable and inventory.

C.4.4 Inventory

Section C.2.6 discussed the importance of reducing assets to a minimum, and inventory is an important asset. Companies seldom appreciate how expensive inventory is. It costs money to store and handle inventory, and it becomes obsolete very quickly. Demonstration inventory is often written off in four years or less, so that its amortization costs could be 25% per year or higher. Other inventory could depreciate even more quickly. A depreciation figure of 50% per year is possible. In the example, the inventory could have been valued at 2200/0.66 or $3,300K before depreciation, so that the total depreciation was $1,100 for the year. Without this depreciation, the PBT would be $2,250K rather than $1,150K!

Inventory is one of the major assets in which a company invests and the one over which it has the most day-to-day control. It is perhaps second in importance only to the investment in people. As a company grows, develops more products, and engages competition, top management finds it increasingly difficult to supervise the details of the organization, and inventory management becomes just another function in the overall organization. Quite often it is a subfunction of finance, production, or purchasing.

Inventory includes all the material, parts, work-in-process, and finished goods purchased or manufactured by the organization and not yet shipped or billed to the customer. It can constitute a very sizable investment, many millions of dollars in large companies. The cost of this inventory comes from outside investment, borrowed funds, or profits from the company's previous revenues, usually a combination of all three. In addition to the direct cost of the inventory, there is the sizable operational overhead cost of personnel who purchase the materials, shipping charges, warehouse personnel, and storage facilities. As an investment in assets and a controllable operational cost, it is management's responsibility to keep the value of the inventory and the costs to maintain it at a minimum that is consistent with sales.

Fighting for new orders, the sales department is often under pressure to promise quick delivery; sometimes the customer doesn't really require it, but uses delivery timing in negotiating for other concessions. Conversely, sales might promise unusually short deliveries as a competitive edge when lacking other advantages. Thus the sales function is pressured and biased toward demanding increased inventory for competitive purposes.

Those responsible for inventory management are also faced with pressures that tend to increase inventory, such as unreliable material supplier and volume discounts. Further, a production line that doesn't receive materials in a timely manner operates very inefficiently. Sometimes, during a business downturn, company management might decide to continue production of finished goods simply because it might be less costly than the redundancy payments (and loss of skilled workers) that result from production layoffs. All these factors tend to result in increased inventory. The only off-setting pressure comes from those directly responsible for asset management, often the financial department.

Inventory is truly the responsibility of a team that crosses all organizational lines of a company; finance, production, and purchasing involvement are all important. Nonetheless, ultimately, inventory levels are driven by the sales department. The marketing and sales departments provide the two most important ingredients that determine levels and effect efficient inventory control: (1) the sales forecast of volume over time and (2) a realistic evaluation of the customer and competitive demands influencing the time lapse between order and delivery.

Marketing and sales must also be realistic in their demands for and management of the inventory of finished goods they use in demonstrations and loan to customers. Products used in promotion are generally transferred from inventory to fixed assets and amortized or depreciated relatively quickly. This transfer affects both income and balance sheet statements. Demonstration and loan units can be very valuable sales tools, but if they are used indiscriminately, that product consumption can adversely affect the financial success of the whole corporation.

C.4.5 Marketing Costs

A cursory examination of financial statements is insufficient to determine whether the expenditures here are too little or too much. However, comparison of these expenditures with those of successful competitors is helpful in such an assessment. A reduction in the costs of marketing and R&D would clearly have a positive effect on PBT, if the same sales level could be maintained in the long run. Even in the short term, with sufficient backlog, such a reduction might show increased profitability, and management might be tempted to reduce marketing expenditures.

The largest component of marketing costs is the cost of labor. A reduction in these costs usually involves a reduction in the work force. Such a reduction is seldom easy to effect without substantial redundancy payments to employees who lose their jobs. Furthermore, any such reduction causes a transient that might have a negative effect on profitability. Also, it is clear that there is a correlation between marketing expenditure and order rate. Still, an inefficient marketing organization must be overhauled, or profitability might continue to be unsatisfactory. The best policy is to maintain a lean but highly motivated and effective marketing organization commensurate with order expectations.

But how does one judge whether a marketing organization is effective? One way is to determine the total yearly orders per salesperson and compare the results with results from successful competitive companies. Figures of 1–10 million U.S. dollars per salesperson are common in high-tech companies. The remainder of the marketing organization, including sales support and overhead, should be as Spartan as possible while still maintaining a high efficiency.

In the sample company, which could represent a high-tech instrumentation company, marketing costs are $2,500K. If 50% of the costs were for sales representatives and their expenses (estimated at, say, $150K per person), then there could be room for ($1,250K)/($150K) or just over 8 sales representatives. The total order value for the year is shown as $13,000K, so each sales representative is responsible for, on the average, ($13,000K)/8 or about $1,600K per year. (The estimates in this paragraph are not meant to be norms but rather indications of the arithmetic involved.)

C.4.6 Research and Development Costs

There is often a tendency on the part of SBU managers (and even overall management) to reduce R&D expenditures to increase profitability. The effect of such a reduction is quickly noted in increased profits, but the long term effect might be suicidal. Unless new products are developed with shorter and shorter time intervals between their introduction, a company might well stagnate, and be overtaken by its competition.

C.4.7 Accounts Receivable

In the company this chapter is examining, the accounts receivable are $5,200K, compared to yearly sales of $12,000K. The accounts receivable result from sales, and in this case, the average number of days of sales represented by these accounts receivable is (5200/12000) x 365, or 158 days. Considering that 30 days is often the time given by a supplier for payment of invoices, 158 days certainly seems excessive. Ninety days could possibly be acceptable, although 60 days would be better. If the company achieved a goal of 90-day sales, then at the sales level of $12,000K per year, the accounts receivable would be about $3,000K. This is a reduction of $2,200 in accounts receivable, more than enough to reduce borrowing to zero! To reduce accounts receivable is one of the best answer to the problem of finding cash to finance expansion.

High accounts receivables are usually the result of mismanagement, often by the marketing organization. The sales representatives who grant their customers easy (long) payment terms because they find it easier to sell this way, might be costing the company a lot of money.

C.5 SUMMARY

This appendix only scratches the surface of finances; however, even this cursory examination might help marketers understand some of the business goals of their companies and how they can further those goals.

Appendix D

Suggested Readings

Allen, Peter, *Selling: Management and Practice*, 3rd ed., London: Pitman Publishing, 1989.

Bradley, Frank, *International Marketing Strategy*, Cambridge: Prentice Hall, 1991.

Branch, Alan, *Elements of Export Marketing and Management*, London: Chapman & Hall, 1990.

Buzzell, R. D., and Gale, B. T., *The PIMS Principles*, New York: The Free Press, 1987.

Buzzell, R. D., and Quelch, J. A., *Multinational Marketing Management*, Boston: Addison-Wesley, 1988.

Davidow, William, *Marketing High Technology*, New York: The Free Press, 1986.

Doyle, Peter, and Hart, N. A., *Case Studies in International Marketing*, Oxford: Heinemann Professional Publishing, 1990.

Harvey-Jones, John, *Making it Happen*, London: Harper Collins, 1989.

Henderson, Bruce, *On Corporate Strategy*, Cambridge: Abt Books, 1979.

Leader, W. G., and Kyritsis, N., *Marketing in Practice*, Cheltenham: Stanley Thornes, 1990.

Levitt, Theodore, *The Marketing Imagination*, expanded ed., New York: The Free Press, 1986.

Mack, Manfred, *L'Impératif Humain*, Paris: Masson S.A., 1992.

McKenna, Regis, *Relationship Marketing*, London: Century Press, 1992.

Miller and Heiman, *Strategic Selling*, New York: Warner Books, 1985.

Morita, Akio, *Made in Japan*, Hammersmith: Fontana, 1988.

Mott, Graham, *Accounting For Nonaccountants*, 3rd ed., London: Kogan Page, 1990.

O'Reilly, J. A., *International Marketing*, Estover: Macdonald and Evans, 1985.

Paliwoda, S. J., *International Marketing*, Oxford: Heinemann Professional Publishing, 1990.

Peters, T. J., and Waterman, R. W., *In Search of Excellence*, New York: Harper and Row, 1982.

Porter, Michael, ed., *Competition in Global Industries*, Cambridge: Harvard Business School Press, 1986.

Porter, Michael, *Competitive Advantage*, New York: The Free Press, 1985.

Rodgers, Buck, *The IBM Way*, New York: Harper and Row, 1989.

Sherlock, Paul, *Rethinking Business to Business Marketing*, New York: The Free Press, 1991.

Simmonds, Kenneth, *Strategy and Marketing, a Case Approach*, second edition, Hemel Hempsted: Philip Allen, 1986.

Thorelli, Hans, and Becker, Helmut, eds., *International Marketing Strategy*, revised ed., Pergamon Press, 1988.

Townsend, Peter, *Up The Organization*, New York: The Free Press, 1987.

Walsh, L. S., *International Marketing*, 2nd ed., London: Pitman Publishing, 1992.

Index

The Artech House Professional Development Library

Preparing and Delivering Effective Technical Presentations, David L. Adamy
Writing and Managing Winning Technical Proposals, Timothy Whalen

For further information on these and other Artech House titles, contact:

Artech House
685 Canton Street
Norwood, MA 01602
(617) 769-9750
Fax:(617) 762-9230
Telex: 951-659

Artech House
6 Buckingham Gate
London SW1E6JP England
+44(0)71 630-0166
+44(0)71 630-0166
Telex-951-659